THE IGNORANCE EXPLOSION

Understanding Industrial Civilization

JULIUS LUKASIEWICZ

Carleton University Press
Ottawa, Canada
1994

Printed and bound in Canada

Canadian Cataloguing in Publication Data

Lukasiewicz, J.
The ignorance explosion : understanding industrial civilization

Includes bibliographical references and index.
ISBN 0-88629-234-4 (bound) –
ISBN 0-88629-237-9 (pbk.)

1. Technology – Social aspects.
2. Civilization, Modern – 20th century. I. Title.

CB78.L85 1994 303.48'3 C94-900171-6

Carleton University Press
160 Paterson Hall
Carleton University
1125 Colonel By Drive
Ottawa, Ontario
K1S 5B6
(613) 788-3740

Distributed in Canada by

Oxford University Press Canada,
70 Wynford Drive,
Don Mills, Ontario,
Canada. M3C 1J9
(416) 441-2941

Cover concept: Julius Lukasiewicz
Cover design: Y Graphics, Julius Lukasiewicz
Typeset by: Carleton Production Centre, Nepean

Acknowledgments

Carleton University Press gratefully acknowledges the support extended to its publishing programme by the Canada Council and the financial assistance of the Ontario Arts Council.

The Press would also like to thank the Department of Canadian Heritage, Government of Canada, and the Government of Ontario through the Ministry of Culture, Tourism and Recreation, for their assistance.

[redacted]

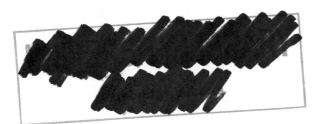

To the memory of my wife

HALINA

Contents

List of Illustrations

List of Tables

List of "Boxes"

Designation of References

References are listed following a chapter in alphabetical order according to the senior author, and in chronological sequence for each author. References are designated in the text by the author's name and the year of publication; when in the same year more than one reference appears by the same author, it is given a letter following the year (e.g., Brown 1988a, Brown 1988b).

Abbreviations

AI	artificial intelligence
ASEAN	Association of Southeast Asian Nations
CFC	chlorofluorocarbon
CIS	Commonwealth of Independent States
DNA	deoxyribonucleic acid
EEA	European Economic Area
EEC	European Economic Community
EFTA	European Free Trade Association
ESA	European Space Agency
GATT	General Agreement on Tariffs and Trade
GDP	gross domestic product
GNP	gross national product
IBM	International Business Machines Co.
ICBM	intercontinental ballistic missile
IVF	in-vitro fertilization
LDC	less developed country
MAD	mutually assured destruction
MNC	multinational corporation
NAFTA	North American Free Trade Agreement
NASA	National Air and Space Administration (USA)
R&D	research and development
SDI	Strategic Defence Initiative
SI	Système International d'Unités
SST	supersonic transport
TGV	Train à Grande Vitesse
TV	television
UN	United Nations
VCR	video cassette recorder
VR	virtual reality

Preface

The post-world War II years saw a rate of scientific and technological progress that even today would be difficult to match. Within only a few decades several major advances were made. They included supersonic and space flight, satellite communications and sensing from orbit, solid state electronics and computers, nuclear reactors, thermonuclear explosives, lasers, and the discovery of DNA (the fundamental genetic material); by 1969 man had landed on the Moon and millions on Earth had watched him walk on the lunar surface and heard him talk.

Western society became supremely confident in its ability to tackle technical problems: if resources were not lacking, there seemed to be no limit to ever more sophisticated technical achievements. This was certainly the feeling that I had gained through twenty-five years of experience in the forefront of aerospace research and development.

It was also a period of fast industrial growth in the West and unprecedented rise of affluence, as well as the appearance of social and environmental problems on a scale not noted before. It became evident that the political, ecological, economic, psychological and cultural consequences of industrialization were infinitely more complex than the most difficult technical tasks that could be envisaged. No wonder that attempts to perform "social engineering" and apply a "systems approach" met with little success; no politician or ideology could offer effective remedies.

Moreover, as noted by Marshall McLuhan in his July 1966 *Vogue* article, "We do not know who discovered water, [but] it was almost certainly not a fish. Anybody's total surround, or environment, creates a condition of non-perception." This was the condition of Western societies, totally immersed in the artificial environment of industrial civilization.

It was a curious situation: a society which had been extraordinarily successful in pursuing scientific and industrial development found it difficult to cope with its own success and manage effectively the environment it had created. To explore the underlying causes of this condition was a challenge that intrigued me and eventually led to a wide-ranging examination of the nature of technology and industrial civilization.

My interest was further kindled when my late wife Halina presented me with a copy of Marshall McLuhan's *Understanding Media* (1964). Here was a cultural historian, already known to me as the author of *Mechanical Bride: Folklore of Industrial Man* (1951), who not only appreciated the purely technical attributes of technology, but also offered original and profound insights into its less direct but far-reaching and highly significant impacts.

Lewis Mumford's *Technics and Civilization*, a pioneering work first published in 1934, provided additional stimulus. *Technics and Civilization* "broke with [the] traditional neglect of technology: it not merely summarized for the first time the technical history of the last thousand years of Western civilization, but revealed the constant interplay between the social milieu ... and the more specific achievements of the inventor, the industrialist and the engineer" (Introduction, Harbinger Edition, 1963).

Mumford's approach was outlined earlier in "The Drama of Machines," an essay published in *Scribner's* magazine, August 1930.

> If we wish to have any clear notion about the machine we must think about its psychological as well as its practical origins; and similarly, we must appraise its esthetic and ethical results. For a century we have isolated the technical triumphs of the machine; and we have bowed before the handiwork of the inventor and the scientist; we have alternatively exalted these new instruments for their practical success and despised them for the narrowness of their achievements.
>
> When one examines the subject freshly, however, many of these estimates are upset. We find that there are human values in machinery we did not suspect; we also find that there are wastes, losses, perversions of energy which the ordinary economist blandly concealed. The vast material displacements the machine has made in our physical environment are perhaps in the long run less important than its spiritual contributions to our culture.

My concern with the nature of industrial civilization led me to develop at Carleton University, starting in 1971, a program of Technology, Society and Environment Studies and graduate seminars on Science, Technology and International Affairs. This is where some of the themes, here included and expanded, were first addressed.

I am greatly indebted to Dr. Robert Morrison, to many members of the Carleton University faculty and others who encouraged these academic endeavours and participated in them; I have profited from their knowledge and wisdom. I owe much to Philip Pocock for many stimulating discussions of the themes addressed in this book and for his contribution of several photographs. I am particularly grateful to Dr. Lionel Rubinoff,

Professor of Philosophy and Environmental Studies at Trent University in Peterborough, Ontario, and to Dr. Patrick van der Puije, Professor of Electronics at Carleton University, for their most valuable, critical and constructive reviews of the manuscript.

I also wish to thank Mr. Anthony Jenkins, whose art the readers of *The Globe and Mail* have enjoyed for many years, for his interest in this work and the incisive cartoons he created for the cover and several chapters.

Notwithstanding word processing and computer typesetting, the task of editing and producing a book remains complex and tedious.

My thanks to my son Mark, who assisted in the early stages.

Ms. Kristin Cooper typed the text, handled the bibliographical data, and contributed in many other ways to the completion of this book. My thanks go to her for her careful and fast work, and for her patience.

To Professor Michael Gnarowski, the former Director, to Dr. John Flood, who succeeded him, and to the Staff of the Carleton University Press, I would like to express my appreciation for their high standards in accuracy and efficiency, and for their wholehearted co-operation in seeing this endeavour successfully completed.

J.L.
Ottawa, August 1994

Acknowledgements

The sources of excerpts quoted in this book and of the illustrations are given with each item or in the References. Grateful acknowledgement is made to the publishers and authors for their permission to include these materials. Every effort has been made to trace all the copyright holders, but if any has been inadvertently overlooked, the author and the publisher will be pleased to make the necessary arrangements at the first opportunity.

Introduction

The object of this study — industrial civilization — is enormously complex and the views on technology — the underpinning of industrial civilization — highly controversial. It will be therefore useful to define first the basic premises and the scope of *The Ignorance Explosion*.

It is essential to recognize that technology (and hence industrialization) is unique to human species. An expression of creativity, it is a facility with which only humans are endowed. As Marshall McLuhan observed, we are "the sex organs of the machine world" (McLuhan 1964, 46).

Technology is most adequately defined as an extension and expansion of our natural, biologically determined capabilities. It is therefore inexorably and most intimately involved with our lives and all spheres of human activity.

Technology is us.

Curiously, this is not the view held by many critics of industrial civilization, who deny the supremely human nature of technology. They see technology as an "autonomous" force with its own dynamics, *separate* from and even *hostile* to people.

They blame technology for what they consider the failings of industrial civilization, instead of blaming a society which, while responsible for the development of technology, is often unwilling to control its application and unable to foresee the consequences of its massive deployment.

If industrial civilization is a true reflection of human nature, the result of what we like to do, experience, and own, if it is the direction in which societies evolve all over the world — then to question industrial civilization is to question human nature itself, a task for moral philosophers to ponder.

The goal of *The Ignorance Explosion* is to identify and analyze the fundamental characteristics and manifestations of technology and industrial civilization, to consider the mechanisms that drive their growth, to explore their ultimate limitations which reflect our own, biological constraints, and to note the trade-offs that adoption of a technology inevitably involves.

The intent is not to oppose or advocate industrial civilization, but merely to explain and to comprehend it better. Nevertheless, undoubtedly there will be those to whom this study will appear biased, an expression of faith in the pursuit of physical sciences and technological rationality.

But this is not so.

The Ignorance Explosion starts with the observation that, paradoxically, in moving from the primitive to the industrial society (or from the natural to the artificial environment), we have merely exchanged one set of difficulties for another: our gains in comprehending the natural world did not equip us to deal with the problems created by industrialization. Indeed, the complexity of industrial society exceeds our ability to manage and control it.

This is the story of the mythical Prometheus, who brought fire and technology to Earth for the benefit of mankind, and Pandora, the woman from whose jar—the so-called "Pandora's box"—evil, toil, and disease escaped to wander among people. Fire and civilization had ended by blighting both people and nature.

Knowledge is the basis of industrial civilization. But to guide the development of industrial civilization beyond "Faustian" objectives, beyond the achievement of technical perfection, economic efficiency, material wealth and creature comforts, wisdom—rather than knowledge—must be found.

This issue is not debated in *The Ignorance Explosion* except to note that traditional ideologies and world-views, which used to be the sources of wisdom, have become irrelevant; they are no longer adequate to cope with the complexities of industrialization. Neither are conventional ethics and politics, which are concerned with the present rather than with the future of mankind and nature.

Can industrial civilization be sustained in the face of increasing population, deterioration of the environment, depletion of resources, erosion of moral standards and highly disparate levels of development (intellectual, social, economic) among societies of the world? These challenges to industrial civilization are a matter of much speculation and uncertainty; they are only peripherally addressed here.

1

The Paradox of Human Progress

WHAT is human progress? By what criteria should it be judged?

Today, progress is universally identified with the growth of material affluence and expansion of social services, with the ability of a society to create knowledge and to innovate through the adoption of the latest state-of-the-art technology in every field. In this prevailing Western view, a high standard of living and efficiency, or more simply, ever-growing productivity, are the hallmarks of progress.

This is a narrow view: it merely reflects the unprecedented development of Western societies since the Industrial Revolution, over a period of hardly a moment's duration in the time scale of human history. It is also a superficial view. While it addresses the most visible manifestations of industrial civilization, it neglects the more subtle, more fundamental aspects of the human condition.

Taking a broader view, progress would be gauged by man's[1] capacity—physical, intellectual, and emotional—to cope with his environment as it evolved from the natural to the artificial.[2] Such examination of progress points to a significant parallel between industrial society and our primitive forebears, and illuminates the essential predicament of humans in the industrial age.

Primitive people had only a very limited understanding of nature. Their ability to exploit and control their surroundings was minimal. Consequently, the primitive environment was a natural one. Unable to influence it, primitive societies adapted to it as best they could. Lacking comprehension of their physical world, primitive men and women turned to the supernatural in an attempt to gain control. Appeal to gods and placation of spirits were the only recourses available to them.

Society, the other component of the primitive environment, was small in size, its members arranged in groups which tended to be closed rather than open, with almost all interpersonal relations being face-to-face (and no impersonal day-to-day contacts), with small units (such as a family or a household) being the basis for economic co-operation and with little occupational specialization. This was a relatively static society which behaved according to a traditional and therefore predictable pattern; there was no need to devise theoretical socio-economic models to understand and forecast its operation. Beyond the level of immediate experience, religion and tradition shaped the primitive's view of the world and its structure.

Progress through several civilizations has brought radical changes to our physical and social environments.

We have gained an understanding of nature, the very knowledge our primitive ancestors lacked. The physical and life sciences have provided us with models which describe our habitat accurately. Through the ingenious application and exploitation of these models we have been able to achieve a significant measure of control over nature and to create a physical environment of our own design. Thus nature's constraints on our condition have gradually been eroded until, in this century, Western societies have all but replaced their natural surroundings with an artificial environment.

The creation of an artificial environment is a fundamental and inescapable consequence of technological development. The output of industry surrounds us with a multitude of artifacts, which extend our physical capability and sensory perception beyond their biological limits. They govern our behaviour by forcing us to accord with the requirements of technologies we rely upon. After some 250 years of intensive industrialization, Western societies live almost totally immersed in and conditioned by the artifacts born of their imagination and insatiable curiosity. What is more, the human quest for knowledge and innovation, for the satisfaction of material needs and creature comforts, has no obvious limits.

Our escape from the natural world has been so complete, we feel a need to recreate it. The best illustration: Disneyland created in 1955 as a "wonderworld" where the artificial has been used to recreate a "natural nature" and even to improve upon it. At Disneyland, the inconvenience of time and distance has been abolished: extinct dinosaurs appear side-by-side with contemporary species from all over the Earth, and are just as real.

Indeed, it may not be long before we will be producing "unnatural nature" and populating the Earth with totally new forms of animal and plant life. In 1988 the first patent for a genetically engineered animal — a "transgenic" mouse — was granted in the United States. In addition, 21 applications for patents on higher life forms, more complex than microorganisms, were pending. The disappearance and appearance of species has been a natural process, now accelerated through man's intervention. The distinction between natural and artificial will progressively be eroded and will eventually lose much of its present significance.

With the development of virtual reality technology,[3] the users experience simulated three-dimensional worlds of sight, sound, motion and, soon, touch and smell, as if they have physically become part of the computer created environment. They can do those things that come naturally — walking, looking, listening — and interact both with the environment and other users. They can also perform feats of fantasy. Liquid crystal screens in a headset, stereophonic sound, a system to track head movements, an electronic glove or joystick to control the action, and a computer make all of this possible.

Before doing things in a world of real artifacts and nature, people can experiment and train in the simulated world of virtual space. Architects can try new building schemes, designers can check out projects, pilots can learn aircraft operations, the military can test new weapons in a battlefield situation. The whole objective of VR is to erase all differences between the real and the simulated, and then to create experiences beyond the reach of the real world.

And even as industrial "progress" brought about a new physical environment, our social environment evolved in parallel. Traditional and relatively static forms of social organization gave way to a highly complex and dynamic industrial society.

But there is a paradox. We are finding that we lack the tools needed to gain an understanding of the environment we ourselves have created. Our ignorance has become apparent on several levels — from the impact of industrialization on the natural environment, to industrial artifacts as elements of the physical environment, to the overall complexity of industrial society.

In short, the knowledge which has allowed us to exploit nature on a grand scale has not been adequate to the task of plotting the course of that exploitation, and its effects on the Earth's ecosystem and its human inhabitants.

Given enough political will, we have proven capable of coping with environmental problems of limited scope, such as the pollution of individual rivers or the damaging impact of specific chemicals on wildlife. In these cases, the physical and life sciences provide us with appropriate and adequate models of nature. But we lack the much more complex, global models of the Earth's ecosystem needed to evaluate the long-term effects of our activities. The problems which arise from the pollution of the Earth's atmosphere illustrate the point.

We know that pollution of the atmosphere with carbon dioxide and other gases impedes the Sun's energy from being re-radiated from the Earth's surface back into space. It is widely held that this phenomenon, known as the *greenhouse effect*, if allowed to run its course, will cause expansion of arid regions and loss of wildlife, melting of the polar ice caps and inundation of coastal cities. But in reality, we are not able to estimate with any certainty the magnitude and the rate of global warming; nor can we determine precisely how the greenhouse effect relates to changes in the Sun's activity and to the vast natural climatic changes which are known to occur in 100,000 year cycles, with warm interglacial periods of some 10,000 years duration. Neither can we assess with any certainty the role of the atmospheric ozone layer and its depletion through chlorofluorocarbon (CFC) pollution.[4]

As for the theory of desertification, which holds that deserts are expanding, it has been questioned following recent studies of Sahel, the drylands on the southern border of the Sahara. Satellite and air observations appear to indicate that the desert boundary did not move steadily south but shifted back and forth in conjunction with rainfall.

As for industrial artifacts, we have specialists or teams of experts who comprehend their design and inner workings. But an average member of our industrial society, although capable of making use of the artifacts that surround him, lacks such comprehension, just as primitive men and women lacked an understanding of the workings of nature. Automobiles, jetliners, satellites, telephones, radios, rockets, televisions, microwave ovens, computers, calculators, cameras, electronic watches, copiers—are all "black boxes" whose contents, the materials they are made of and the processes responsible for their production, are an utter mystery to the vast majority of those who use them.

85 per cent of people in the United States are technologically illiterate

"How does a telephone work? What are DNA and GNP?" These and many other basic science questions are Greek to most Americans, according to a Northern Illinois University poll that says 85 per cent of people in the United States are technologically illiterate.

"Something travels along a wire, but I'm not sure what it is," one respondent said when asked how the telephone works. Another answered: "I can't really say. I dial and it usually works."

Some respondents were sure a molecule was a one-celled animal, while others defined it as a unit of energy or a "very tiny particle of something," said Jon Miller, director of NIU's Public Opinion Laboratory.

Mr. Miller said perhaps the most disturbing finding in his telephone poll of 1,992 people late last year was that recent high school graduates know less about technology than most other adults.

"How can a citizen who does not understand the nature of radiation participate usefully in a discussion of the disposal of nuclear power plants?" he asked. "How can a citizen who does not understand the idea of GNP (gross national product) evaluate the arguments of candidates about the rate of economic growth?"

Over all, the men polled were more technologically literate than the women, Mr. Miller said.

(Associated Press, 18 March 1986)

Today, with the advent of microprocessors, the operational complexity of many consumer products also exceeds their users' ability to efficiently work the electronic gadgetry.[5] As noted by Amy Willard, a Toronto writer who is outwitted by a toaster and an answering machine—:

> All over the place microwaves and VCRs flash 12:00 around the clock—never reaching 12:01. That perpetual midnight represents the scarlet letter of technical ineptitude. Although owned by many, the Very Complicated Recorder or VCR thwarts all but a few. A totally unscientific poll using no technology whatever surveyed 15 people in four major cities. Only 26 per cent—or four of them—could program the machine to perform its intended function: tape a show while doing something else. Not just humanist boobies were confused, a physicist and an engineer admitted to VCR ineptitude. Like Third World jokes about the first family in the village to have TV but no electricity, possession is nine-tenths of the thrill. Although most computerphiles insist on top-of-the-line ware, most use their machines as glorified typewriters. People love what they can't understand. (*The Globe and Mail*, 9 August 1990, A18)

On another and more significant level, the complexity and the dynamic character of our industrial society increasingly exceed our ability to manage and control it. With physical and mental tasks largely performed by machines, our environment is characterized by an ever-increasing volume of data and information. The effect—as demonstrated in Chapter 4—is that the human being of industrial age, overwhelmed by information, is experiencing an "ignorance explosion."

The complexity of the industrial environment reflects the influence of an infinity of factors, all of them more or less interdependent and subject to a high rate of change (on the time scale of the human life span). This accounts for unpredictability of our environment and precludes the development of long-term, multigenerational solutions.

Such difficulties do not arise in the natural environment, nor do they arise in primitive society, which are essentially static or operate on cyclic time, with behaviour conforming to constant laws and the future being largely preordained. The predictable influence of the "invisible hand of nature" has no counterpart in industrial society which—in a free, capitalist economy—is subject to the invisible, and unpredictable, "hand of the market."

Industrial societies have been only marginally successful in tackling socio-economic problems, such as urban crime, homelessness and poverty, economic crises, inflation and unemployment, etc. So-called progress which allowed us to understand and exploit nature did not equip us for dealing with some of the important negative effects of industrialization.

Traditional approaches have been of little help in prescribing remedies for the ills of the industrial age. Ideological platforms, whether of the left, centre, or right, do not provide effective guidance. Similar difficulties seem to beset all industrialized societies, irrespective of the ideological bent of their governments.

Rather than to address the basic causes of undesirable socio-economic phenomena, the response has been to treat the symptoms through the establishment of extensive social safety nets and the application of short-term pragmatic measures.

This is probably the most we can hope for.

The social sciences — sociology, economics, political science, psychology — have not been of much assistance either. They have been useful in analyzing the past rather than in coping with the present and providing guidance for the future.

There have been attempts to imbue the social sciences with the exact, mathematical tools of the physical sciences, but these have not resulted in significant gains. Nor has there been success in the oft-repeated attempts to construct mathematical models of our complex socio-economic systems. The dream of Enlightment to restore man to an earthly paradise through great miracles of applied science, was reborn in the 1960s as the dream of overcoming social ills through "technology fixes." With "goal directed" research and a comprehensive "systems approach" — the techniques so successful in making the atomic bomb and taking man to the Moon — optimum solutions would ultimately be found.

Today, such views are generally recognized as naïve and simplistic. But it is not generally realized that a more profound truth is at work here: that in moving from the natural environment to the artificial, from the primitive to the industrial, we have merely exchanged one set of intractable difficulties for another. And we must ask the question: is this progress?

Consider it: just as primitive man lacked models of his world, so now industrial man lacks models of his. Despite the ever increasing sophistication of our knowledge in the physical sciences, we have no global models of physical environment that are adequate to evaluate the long-term impacts of industrialization. And in the social sciences precision eludes us. We have repeatedly attempted, and repeatedly failed, to describe and predict our world's behaviour in economic, political, social, and psychological terms. There is no counterpart to mathematics, physics, chemistry, and biology in the realm of social sciences.

So far, the consequences of this reality have been much less serious for humans in the industrial age than they were for our primitive ancestors. But potentially, the opposite is true.

Until now, industrial development has, for the most part, provided benefits. It has eliminated sweat and toil from human labour; it has reduced work and increased leisure; it has generally freed us from the physical struggle for survival and enabled us to evade the dangers that are inexorably a part of nature. Science and technology have increasingly shielded us from the extremes of weather, sickness and famine. Our advances in coping with the adversities of the natural environment have been truly remarkable, and these advances can be expected to continue as our understanding of the physical world deepens and broadens.

Some analysts, impressed by such spectacular progress, have predicted the emergence of a golden age of economic plenitude and idle luxury. As all utopias, this one is static and incompatible with change, which puts it at odds with the very essence of an industrial society. A more probable scenario is that our growing preoccupation with the problems created by high automation and productivity will prevent the arrival of idle luxury.

Moreover, at least potentially, we face a much greater danger than our primitive ancestors ever faced. It was a danger recognized as early as 1930 by Sigmund Freud, who wrote in *Civilization and its Discontents*:

> Men have gained control over the forces of nature to such an extent that . . . they would have no difficulty in exterminating each other to the last man. They know this, and hence comes a large part of their current unrest, their unhappiness and their mood of anxiety."

Indeed, the outcome of our exploitation and manipulation of nature may exceed by far any natural disasters primitive society had to cope with. Thanks to the spectacular achievements of science and technology, we have somehow gained the ability to destroy our environment but not to manage it.

In this century, humans acquired for the first time the capability of waging environmental warfare on a global scale. The technology of modern weapons — of nuclear explosives and long-range aerospace delivery systems — makes it possible to destroy life altogether and condemn the planet to a "nuclear winter." Chemical and biological warfare could have equally devastating effects on a global scale.

But let us assume for the moment that Western civilization will not vanish in a nuclear holocaust. If not, it is quite possible that the next step could be the creation — with the help of genetic engineering — of a superhuman. It would be presumptuous of merely human designers to predict the nature of such a species, but, as discussed in Chapter 4, it is nevertheless unlikely that superhumans would be more successful in coping with their environment than we have been in coping with ours.

Human progress, when viewed in the broad perspective adopted here, loses some of its lustre. In some important respects, we appear to be just as helpless as our primitive ancestors. Progress has made the environment of industrial humans radically different from the environment of primitive societies, but paradoxically, our respective relationships with our environments are fundamentally the same. Indeed, the condition of industrial men and women closely parallels that of their primitive predecessors: despite progress, we remain severely limited in comprehending our world.

As suggested in Chapter 4, this was to be expected. Despite progress, the complexity of the human environment has always, and will always, overwhelm the intellectual prowess of men and women.

It is interesting to note that the predicament of industrial humans outlined here closely parallels the biblical explanation of man's downfall from the innocence and state of bliss in which he was created.

Not content with obedience to the will of God, Adam and Eve broke the only restraint placed upon them in the garden of Eden and ate the fruit of the tree of knowledge of good and evil. This sinful act brought punishment from God: Adam and Eve lost immortality and had to till the earth which was henceforth cursed. The knowledge, which would bring man to an equality with God, brought only the discovery that man was naked.

For us, knowledge has created problems which we find difficult to tackle, and has opened up the possibility of a global calamity comparable in its consequences to man's expulsion from the garden of Eden.

We are the only animal capable of destroying our planet; are we capable of saving it?

Notes

1. In this work "man" is often used in its traditional sense as referring to all people; the context makes this clear.
2. The generally accepted usage of "artificial" for "man-made" is inaccurate and unfortunate. To consider as "natural" only what is devoid of human intervention is to exclude man from nature and to view as unnatural the results of activities which are the very expressions of his nature.
3. Virtual reality technology grew out of aircraft flight simulators and head-mounted display systems developed for the U.S. military.
4. Heavy depletion of the ozone layer and dangerous levels of ultraviolet radiation, predicted for the summer of 1992, did not materialize. Recent (1993) research by the U.S. National Aeronautics and Space Administration indicated that atmospheric concentrations of CFCs will peak before the end of this century and the ozone layer will slowly recover over the next 50 to one hundred years.
5. Incidentally, one should note that it is often the instruction manual that causes the difficulty. The following instruction for tuning a VCR is typical:

   > After pre-tuning, if you wish to change the real channel number to correspond to the actual pre-tuned station, press the CH NO. SET button after calling up the corresponding channel position number on the display and enter the desired channel number using the READ OUT buttons ("10" and "1"). The "1" button changes the figures of the units digit: numerals 0 to 9 are available. The "10" button changes the figure of the tens digit: blank, numerals 1 to 9, U and C are available. (*Business Week*, 29 April 1991)

   Evidently, such instructions are written by designers with no concern whatsoever for the users.

2

Humanities, Social and Physical Sciences: The Two Cultures

(David Austin, *New Scientist,* 11 December 1986)

Any cocktail party will provide you with evidence of the anti-science culture: you only have to admit to being a scientist and the conversation is very likely to freeze. Even now, to be scientifically illiterate is socially quite acceptable; to admit ignorance of poetry and literature is to risk ostracism. (John Holman, *New Scientist,* 12 November 1987)

The Cultural Gap

C.P. Snow touched a sensitive chord when he gave the Rede lecture at Cambridge University in 1959 on *The Two Cultures and the Scientific Revolution*. First published in 1959 and, after many reprints, issued in 1964 in an expanded version as *The Two Cultures and a Second Look* (Snow 1969), Snow's analysis met with a flood of comment and criticism.

The issue of the two cultures, as seen by Snow, concerns the communication gap between scientific and non-scientific cultures.[1]

> In our society (that is, advanced Western society) we have lost even the pretence of a common culture. Persons educated with the greatest intensity we know can no longer communicate with each other on the plane of their major intellectual concern. This is serious for our creative, intellectual and, above all, our normal life. It is leading us to interpret the past wrongly, to misjudge the present, and to deny our hopes of the future. It is making it difficult or impossible for us to take good action. (Snow 1969, 60)
>
> It is dangerous to have two cultures which can't or don't communicate. In a time when science is determining much of our destiny, that is, whether we live or die, it is dangerous in the most practical terms. Scientists can give bad advice and decision-makers can't know whether it is good or bad.[2] On the other hand, scientists in a divided culture provide a knowledge of some potentialities which is theirs alone. All this makes the political process more complex, and in some ways more dangerous, than we should be prepared to tolerate for long, either for the purposes of avoiding disasters, or for fulfilling — what is waiting as a challenge to our conscience and goodwill — a definable social hope. (Snow 1969, 98; ©1959, 1964, Cambridge University Press)

The same concern was expressed by S. Andreski in his critique of social sciences. Although theology, classics and metaphysics have been displaced by natural sciences and

> abandoned as a tool for controlling nature, incantations remain more effective for manipulating crowds than logical arguments, so that in the conduct of human affairs sorcery continues to be stronger than science. (Andreski 1974, 98–99)

Since Snow's seminal lecture the cultural gap has been narrowed but not eliminated. The scientists and engineers have become much more aware and concerned with the consequences — physical as well as social — of the fruits of their labours, while the non-scientists have developed considerable interest and appreciation of the social and environmental impacts of science and technology.

Scientists' concern with the morality and social value of their activities gave rise to organizations (such as Scientists Against Nuclear Arms or Physicians for Social Responsibility) which advocate social and ethical responsibility of professionals. The literature on ethical, socio-political, economic, and environmental aspects of science and technology has proliferated, including the appearance of several multidisciplinary journals. All levels of government became concerned with the environmental issues, and bureaucracies were established to monitor and control environmental quality and impact of technology. In the academia, interdisciplinary courses and symposia on such topics as "science and society," "technology, society and the environment," "science and values" have been set up in an attempt to expose students and faculty of all disciplines to the multifaceted impacts of science, technology, and industrialization.

Nevertheless, in spite of a considerably broader awareness of science and technology by both cultures, the cultural gap — as perceived by C.P. Snow — is likely to persist. As the pace of scientific and industrial development is accelerating and specialization augmenting, the bridging of "the gulf of mutual incomprehension" which separates the physical scientists and engineers from the literary intellectuals who "represent, vocalise and to some extent shape and predict the mood of the non-scientific culture" — continues to be difficult (Snow 1969, 4, 61).

A controversy which shook Princeton's Institute for Advanced Study in 1973 provides an excellent and unambiguous illustration of the problem of the two cultures (Shenker 1973). The nomination of sociologist R.N. Bellah to become a permanent professor at the Institute polarized the faculty. The split led Professor Bellah to withdraw his acceptance of the appointment.

While prominent sociologists judged Professor Bellah to be "one of the leading historical sociologists in the country, if not the leading one," "a man of extraordinary depth and scholarship," a famous mathematician considered Professor Bellah's publications to be "worthless" and reading them "an utter waste of time." A distinguished logician questioned "the truth . . . of Professor Bellah's 'sociological assertions.' "

In an incisive comment on the Princeton dispute, Professor Washburne, a sociologist at Rutgers University, noted that mathematicians never have to suffer the indignity of having their works judged by sociologists, since sociologists admit that they are not competent to do so. However, mathematicians and logicians seem to assume that the problems of sociology are so simple that they are capable of judging the work of sociologists. In fact, sociology is an incredibly difficult field. If a sociologist's work is good, it is controversial (Washburne 1973).

The Issue of Accessibility

The Princeton controversy brings out a number of important aspects which separate the two cultures. The difference in their relative accessibility is one of them.

Mathematics and physical sciences are largely inaccessible to members of the non-scientific culture. These disciplines require a working knowledge of mathematics beyond the elementary and familiarity with highly specialized terminology; without mathematics, a solid background in physical sciences cannot be acquired. The "language" of physical sciences must be learned as part of formal education; to acquire it later is for most people a prohibitive effort. It follows that the scientific culture is effectively closed to those who have not been raised in it, i.e., to humanists and social scientists.

The opposite is not true: members of the scientific culture face no insurmountable obstacles should they wish to gain knowledge of social sciences or humanities. Ordinary, relatively unspecialized language is the medium of non-scientific culture; at worst, the newcomer can be discouraged, but not stopped, when he encounters excessive doses of jargon which is supposed to bestow a scientific aura on concepts more clearly expressed using every day vocabulary. An engineer or a biologist, should he so desire, can become well versed in literature, history, films, or theatre, or can educate himself — to the extent of his interest — in economics or sociology.

Indeed, it is no accident that the issue of the two cultures was broached by C.P. Snow, by training — a scientist, by vocation — a writer. As a physical scientist he could appreciate the cultural gap and could bridge it — and feel comfortable in doing so.

It is among the physical scientists and mathematicians that one finds individuals whose interests range from sciences to humanities, from physics and astronomy to music and literature. Albert Einstein — like many mathematicians — was an accomplished violinist and wrote on the music of Mozart. Aleksandr Borodin, the nineteenth century Russian composer, taught chemistry for a living. Aleksandr Solzhenitsyn taught physics and chemistry before becoming famous as a writer (Dunbar 1988).

The difference in the accessibility of the two cultures is reflected in the qualifications required to evaluate their respective achievements.

To pass judgment on scholarly works in mathematics, physical sciences and engineering, one must be working in the same field; a critic of science or technology must necessarily also be a practising scientist or engineer. While the same may hold, albeit to a lesser extent, in the field of social sciences, it does not apply to humanities and arts. Reviewers of fiction, plays, and poetry need not be prominent authors, playwrights, and poets. Being a dance critic is not contingent on being a dancer; art, film, music, and theatre critics are seldom painters, movie directors, composers, musicians, and actors. To evaluate their endeavours one need not be one of them; being a connoisseur of their productions is all that is required. But there can be no professional critics of physical sciences; only dilettantes can attempt to fill this role, and must necessarily fail.

Technologically challenged

My father you see really needs me . . . I . . . have to explain why TV stations come in through a cable converter on different numbers than those listed in the *TV Guide.* I help adjust the volume during a baseball game so that he can sleep comfortably. I load and program the VCR. I get to show him again and again what it means to have an auto-reverse tape deck in your car. Also I can explain why it does matter which way the print faces when you send a fax.

My father is technologically challenged.

He types with two fingers and he types hard and a period ends the sentence best when it authoritatively punches the page. A few years ago a very important day passed for my father although it was unmourned, even unnoticed by the rest of the world. Olivetti put together its last manual typewriter. My dad had to go electric. These new machines aren't built to withstand his heavy touch. The letters that were stencilled onto the keyboard wore off completely within a week. So every morning he would write them in himself with a supposedly indelible marker. Looking at his inky fingers one afternoon I had to ask him a question. "Dad," I said "don't you know where the letters are by now?"

(Jacob Richler speaking about his father at the "Roast of Mordecai Richler," held at the Carleton-Ritz Hotel in Montreal on 9 May 1993 and broadcast on the CBC Radio *Morningside* program on 12 May 1993)

The Psychological Gap

Perhaps the most fundamental aspect of the cultural gap, and also the one most difficult to bridge, is the basic difference in the psychological makeup of members of the two groups, their temperaments, interests, and perceptions of values.

As noted by Snow, scientists and engineers are concerned with the physical world and practical solutions, i.e., with "things"; they are activist, have a "can do" mentality, are good planners and hard workers, think that most problems can be solved, are concerned with innovation, and "have future in their bones."

At the other end of the spectrum, humanists are concerned with people as individuals, operate in a reflective, rather than activist, mode, are interested in emotions, feelings, and symbols rather than in a rational and logical approach, in the theory rather than practice, have a tentative attitude to evaluation of problems, are not affected by practical constraints (such as deadlines), have no interest in technology or physical work, are pre-occupied mostly with the past, and "wish future didn't exist."

Social scientists belong between the two extremes: they are interested in society and people "as things" and attempt to apply scientific and quantitative methods to phenomena related to people. Nevertheless, as noted below, social sciences have, in fact, little in common with the physical sciences.

Short of resorting to such drastic means as genetic engineering, there can be little hope of narrowing the "psychological gap" between the two cultures. Other causes of the cultural gap, as suggested by several authors including C.P. Snow, could be influenced by a reformed and innovative education, but the extent to which education could unify the two cultures seems limited.

Traditional Culture and Education

The appearance of the cultural gap is a relatively recent development in Western civilization; it reflects the rapid growth of physical sciences and industrialization since the eighteenth century. However, our education still reflects a cultural tradition that emphasizes political history and literature rather than the history of science and technology, the developments largely responsible for the present condition of Western society. As Lynn White Jr. noted, "the better we are educated, the more we are fitted to live in a world that no longer exists" (White 1968, 135).

To test the general awareness of significant scientific and technological developments as compared to knowledge of important events in the realms of politics and economics, a quiz was conducted among students and faculty who participated in an interdisciplinary course on "Introduction to the study of major problems of industrial society," first offered at Carleton University in Ottawa in 1971–72 (Lukasiewicz 1972). The following were some of the typical questions (here listed with answers) tackled by 110 students from Arts, Engineering, and Science faculties.

1. An invention which was perfected by 1450 played a decisive role in the development of an important movement in Europe in the 16th century. Name the invention and its inventor, the movement and its originator.

   Movable type — *Johann Gutenberg (c. 1398–1468)*
   Reformation (1517–) — *Martin Luther (c. 1483–1546)*

2. The term REVOLUTION is used to describe periods of vigorous, often violent change. Name revolutions which are usually associated with the following dates:

1775–1781	*American*
1780–1795	*French*
1750–1830	*Industrial*
1917–1921	*Russian*
1966–1971	*Great Proletarian Cultural Revolution, China*

3. Name and comment briefly on important events in the realms of politics, physics and technology which are associated with the year 1939.

Politics:	*Outbreak of WW II (1 September 1939)*
Physics:	*Publication of discovery of uranium fission, which led to the development of nuclear weapons and energy.*
Technology:	*First flight of a jet-propelled aircraft (on 27 August 1939 in Germany).*

4. Name and comment briefly on important events in the realms of politics, economics and technology which are associated with the year 1776.

Politics:	*Declaration of Independence (separation of 13 colonies from Great Britain, approved on 4 July 1776 by the Second Continental Congress in Philadelphia).*
Economics:	*Publication of "The Wealth of Nations" by Adam Smith: advocated laissez-faire, free competition economy and freedom from government interference; recognized benefits of division of labour.*
Technology:	*James Watt (1736–1819) develops improved steam engine which becomes the main prime mover of industry.*

5. Many years before 1861, an invention was made which, by stimulating the expansion of a declining economy and social system, contributed to bringing on of a major social and military conflict. Name the invention and describe briefly its purpose, state its date and the name of its inventor, and the conflict. Can you recall another important technological development due to the same man?

Invention:	*Cotton gin.*
Purpose:	*Separation of seeds of short staple, green cotton (which grew in the Southern U.S.) from lint.*
Date:	*1793*
Inventor:	*Eli Whitney (1765–1825)*
Conflict:	*American Civil War and slavery.*
Development:	*American system of manufacture (1798: early large scale application of mass production; contract for 10,000 muskets).*

An analysis of the response to the quiz indicated

- a relatively high degree of awareness of political and recent technological developments among students of all faculties;
- a negligible awareness (among all students) of early technological and scientific developments;

- a low awareness of social impact of technology among Engineering and Science students, and a much higher awareness (50%) among Arts students;
- a very limited knowledge of basic analytic models (exponential and logistic functions) not only among Arts students, but surprisingly also among Engineering and Science students;
- similar results were recorded for the small sample (12) of the faculty who participated in the quiz.

Knowledge of physical sciences, engineering and technology, or merely of their history, is still not considered a "cultural literacy" prerequisite for Americans. Among some five thousand terms that, according to Professor E.D. Hirsch, Jr., "every literate American should know," the great majority refer to literature, art, political history, and geography, and only very few to physical sciences, engineering and technology (Hirsch 1987). Condom, jet engine, Kleenex, Kodak, microwave, microprocessor, rocket, VCR, video, word processor and xerox are not on the literacy list; neither are the names of such giants of science and technology as Carnot, Diesel, Fourier, Leibniz, Mach, Marconi, Otto, Roentgen, Stephenson, von Ohain, Watt, and Whittle.

The tremendous emphasis on traditional culture is also evident in *The Dictionary of Cultural Literacy* (Hirsch et al. 1988), a companion volume by Hirsch (English scholar), J. Kett (historian) and J. Trefil (physicist). Of the 536 pages of entries, 80 percent are devoted to humanities (61 percent) and social sciences (19 percent); technology occupies a mere 2.4 percent! As compiled, the dictionary is a monument to cultural illiteracy in the industrial age.

But, in any event, given our finite intellectual capacity, there is no possibility of ever producing, irrespective of the system of education, broad generalists who could straddle most of the territory occupied by the two cultures. A Renaissance man, who knew most what has been known in his time, is today an extinct species. As a limited but more practical approach, it has been frequently suggested that education in each culture should provide a significant degree of literacy in the other. For this to occur, the public must recognize that mathematics, science, and technology belong in the core of a liberal education, just as the study of humanities and of the socio-economic impact of science and technology should form part of science and engineering curricula.

The Inescapable Predicament of Social Sciences

The attitudes of physical scientists and non-scientists to each other and to their respective fields of endeavour, attitudes which figured prominently in the Princeton controversy, represent yet another dimension of the cultural gap. Inaccessible and highly specific, the physical sciences are regarded by the traditional culture as "hard" and difficult; conversely, the physical scientists view the humanities and social sciences as descriptive and speculative, and therefore "soft" and easy. These popular and generally accepted perceptions are highly misleading; in fact, the opposite holds true.

Two fundamental difficulties confront the social sciences.

The first one concerns human actions which, unlike physical phenomena, are not governed by immutable laws and are not like stimulus-response behaviour of animals.

Attempts by "scientists of the mind" — psychologists and psychiatrists — in predicting human behaviour have not been successful. A recent study (Faust and Ziskin 1988) has found a poor match between predicted and actual behaviour. In screening for brain damage, "professional psychologists performed no better than office secretaries"; in predicting violence, the experts "are wrong at least twice as often as they are correct ... the amount of clinical training and experience are unrelated to judgemental accuracy."

Our religion, our views on sex, ethics, or economics do not reflect logical and rational thought. The behaviour of people reflects perceptions, values, and beliefs that vary between individuals, nationalities, cultures, and civilizations, and therefore cannot be accounted for by any general scientific theory. Just as the society they study, the social scientists are themselves subject to the same influences and limitations. Their perception of society cannot be objective but must necessarily be biased, reflecting their own beliefs and ideological inclinations.[3]

Sociology at cross-purposes

The fundamental contradiction of the science of sociology is captured in this definition which sees sociology as "a misguided attempt to provide rational explanation for irrational motives."

Social science turns to mud pies

Psychologists Sheri Berenbaum of Chicago's University Health Sciences and Melissa Hines of the University of California at Los Angeles School of Medicine have studied the toy play of children afflicted with congenital adrenal hyperplasia (CAH). This rare genetic disorder results in production of abnormally high levels of the masculinizing hormone androgen.

Once the condition is diagnosed after birth, doctors give corticosteroids to normalize hormone levels. Previous studies have suggested that nonetheless CAH girls are more aggressive and tomboyish and prefer boys' toys over girls' toys.

Now the wise child among you might exclaim, "But what about guns?" Amazingly, they weren't included among the traditional boys' toys because they were (trite but true) politically incorrect. "I didn't include guns partly because of my own political reasons," admits Dr. Berenbaum. "I don't like guns."

And all the laboriously obtained, objective social science turns to mud pies when it comes to explaining what any given human will do. "On average" hides humanness. Five of the CAH girls basically ignored boys' toys entirely. Two of the control girls spent nearly the entire 10 minutes being toy-boyish. Six of the boys spent most of their time playing with girls' toys. Three of the CAH girls spent almost all their time playing with girl things. Half of the control-group girls scorned girls' toys.

So the truth may be Rabelais' anarchic political message: *"Fay ce que vouldras."* To accommodate our varying male-female selves society should allow as much and forbid as little as possible. Do what you like.

(*Psychological Science*, May 1992, as reported by Stephen Strauss, *The Globe and Mail*, 27 June 1992)

The second basic difficulty of the social sciences is the same one that limits our ability to create artificial intelligence through application of computers. As noted in Chapter 4, this would require "man to lift himself by his own bootstraps, using the mind to understand the mind," a feat, explains Andreski, impossible to perform.

> Understanding is sometimes described as the building of models of external reality in one's brain. This should not, perhaps, be taken too literally; but if we accept the view that conceptual understanding has some physiological counterpart, and bear in mind that the number of configurations of neurons and synapses is finite, though astronomically large, then it follows that whereas the mind might be able to make a perfect model of things simpler than itself, its ability to work out models of objects which are equally or more complex must be subject to severe limitations. It seems impossible therefore that our understanding of other minds and their aggregates could ever reach the degree of adequacy of physics and chemistry, made possible by the simplicity and invariance of their objects.

> Reasoning along these lines, we might also infer that it is logically impossible that anyone could ever acquire an understanding of his own mind which would enable him to make exact predictions about its future states; because, even apart from the question of the knowledge of the future impacts of the environment, the mind would have to contain a model as complex as itself as well as an agency which would draw inferences. In other words, such a faculty would require a part to be as large as the whole and still remain only a part. (Andreski 1974, 18, 25)

The inability of "a system to explain itself" is a very basic limitation which inevitably denies the social sciences the possibility of ever attaining the successes that have been the realm of the physical sciences. But even beyond the two fundamental constraints, the social sciences are subject to a host of related difficulties not encountered in the physical field. Extensively examined by S. Andreski (1974), they are here briefly reviewed.

Exact science of society can never be developed because some kinds of information cannot be obtained; behaviour involving deliberate secrecy or punishable and shameful acts belongs in this category. Thus the extent of corruption, or the amount of tax evasion, or the degree of support that a tyrant enjoys — are intrinsically immensurable.

Because obtaining quantitative data is often difficult or impossible in the realm of social sciences, the information that can be measured may be perceived as more important than that which cannot. (Production and consumption can be measured, but how does one quantify aesthetic and moral values?) Should this happen, quantified data may not give the answer to the most obvious questions. This has been particularly evident in the field of economics.

Labour, land, and capital, which can be easily defined and measured, have been considered to be the major "factors of production"; invention and innovation, not amenable to quantification or prediction but nevertheless the fundamental driving forces of economic growth and productivity, have been treated by economists as "events transpiring inside a black box," to quote Nathan Rosenberg (1982, vii). It is only in the second half of this century that innovation gained recognition as the key factor in economic growth, as opposed to capital investment and labour. Demonstrating that technical change is central to productivity growth won Robert Solow the Nobel prize in economics in 1987 (Marshall 1987; Thurow 1987).

Even more basic than invention and innovation, education as a process necessary to acquire and produce knowledge is yet another intangible and unaccounted for factor of paramount economic importance. Benjamin Franklin, the farsighted American statesman and scientist, noted over two centuries ago that "an investment in knowledge pays the best interest" (Anderson 1989).

The higher the educational level of society, the more inventive and innovative it is likely to be, and the more capable of creating wealth and new jobs. In the United States, about 45 percent of the job growth between 1980 and 1986 was in professional and managerial occupations, and almost 50 percent of the new jobs created between 1983 and 1986 went to people with at least three years of college education (OTA 1988).

Another recent study (Sharp 1985) has shown that where educational level of the work force is high, as in Sweden, Denmark, Switzerland, and the Netherlands, the adaptability is good and advantage can readily be taken of new opportunities; where it is particularly low, as in Great Britain, opportunities are lost through change coming too slowly.

Political Science: the Sovietological profession

How eerily silent in the face of this catastrophe [the collapse of the Soviet Union in 1991] is the Sovietological community which for years has been assuring the world that the Soviet Union and the Communist bloc were solid and popular and, for all their obvious shortcomings, able to teach us a thing or two about social justice. What thoughts cross the minds of the "revisionist" historians who depicted Lenin as the leader of a genuine popular revolution and the father of the country, as they look at photographs showing his monuments razed by furious, truly revolutionary crowds and his severed head dangling from the wrecker's noose?

An analysis of the profession's failure to foresee anything that has happened deserves to be undertaken not only to shame it, but to learn from its mistakes. These had several causes. One was intellectual vanity. With the overwhelming majority of ordinary Americans hostile to Communism, the expert was inclined to take a contrarian view, to argue that reality was different or, at the very least, more "complex." For what would be the point of being an expert if one knew no more than the untutored masses?

To qualify as an expert one also had to travel to the Communist bloc, and this required the kind of access which totalitarian governments granted only foreigners whom it [sic] considered friendly. I heard not a few Sovietologists speak privately of the Soviet regime in terms of utmost contempt, but they never dared to do so in public. By their public silence they became accomplices in the Big Lie.

But the failure of the profession was also and perhaps most of all due to a "social-scientese" methodology which ignored history, literature, witnesses' testimonies, and all else that could not be explained in sociological jargon and buttressed with statistics. Playing scientists, they developed "models" which assumed that all states and societies were fundamentally identical because they were called upon to perform identical functions. Being imponderable and hence unquantifiable, the peculiar features of national culture escaped their attention. So, too, did the moral dimension of human activity inasmuch as scientific inquiry was expected to be "value-free." Human suffering was an irrelevant factor.

The fate of the Sovietological profession, which constitutes only one regiment in the army of social "scientists," should serve as a warning. Science in our day enjoys well-deserved prestige, but its methods cannot be applied to human affairs. Unlike atoms and cells, human beings have values and goals which science is incapable of analyzing because they never stand still and never recur. They are, therefore, the proper province of the humanities, and best studied by the methods of history, literature, and the arts.

They are at sea now, the Soviet experts, confounded by irrefutable realities and abandoned by a regime whose claims to being progressive and democratic they once helped to bolster. They remind one of the 18th-century French adventurer, a contemporary of Dr. Johnson's, George Psalmanazar. Claiming to come from Formosa, he devised a Formosan alphabet and language, an accomplishment that earned him an invitation to Oxford. Psalmanazar also wrote historical and geographical descriptions of his alleged homeland. They became international best-sellers even though everything in them was invented. A group of young Oxford missionaries trained on his manuals travelled to Formosa only to discover that nothing they had been taught bore any relationship to reality. A good part of the "Sovietological" literature of the past 30 years has served us a Psalmanazarian Soviet Union: not totally invented, perhaps, but sufficiently deceptive to cause widespread disbelief once the true state of affairs was revealed.

And so, one fine day, the Communist regimes vanished in a puff of smoke. And what remained? A tormented people who the Sovietologists had not even noticed were there.

(Richard Pipes: "Russia's Chance," *Commentary*, March 1992, 32–33; reprinted by permission; all rights reserved.)

The constraints on information accessible to social sciences have sometimes caused the use of empirical data of inadequate accuracy in sophisticated mathematical models. Such models have often been endowed with exactitude and significance which exceed by far the limitations of the data.

This situation, recently examined by Kolata (1986), has drawn severe criticism from Wassily Leontief, Nobel laureate in economics.

> Not having been subjected from the outset to the harsh discipline of systematic fact-finding, traditionally imposed on and accepted by their colleagues in the natural and historical sciences, economists developed a nearly irresistible predilection for deductive reasoning. As a matter of fact,

many entered the field after specializing in pure or applied mathematics. Page after page of professional economic journals are filled with mathematical formulas leading the reader from sets of more or less plausible but entirely arbitrary assumptions to precisely stated but irrelevant theoretical conclusions.

Year after year economic theorists continue to produce scores of mathematical models and to explore in great detail their formal properties; and the econometricians fit algebraic functions of all possible shapes to essentially the same sets of data without being able to advance, in any perceptible way, a systematic understanding of the structure and the operations of a real economic system. (Leontief 1982, ©AAAS)

Leontief's views were corroborated by Richard A. Staley who wrote:

> Having trained as both engineer (mechanical) and economist, I am particularly upset by the lack of substance and precision in much current economic literature. I once described this phenomenon to some graduate students as a procedure of piling estimate on top of conjecture, declaring the whole to be an axiom based on the author's reputation, and then using this "base" to launch still further estimates and pseudo-precise conjectures. A harsh appraisal but I fear not an inaccurate one. (Staley 1982, ©AAAS)

Yet another fundamental difficulty faced by the social sciences is the dynamic character of the phenomena they address—as opposed to the physical sciences, which deal with a permanent system, a system not only measurable but also verifiable and predictable, and therefore amenable to highly accurate observation. This is not true of people and society: their behaviour does not provide exact recurrences and does not allow controlled experimentation.

Clearly, it is not possible to apply policies based on different social and economic theories to identical and isolated groups of people, yet this is precisely what would be required to determine the correctness of such theories. Given the dynamic nature of society, particularly of modern industrial society, it is not even possible to repeat a social experiment under identical conditions. The possibility of verification denied, the correctness or falsehood of a theory cannot be easily proven.

The fact that human beings react to predictions of events is another, and a most fundamental obstacle to the development of an exact science of society. Since groups and individuals may be deliberately supporting or opposing such predictions, the effect of predictions on future events may be self-negating or self-fulfilling.

Should an undesirable development be predicted, steps will be taken to prevent its occurrence. Should a socio-economic theory or ideology be advocated, its supporters will do everything possible to make it come true, whereas its opponents will make every effort to prevent its fulfilment. In such circumstances, there can be no objective proof of the correctness of a socio-economic theory, but only a historical assessment of its success or failure. The story of Marxism is a case in point: it illustrates well the continuing attempts to fulfil or negate its predictions.

The operation of a stock exchange in a capitalist free market economy is perhaps the ultimate illustration of the fundamental limitations of social sciences.

The stock exchange provides a mechanism through which the worth of business enterprises (in terms of current value and future potential) as perceived by the society is established. Clearly, were it possible on the basis of a socio-economic theory to predict, with a fair degree of accuracy, the market value of the shares, there would be no stock exchange since it could not serve a useful purpose.

Indeed, although economic forecasting is a major activity in the industrialized West, its track record hasn't been good. Examination of material published in the Canadian daily *The Globe and Mail* (Sheppard 1990) shows that over a period of 13 years (1978 to 1990), economists as a group have been surprised about something on at least 257 occasions, or almost twice a month. It has been said that "economists exist to make weather forecasters look good."

With exactness, verifiability, and predictability being largely out of reach of the social sciences, it has been possible to maintain unreasonable or even absurd views with impunity, to supply information that the recipient wants to hear and to seek a scientific aura through verbal innovation which amounts to no more than to the deliberate use of an obscure jargon.

That social sciences face such perils was already recognized three centuries ago by Isaac Newton, who wrote in the introduction to *Principia* (first published in 1687): "Nature is pleased with simplicity and effects, not the pomp of superfluous causes." H.G. Wells (1984) expanded on this fundamental characteristic of natural sciences.

> Scientific truth is the remotest of mistresses, she hides in strange places, she is attained by tortuous and laborious roads, but she is always there! Win to her and she will not fail you; she is yours and mankind's for ever . . . You cannot change her by advertisement or clamour, nor stifle her in vulgarities. Things grow under your hands when you serve her, things that are permanent as nothing else is permanent in the whole life of man. That, I think, is the peculiar satisfaction of science and its enduring reward.

The late Joan Robinson (1973), a renowned Cambridge economist, noted that "in the natural sciences, honesty is the best policy because if you start fudging you will very soon be caught out. Unfortunately, this is not the case in the social sciences . . . "

In engineering and technology, fudging may have tragic consequences. It was ultimately responsible for the explosion of NASA's space shuttle *Challenger* in January 1986, the death of seven astronauts and serious disruption of the U.S. space program. "For a successful technology, reality must take precedence over public relations, for nature cannot be fooled," wrote the late Richard Feynman, a highly esteemed physicist, in the final report of the inquiry into the *Challenger* disaster (Lewis 1988).

With verification difficult or impossible, the desire to please or to follow the fashion may exert a strong influence on the practitioners of social sciences. Maximization of mental comfort — as opposed to mental effort — through believing what we would like to be true is often the guiding principle. Unlike nature, people and societies can be brainwashed and manipulated.

The use of pseudo-scientific instead of ordinary vocabulary serves two purposes: it invokes the magic of science to hide the lack of substance, and facilitates advancing arguments and ideas by expressing them so that they cannot be clearly understood. Impressive sounding terms are used instead of common ones. And so unintended effect becomes a "latent function," incentive is a "positive reinforcer," deterrent is an "aversive reinforcer," teacher is a "facilitator of learning," useful is "functional," real reason is "manifest," and assassination team, a "health alteration committee." Some other gems of obfuscatory jargon are reproduced in the Appendix to this chapter.

Advancement of science?

"Sexual and reproductive behaviour among a sample of female drunk drivers" — A paper presented in February 1993 in Boston at the meeting of the American Association for the Advancement of Science.

It is not surprising that, given the difficulties, social sciences have been sometimes concerned with investigations of straightforward phenomena only to produce common sense and obvious, albeit well documented, answers. For example, a recent study of migration from Mexico to the United States (Massey and Espana 1987a, 1987b) has discovered that

> after pioneering migrants settle in a new place, friends and relatives from the home community feel encouraged to follow; for each new wave of migrants, the process becomes simpler because of the assistance ...

> received from the earlier migrants. Surveys ... indicated that, in those households or communities that had ties to [migrant] networks, the likelihood was greatest that other members of the community would migrate. Eventually the process develops an internal momentum and is self-perpetuating ...

In 1983, a psychologist at the University of Windsor (Ontario) found from a survey of two thousand grade 10 and 12 students that students in single-sex schools were much more likely to believe that getting high grades was an important way of achieving status among their schoolmates.

Students from coed schools, on the other hand, placed more emphasis on good looks, good personality, and having money as routes to status (*G&M* 1983).

Could anyone expect these investigations to produce different answers?

In search of wisdom

A Michigan judge ordered the University of Michigan yesterday to pay $1.2 million in damages to a scientist after a jury found that her supervisor had stolen credit for her research and that the university had failed to investigate properly.

The suit was brought by Dr. Carolyn Phinney, a research psychologist who had worked on how to define wisdom and measure its accumulation as people age. She conducted interviews in which she asked subjects whom they considered wise and what qualified those on their lists. She found that wise people are commonly identified as those who avoid unwise and destructive actions.

(P. Hilts, *The New York Times*, 22 September 1993. Copyright ©1993 by the New York Times Co. Reprinted by permission.)

The Ineradicable Gap

The picture which emerges from the foregoing *tour d'horizon* of the two cultures is not encouraging: only limited progress in bridging of the culture gap can be envisaged. The scientific culture is largely, and inevitably, inaccessible to the non-scientific one, and members of the two solitudes represent radically different and incompatible attitudes and values. The possibility of overcoming the culture gap is ultimately and inexorably frustrated by our limited intellect and hence unavoidable specialization.

The examination of salient characteristics of physical and social sciences shows that the development of the latter is severely constrained by inherent and inescapable difficulties. Concerned with the behaviour of man and society, social sciences suffer from the inability of a system to explain itself and attempt to analyze and rationalize an environment which is highly unpredictable and dynamic, difficult to experiment with (repetition of experiments under identical conditions is seldom possible) and quantify, where theories cannot be verified and can influence the phenomena under study.

In the face of such fundamental obstacles, the contribution of social sciences to the understanding and managing of an industrial society is necessarily severely limited. The abuse of pseudo-scientific jargon as a means of bestowing a scientific aura on the social sciences has only helped to denigrate the field in the eyes of physical scientists.

Notes

1. The term *scientific*, as used here, refers to mathematics, computer science, physical sciences (including life sciences and medicine) and engineering; *non-scientific* comprises social, or more accurately, behavioural sciences (sociology, economics, political science, history, psychology, anthropology) and humanities.
2. A recent typical example of this situation was President Reagan's Star Wars initiative, described in Chapter 7. Bad scientific advice, undoubtedly politically motivated, supported a misguided project which was abandoned after ten years and $30 billion.
3. This is not necessarily acknowledged by social scientists. A prominent psychologist expressed recently the hope that, "possibly, behind the diverse behaviours of humans and animals, as behind the various motions of planets and stars, we may discern the operation of universal laws" (Shepard 1987, 1323).

References

Anderson, A. 1989. "Against the Forces of Corporate Ignorance," *New Scientist* (18 February): 59–60.

Andreski, S. 1974. *Social Sciences as Sorcery*, Harmondsworth, England: Penguin Books.

Dunbar, R. 1988. "Polymaths of Science," *New Scientist* (18 February): 69.

Faust, D., and Ziskin, J. 1988. "The Expert Witness in Psychology and Psychiatry," *Science* 241 (1 July): 31–35.

G&M. 1983. "Teens Prefer Coed Schools," *The Globe and Mail*, 18 August 1983.

Hirsch, E.D., Jr. 1987. *Cultural Literacy: What Every American Needs to Know.* Boston: Houghton Mifflin.

Hirsch, E.D., Jr., Kett, J.F., Trefil, J. 1988. *The Dictionary of Cultural Literacy.* Boston: Houghton Mifflin Co.

Kolata, G. 1986. "Asking Impossible Questions about the Economy and Getting Impossible Answers," *Science* 234 (31 October): 545–46.

Leontief, W. 1982. "Academic Economics," Letters, *Science* 217 (9 July): 104, 107.

Lewis, R. 1988. *The Final Voyage*. New York: Columbia University Press.
Lukasiewicz, J. 1972. "An Introduction to the Study of Major Problems of Industrial Society," Report on Interdisciplinary Course Engineering 90: 300, 1971–72, Ottawa: Carleton University.
Marshall, E. 1987. "Nobel Prize for Theory of Economic Growth," *Science* 238 (6 November): 754–55.
Massey, D.S., and Espana, F.G. 1987a. "Migrant Networks," *Science* 237 (14 August): 703.
———. 1987b. "The Social Process of International Migration," *Science* 237 (14 August): 733–38.
OTA. 1988. Office of Technology Assessment. *Technology and the American Economic Transition*. Washington, D.C.
Robinson, J. 1973. "Of Economics, Politics, Morality and Tea," *This Week Times Two* 6, no. 10, Carleton University (14 June): 1.
Rosenberg, N. 1982. *Inside the Black Box: Technology and Economics*. Cambridge: Cambridge University Press.
Sharp, M., ed. 1985. *Europe and New Technologies*. London: Frances Pinter.
Shenker, I. 1973. "Dispute Splits Advanced Study Institute," *The New York Times*, 2 March 1973.
Shepard, R.N. 1987. "Toward a Universal Law of Generalization for Psychological Science," *Science* 237 (11 September): 1317–23.
Sheppard, R. 1990. "How Well Can Cabinet Ministers Count?" *The Globe and Mail*, 19 July 1990, A17.
Snow, C.P. 1969. *The Two Cultures and a Second Look*. Cambridge: Cambridge University Press.
Staley, R.A. 1982. "Nonquantification in Economics," *Science* 217 (24 September): 1204.
Thurow, L.C. 1987. "A Weakness in Process Technology," *Science* 238 (18 December): 1659–61.
Washburne, N.F. 1973. "Indignity at Princeton's Institute for Advanced Study," Letters to the Editor, *The New York Times*, 13 March 1973.
Wells, H.G. 1984. Quoted in *Canadian Aeronautics and Space Journal* 30, no. 4 (December): 299.
White, L., Jr., 1968. *Machina Ex Deo: Essays in the Dynamism of Western Culture*. Cambridge, Mass.: MIT Press.

Appendix to Chapter 2

Some Gems of Obfuscatory (Sociological and Other) Jargon

For the reader who doubts the extent of abuse of jargon, a few gems of this practice are reproduced here. They belong mostly, but not uniquely, to the field of sociology.

The following is one of the more lucid, simple sentences from a five-hundred page sociology textbook: *The Canadian Corporate Elite* by Wallace Clement (quoted by Barbara Bayne, *The Globe and Mail*, 26 October 1976).

> The concept comprador elite is operationalized as those members of the elite who identify their main corporate affiliation as a Canadian subsidiary of a foreign controlled parent, or in a few cases where the 'principal operation' was other than corporate, as in the case of a law firm, the designation was based on which country of control the individual held the majority of his dominant directorships.

Sociological jargon makes for difficult communication even among sociologists, as noted in *The Globe and Mail* editorial of 2 January 1978, reprinted below.

Fondling a Gordian knot?

> Although the difficulties sociologists have in communicating with the outside world are pretty severe, we had always assumed that they could console themselves with the thought that at least they could chat freely and intelligibly among themselves. They did, after all, appear to be homogenized by training to the point at which they could chat endlessly to each other about treatment modalities and the operationalizing of roles without drawing blank stares.
>
> We admit to being wrong, now that we know of the plan to provide civil servants in Ontario's Social Services Ministry with a dictionary designed to help them understand what they are talking about. (They are reported to be having trouble coping with sociological jargon.)
>
> This can only be a useful first step toward helping 'us' understand what they are talking about. In the basic language sense, that is; they may still fail to make any other kind of sense.
>
> The dictionary idea, we are bound to point out, is not new among the servants of the people. We have seen a slim volume entitled *Glossary of Educational Key Words* intended to help the outsider understand that a 'facilitator of learning' is actually a teacher — though not to explain why anyone in his right mind would choose one expression over the other.

The foreword contains a priceless sample of jargon:

> "Consequences of responses which satisfy the prevailing motivation condition strengthen directly the situation-response relationship they follow." This means: if one enjoys doing something, one is likely to do it again.
>
> There is no promise that the sociological dictionary will condense and clarify in this manner. It may serve merely as a cross reference linking new jargon to old jargon — and leaving us out in the cold again.
>
> This all means that we are trying to keep up with efforts now under way in the United States to ensure that official utterances are allowed to be neither unwittingly nor deliberately obscure. Out of the phrases that helped inspire the movement was a Central Intelligence Agency reference to an assassination team as a 'health alteration committee'.
>
> It's better to know what they are talking about.

Proliferation of social sciences' jargon has been viewed as a form of illiteracy affecting university students, as reported by *The Globe and Mail* of 6 April 1977.

Sound but no Meaning

> Professor J.M. Carmeron of St. Michael's College fears today's students are slipping into a fate worse than illiteracy, a habit of talking an unintelligible polysyllabic jargon borrowed from the social 'sciences', the shallower forms of mysticism and — although he did not mention it by name — the Ontario Institute for Studies in Education. The trouble with this jargon, which he calls para-sense, is that it has sound but no meaning.
>
> Thus the meaningful verbalization of conceptual improvisation at the interpersonal interface is contra-indicated by frustrations arising from idiosyncratic linguistic actualization, vocabulary-wise, so that the verbalized formulations of the initiating consciousness actuate the latent rejection mechanisms of the consciousness designated as the countervailing component of the envisioned dialogue so that the anticipated sharing of mutual affect-patterns and cross-fertilization of conceptual preferences is reflexively aborted and not a damn thing gets through.

You can't see the woods for the treatise

The use of jargon — the expression of our penchant for muddled thinking — is practised by many professions. This is how Mr. Gordon Baskerville, Dean of Forestry at the University of New Brunswick, evaluated the way the Ontario government manages its forests:

The proposed tools for implementing the plan were examined for adequacy relative to the logistical task of implementation, and evidence was sought with respect to the manner in which efficacy of management as it occurred in the forest was evaluated, and used as feedback control to improve the overall performance of the management process. (*The Globe and Mail*, 13 September 1986)

3

Technology: The Land of Many Faces

"The belief in a supernatural source of evil is not necessary; men alone are quite capable of every wickedness."

(Joseph Conrad, *Under Western Eyes*, 1911)

"... all 'inhuman' behaviour is always human. The enemy is not a devil out there called technology—he is Man, the creature we are trying to save. Only because he has become more conscious of his powers is he capable of so much folly and evil."

(Muller 1970, 331)

The Critics of Technology

SINCE the Scientific Revolution of the seventeenth century and the Industrial Revolution of the eighteenth and nineteenth centuries, Western societies have been increasingly immersed in scientific and industrial activities. Today the results of these endeavours literally permeate all aspects of life in the West, and increasingly influence life on the rest of the planet. Science and technology are the pillars of our contemporary Western society; in no civilization known to us have they wielded a greater influence.

It is not surprising that, in view of its tremendous impact, the process of industrialization has met with severe criticism and outright opposition. The most prominent among the early critics was Karl Marx (1818–1883). At a time when Great Britain and Western Europe had already almost a century of intensive industrialization behind them, Marx became deeply preoccupied with social consequences of technology. Another hundred years were to pass before a second major wave of concern with technology emerged and gave rise, in the second half of this century, to a vigorous anti-technology movement. And yet, in spite of much critical analysis and study, our view of technology as it relates to people lacks clarity: it tends to reflect the ideological bent of the student rather than an impassionate examination.

Marx's critique was focused on the socio-economic system within which industrialization was taking place. In formulating his theory of the alienation of labour, Marx contended that, under the capitalist industrial system, work was no longer a means of self-expression but "the dull routine of ceaseless drudgery and toil," the worker "a mere living appendage" of the machine which "does not free the worker from his work but merely deprives his work of interest." In 1867 Marx wrote in *Das Kapital*:

> All kinds of capitalist production, in so far as they are not merely labour processes, but also processes for promoting the self-expansion of capital, have this in common, that in them the worker does not use the instruments of labour, but the instruments of labour use the worker. (Marx 1867)

Marx's remedy for the alienation of labour—which, to the extent that it really exists is obviously the result of the fragmentation of the work process through division of labour—was not to denounce technology and advocate return to nature and to an individual craft system of production, but to impose a new social and economic order. Under the Marxist, i.e., the communist system, the control of industry would be removed from the capitalist class and the product of labour would belong to the worker. Only then would the alienation of the worker from the product of his labour be overcome. In an industry freed from the imperative of capitalist profit, the worker would not be tied to one particular occupation, but would be able to change jobs and participate in all phases of production. "The divorce of intellectual powers of the process of production from the manual labour" would no longer take place, the worker finding new interest and satisfaction in his occupation.

The experience since Marx's days does not support his diagnosis and cure. Although Marxist ideology, as well as less radical socialist movements have been effective in curbing the excesses of early capitalism, promoting social justice, and strengthening the workers' cause, alienation of labour and class struggle did not prove to be the crucial issues among the industrialized capitalist societies.

Marx, as a social ideologue and revolutionary, mistakenly felt that the impact of the productive process on people is governed by the socio-economic system within which it occurs rather than by the immutable objective requirements of the process itself. Indeed, on the technical side the systems of production in countries which attempted to practice Marxist ideology turned out to be no different from those in the capitalist ones, with the workers in the communist countries having less—rather than more—control over the industrial activities and economy than their confreres in the capitalist West.

Marx did not appreciate that specialization (i.e., division of labour) is dictated by our biological limitations (both physical and intellectual) and is therefore an unavoidable adjunct of high productivity; it has been growing as mechanization and automation progressed.

The performance of physical tasks has been increasingly relegated to machines and has been giving way to generation and handling of information. This process has resulted in elimination of much of the toil and drudgery, in less physical and more mental effort, in a higher level of workers' education and sophistication, a shorter work day and work week, a growing standard of living, and as a result, in alleviation of the alienation problem. In many modern Western enterprises the role of the worker has been elevated from that of a mere performer of assigned routine physical tasks to one which offers the opportunity to contribute to the improvement—both technical and managerial—of the whole production process. Modern industrialization — and not state ownership — is leading to the disappearance of Marx's worker class and to the emergence of a relatively classless society in which co-operation between workers and managers plays a significant role.

In future, as generation and handling of information becomes the main preoccupation of industrial society, traditional work will give way to complete involvement. This has been suggested by Marshal McLuhan, author of *Understanding Media*.

> Work does not exist in a nonliterate world. The primitive hunter or fisherman did no work, any more than does the poet, painter, or thinker of today. Where the whole man is involved there is no work. Work begins with the division of labour and the specialization of functions and tasks in sedentary, agricultural communities. In the computer age we are once more totally involved in our roles. In the electric age the 'job of work' yields to dedication and commitment, as in the tribe. (McLuhan 1964, 138)

Although Marx's expectations of the dire impact of "capitalist technology" did not materialize, a hundred years later much more basic and far reaching objections to technology were being voiced. The modern anti-technologists not only opposed — as Marx did — the socio-economic system under which technology was developed and deployed, but they also denounced the very concept of technology. They saw science and technology as autonomous and deterministic forces that have an existence of their own, beyond society's control. In demanding deliberate and rational behaviour, a high degree of efficiency and organization, technology has been fundamentally dehumanizing, destroying the quality of life, dominating people, cutting them off from the natural world, and inhibiting their emotional development.

Jacques Ellul, a French sociologist and theological philosopher, one of the founders of the contemporary anti-technology movement, views "technique" — a term he uses for broadly defined technology — as a demonic force that is totally out of hand, a system completely separate and independent of people. "Technology ultimately depends upon itself, it maps its own route, it is a prime and not a secondary factor, it must be regarded as an 'organism' tending toward closure and self-determination; it is an end in itself" — writes Ellul in *The Technological System*, a volume that followed in 1980 *The Technological Society*, a massive work first published in 1954. According to Ellul, "Man is absolutely not the agent of choice. He is an apparatus registering the effects, the results obtained by various technologies, and the choice is not based on complex or in any way human motives; man decides only in favour of whatever gives the maximum efficiency." Everything "occurs as if the technological system were growing by internal, intrinsic force, without 'decisive' human intervention." "Technology is self-determining," "technological progress has its own inner dynamics," "technology develops because it develops"—are some of Ellul's typical assertions.

Ellul's view of technology as a system separate from people clearly neglects the pivotal role of humans in the development of technology[1] and the increasing numbers engaged in this task. Contrary to Ellul's views, invention and innovation—the fundamental ingredients of technological growth—far from being automatic and self-determining processes are totally dependent on our creativity and require our decisive intervention. But, in the end, in seeking ways for people to escape the enslavement by technology, Ellul also has to admit that the impact of technology depends on people. "... if man does not pull himself together and assert himself," wrote Ellul in *The Technological Society*, "technological doom will be humanity's future."

Ellul's bizarre and inconsistent negation of the man/technology relationship is matched by his equally unfounded assessment of human life in a technological civilization as "abdication of [man's] responsibilities with regard to values" and a "trivial existence." Why it is more trivial than in any other civilization we are not told. Obviously, Ellul's views are not shared by the overwhelming majority of members of the industrial society, many of whom find life highly meaningful and the environment stimulating.

Other prominent anti-technologists, such as Charles A. Reich (1970), Theodore Roszak (1972) and, to a lesser extent, Lewis Mumford (1967, 1970) and René Dubos (1968), have echoed Ellul's views. For them, as for Ellul, denaturization and dehumanization is all that industrial civilization has to offer.

Similar criticism of Western technology was offered by E.F. Schumacher in the 1970s, particularly in relation to the less developed countries. In *Small is Beautiful: Economics as if People Mattered* (1973), a moralistic and utopian prescription for development of technology with "a human face," Schumacher argued that technology "tends to develop by its own laws and principles, and these are very different from those of human nature," and "recognizes no self-limiting principle—in terms of size, speed and violence. It, therefore, does not possess the virtues of being self-balancing and self-adjusting." Again, Schumacher viewed technology as an autonomous system separate from people and out of society's control.

With technology viewed as the evil force responsible for our miseries, the apostles of the anti-technology movement have advocated "counterculture" or the return to a simpler and—in their view—a more "genuinely human" mode of life. Only then would we be able to escape "the death-in-life of alienation," recover psychic balance and live again in harmony with nature, the environment in which we have evolved and to which we are well adapted, both physically and socially.

Schumacher advocated "a new life style, with new methods of production and new patterns of consumption; a life style designed for permanence." He favoured decentralization and small scale production "by the masses, rather than mass production." Similar views were expressed by Capra (1981) who urged, among others, development of renewable energy sources (solar and wind) as substitutes for non-renewable fuels (fossil and nuclear).

Such measures, which amount to turning the clock back to the individual craft era, while applicable where the extent of industrialization is small, are unrealistic elsewhere. The manufacturing of sophisticated products of modern industry could not be performed "by the masses," for both economic and purely technical reasons; the energy available from renewable sources is so diffuse and unsteady that it could not become a substitute for conventional sources. "Permanence" or lack of change is incompatible with human creative drive for knowledge and innovation.

Curiously, for the advocates of "counterculture," traditional agriculture and animal husbandry developed in the neolithic period are "natural" ways of life, whereas mechanized farming and genetic engineering of our day are not. More than a century ago, John Stuart Mill, in his essay on nature, provided a persuasive refutation of their naturalistic fallacy:

> If the artificial is not better than the natural, to what end are the arts of life? To dig, to plow, to build, to wear clothes are all direct infringements of the injunction to follow nature.

Every intervention by humans could be criticized as unnatural—but, in fact, the opposite is closer to the truth.

> Whatever we do is in accordance with nature, for it is in the nature of our species to change our natural environment. Science and technology are as natural for mankind as dams are for beavers or honeycombs for bees. (Schafer 1988)

The idea of counterculture is not new, but has become much more popular in our time than a century ago, when it was being developed in America by Henry David Thoreau (1817–1862) and his mentor, Ralph Waldo Emerson (1803–1882). These transcendental philosophers and writers held up people's right to self-culture amidst a society that was being commercialized, and called for a return to self-reliance and creative self-sufficiency. They saw individualism and intimacy with nature, freedom to pursue unique lifestyles and an uncommitted life, leisure, contemplation, and rootedness as the genuine values we should guard and enhance. Mind, not matter, was supreme and human fulfilment was not in narrow specialization but in wholeness of being. Thoreau's experiment in simple living and subsistence farming at Walden Pond in the years 1845 to 1847 (which he described in *Walden* first published in 1854; see Thoreau 1948) was being repeated in the 1960s and 1970s by hippie communes scattered throughout North America. But, by 1980, the movement had lost much of its momentum and many a hippie returned to the reality of industrial civilization.

The proponents of counterculture have nevertheless admitted that its realization would require nothing less than "reshaping the consciousness of people" and a change in human nature (Roszak 1972, 55). In doing so they have demonstrated how badly flawed and inconsistent their ideas are.

Clearly, if "counternature" is required to adapt us to the non-dehumanizing environment and lifestyle the anti-technologists favour, such environment and lifestyle are not "natural" to mankind. Conversely, it must be that industrial civilization reflects true human nature and is not the result of imposition of an "evil and autonomous" technology. The anti-technologists seem to have decided for themselves what is good for people and found that, in order to achieve their design, they would have to mould people to fit. Not surprisingly, they have stopped short of specifying the measures that would be necessary to accomplish this. Ellul invoked God's intervention through which "man's freedom may be saved by a change in the direction of history or in the nature of man" (Ellul 1964, xxx), but rejected it as not amenable to sociological analysis.

Modern anti-technologists have viewed technology as separate and independent from people rather than a manifestation of human creativity. They blamed technology — rather than man's limitations — for what they considered as undesirable consequences of deployment of technology.

Embracing the Unknown

The trouble is not technology per se.

Until deployed, technology is neutral. Its deployment always creates dependence and involves trade-offs, and in this sense technology is deterministic. Indeed, an industrial civilization necessarily reflects the properties of technology on which it relies. In other words, any society which, for example, has universally adopted the automobile, telecommunications, and mass production, is likely to evolve into a civilization similar to our own in the West.[2]

The fundamental trouble is our inability to foresee technological developments and the wide-ranging consequences of their application, and to make — even if we were willing to do so — informed choices.

These are the limitations already noted in Chapter 1: our intellectual prowess, responsible for the creation of industrial civilization, is not adequate to cope with its problems.

One could think here of two broad classes of issues: the current short-term difficulties in managing the industrial society and the guidance of its future evolution.

The first one is considered in some detail in Chapter 4 where it is suggested that the complexity of the artificial environment precludes the exercise of effective control over it by its creators.

As for guiding the future evolution of industrial civilization, this would require making confident prophecies of inventions,[3] their viability, impact and long-term effects, establishing criteria for selection, and mechanisms for adoption. Not surprisingly, the history of industrialization clearly demonstrates that in general this has not been possible. And, as already noted, traditional ideologies are no longer a substitute for forecasts and no longer provide useful direction.

First of all, the invention — the initial step in the process of innovation — is not necessarily the result of systematic or directed research, but often a matter of accident or of an idea which for no particular reason seized the imagination of the inventor; it is therefore highly unpredictable. Eli Whitney's cotton gin of 1793 (which revived the depressed economy of the U.S. South), the textile, metallurgical, and steam power technologies which founded the Industrial Revolution are all in this category, as well as, for example, vulcanized rubber, X-rays, penicillin, and the instant photographic camera. Here also belong innumerable simple but useful devices, from the paper clip and zipper to the paint roller and ballpoint pen.

As for technological forecasts, there have been few successes and many failures. The latter often originated with individuals and organizations who could be expected to command a superior insight into the future of their fields of activity.

Among the brilliant forecasts stand out the 1911 prediction by Charles Steinmetz of General Electric Co. of electric kitchens and appliances, air conditioning, and radio broadcasting, Herman Oberth's accurate descriptions in 1923 and 1929 of interplanetary rocket travel, some 40 years before the fact, general Mitchell's views on the potential of military aviation and his 1925 prediction of Japan's 1941 attack on Pearl Harbor (see Chapter 7, p. 216) and Arthur C. Clarke's communications satellite proposal of 1945, 20 years before commercial satellite communication service began.

The erroneous forecasts concerned such major developments as air and space flight, the jet engine, nuclear energy and xerography, and many others.

Eight weeks before the Wright Brothers first flew in December 1903, a leading U.S. astronomer ruled out flight by heavier-than-air craft. In

1956, one year before the first man-made satellite went into Earth's orbit, the British Astronomer Royal pronounced space travel to be "utter bilge" (he later became a member of the committee advising the government on space research). In 1929, the 22-year-old Frank Whittle conceived of the idea of a jet engine. The Royal Air Force and its expert consultants did not support the new concept; it was only in 1939 that Whittle was allowed to work full time on his revolutionary engine (unbeknown to the British, a German jet had already flown in August 1939). In 1930, R.A. Millikan, Nobel Prize winner, wrote that "it is highly improbable that there is any appreciable amount of available subatomic energy to tap" (Sinsheimer 1978, 24). Three years later Lord Rutherford, who first split the atom, said that "the energy produced by the breaking-down of the atom is a very poor kind of thing. Anybody who expects a source of power from the transformation of the atom is talking moonshine." Nine years later, self-sustaining chain reaction of nuclear fission was achieved; the era of nuclear energy began (Snow 1969, 33; *G&M* 1993).

Chester Carlson invented xerography in 1938. During the next eight years he approached 21 major companies, including such giants as Kodak, IBM, General Electric, and RCA; they all turned him down (Dessauer 1971). Thirty years later no office or industry in the industrialized West could function without a copier (Brooks 1967).

A more critical problem than the unpredictability of invention concerns its immediate and particularly long-term indirect effects.

The use of coal burning fireplaces — a technology among the most ancient — was never considered a danger to human life. But when this practice caused London to remain shrouded in dense smog for five days in December 1952, it resulted in a death rate that was 2.5 times the average of the previous five years. Within a month, the number of dead exceeded the average by 3,500; the majority of the dead were persons with respiratory and heart troubles.[4] The first clean air act was passed in the United Kingdom in 1956 (U.S. federal air pollution legislation dates to 1955).

A housing project for the poor, the Pruitt-Igoe, completed in St. Louis, Missouri, in 1954, was to be a model of slum rehabilitation and racial integration. It consisted of 2,800 apartments in 33 eleven-storey blocks on a 57-acre site.

The Pruitt-Igoe public housing attracted and trapped a poor population without providing jobs, opportunities for economic betterment, and resources for maintenance of buildings. Indeed, it made the area more attractive to the poor, who need more jobs, and less attractive to those who make jobs. It soon became a "chamber of horrors" where vandalism, drugs, muggings, rapes, and murders defied control. Windows, doors, and plumbing fixtures were broken, the walls ripped open for valuable loot — copper pipe.

(Lee Balterman, *Life Magazine,* 5 May 1972 ©Time Warner)

Demolition of the Pruitt-Igoe public housing in downtown St. Louis, Missouri in 1972.

Once there were 12,000 people living in Pruitt-Igoe. By 1976 the vandalized apartment blocks were all demolished.

The St. Louis experience was a classic demonstration of counterintuitive response of a social system to a new environment. As noted by J.W. Forrester, "In complicated situations, efforts to improve things often tend to make them worse, sometimes much worse, on occasion calamitous" (Forrester 1971; Schwartz 1971).

Who would have thought that urban crime is a function of urban design? A 1972 study of crime in New York (Newman 1972; NYT 1972) in 1969 found a significant dependence of crime rate on building height: the higher the building, the higher the crime rate.

In three-floor walk-up buildings, the study found, there were 30 serious crimes for every thousand families. In buildings of six or seven floors, there were 41 serious crimes. In highrise buildings of 13 to 30 floors there were 68. While the total serious crime rate was twice as high in tall buildings as in walk-ups, the rate of crime in public spaces in the highrises was seven times higher. Why? The study offered the following answer:

> In a high-rise, double-loaded corridor apartment tower, the only defensible space is the interior of the apartment itself; everything else is a "no man's land," neither public nor private.
>
> Unlike the well-peopled and continually surveyed public streets, these interior areas are sparsely used and impossible to survey; they become a nether world of fear and crime.
>
> ... in the walk-up buildings, where few families share an entry, the interior public space becomes an extension of the home. And so does the street.
>
> Kids can play outside and still be within calling distance of the window. And as parents supervise their children at play, they also monitor street life. Defensible space is extended. You begin to get safe streets as well as safe buildings.

An old-fashioned key in one's pocket is a better guarantee of privacy than an electronic lock, or some subtle trade-offs of innovation.

Deployment of most technologies involves a trade-off: there is a "price" that must be paid for the intended and realized benefits of innovation.

Medical drugs can be very effective in the treatment of certain diseases or control of their symptoms; but drugs also produce unintended and not necessarily harmless side effects.

Computerization, which allows storage and quick manipulation of enormous amounts of all kinds of information, has rendered operations of many organizations more efficient and more convenient for their clients. But huge computerized personal data banks which, while legitimately acquired by governments, police forces, financial and insurance companies, and many other businesses and organizations, can be used by them without the individual's permission or knowledge for objectionable purposes. Indeed the control of privacy of information presents a major problem.

In many cases, innovation, whose purpose may appear to be completely obvious and straightforward, produces subtle, unexpected, and sometimes undesirable effects. The nature of the "price" and its magnitude are not necessarily appreciated when innovation occurs.

High quality, fast, and cheap copying, which originated with the process of xerography (dry writing) and saw large scale commercialization beginning in the 1960s (see p. 44), belongs in this category. Xerox has virtually eliminated what used to be the *original* (as distinct from *copy*, customarily an easily identifiable carbon copy) and has made it impossible to control the number of copies reproduced and distributed. The process has been further perfected with computer printouts: the notion of a paper original has disappeared, the only "original" being electromagnetically encoded in the computer's memory, and every printout becoming the true "original." Moreover, such "original" of a text or drawing can be easily manipulated and altered without the knowledge of the author, and it requires minute scrutiny to discover which "original" has been changed, how it has been changed and when. To sum up: modern copying/printing, while achieving superb reproduction, results in the loss of information and control: it is no longer possible to distinguish between the original and a copy, and to control their distribution.

Electronically stored information of any kind—as opposed to the so-called hard or paper copy—can be readily manipulated or destroyed. Wiping out a sound tape is easily done, as many investigations, including the Watergate affair which led to the resignation of President Nixon in 1974, have shown. It is also easier than destroying all of the hard copies whose distribution could have been wide and unknown.

Before the advent of computer visualization (or computer processing of images), a photograph was an authentic and true visual record at the instant it was taken. But this is no longer the case: computer processed original photographs or video images can be altered at will and their authenticity is gone. Again, information and control have been lost.

Computer-keyboard-printer systems and wordprocessing programs allow extensive manipulation of text, including its content, format, font, creation of tables, spread sheets, etc. (see Note 13 below). But the filling-out of printed forms cannot be conveniently done with such systems, a task simply performed with a conventional typewriter.

The ease of storing and manipulating information inevitably facilitates its accessibility and causes a loss of privacy. Electronic mail (E-mail), which sends messages instantly over global networks of computers (and often substitutes for telephone conversation), involves storage in computer memories so that messages may be accessible to others than the addressees. Telephone caller identification services, which display the numbers and the names of callers, compromise the confidentiality of the caller and may provide information for purposes objectionable to the callers, such as their inclusion in telemarketing or other data banks. To prevent caller ID may not be free or may require entering a call-blocking code each time a number is dialled. But, even if your number is blocked, the call return feature may allow the other party to call you back.

Encoded cards are convenient to control access but they may also provide a record of who and when entered and left a building, a hotel room or a parking lot, unbeknown to the users. An old-fashioned key in one's pocket is a better guarantee of privacy.

Deployment of a new technology may result in totally unexpected consequences, and adoption of innovation on a massive scale is likely to lead eventually to profound social, environmental, and cultural changes which reach far beyond what was to have been the intended primary objective of the innovation.

While not particularly important, the following two examples illustrate well how utterly surprising the results of innovation can be.

Who could have predicted that the November 1965 power failure (*Time* 1966) which left 30 million people in the north-east United States without electricity would result in a large increase in the birth rate 9 months later? (Was it the lack of light or of television that was responsible?) Or that introduction of matches would change the sexual behaviour in an African community whose members thought it necessary to start a new fire in the fireplace after each act of sexual intercourse? This meant that following each sexual act someone had to go to a neighbouring hut to bring back a burning stick to start a new fire; this meant also that each act of intercourse was publicized and adultery was embarrassingly difficult. Matches changed all this: the fire could be lit without going to a neighbouring hut and privacy of sex (and adultery) were facilitated (Baier & Rescher 1969).

Many of the most significant technological developments have led to similarly unpredictable consequences. This has been true of interference with the ecology of the natural environment as well as of diverse cultural and social impacts. The examples summarized here are typical of such occurrences.

(Digital image by Jack Harris/Visual Logic; original photograph of Abraham Lincoln by Alexander Gardner, Bettmann Archive; original photograph of Marilyn Monroe courtesy of Personality Photos, Inc. *Scientific American*, cover, n. 2, vol. 270, February 1994).

This image was created in a computer by blending an 1863 photograph of Abraham Lincoln with a publicity shot of Marilyn Monroe made in 1955. The ability to transform photographs in this way has brought to an end the 150-year period during which photography seemed unassailable. And it has left us with the task of learning to view photographs with a new wariness.

Digital forgery can create photographic evidence for events that never happened.

The case of the automobile is a prime example of an innovation whose basic original function became incidental and almost irrelevant to the enormous and pervasive influence it brought to bear on every aspect of human activity.

Conceived as a substitute for horse and buggy and first mass produced in 1914 by Henry Ford to provide fast, affordable, and convenient door-to-door transportation, within a period of less than fifty years, while undergoing small changes itself, the automobile has totally shaped the lifestyle and the environment of every industrial society.

A listing of its impacts is staggering. It includes:

- explosion of cities into suburbs and shopping plazas, and decay of city-centres;
- congestion of streets and highways;
- smothering effects of freeways and parking facilities on cities;
- drive-in and drive-through services of all kinds (sleeping, eating, banking, entertaining, marrying,[5] etc., funeral services;
- impact on courting and sex habits, on universal education (school buses), as accessory to most criminal activities;
- licensing, policing, insurance and traffic control, rentals;
- virtual monopoly on inter-city traffic (90 percent), proliferation of highways, degradation of countryside, advertising, reduction of agricultural land acreage;
- prodigious costs in deaths, injuries, and property damage;
- single largest cause of pollution of the atmosphere, pollution of cities and land with hundreds of millions of discarded cars and billions of discarded tires;
- major consumer of gas, glass, and rubber;
- responsible for an estimated 25 percent of GNP (all automobile related activities in the United States).

Clearly the extent of automobile popularity and of its consequences could not have been foreseen in the early stages of car production.

Moreover, even if this were possible, what criteria would guide us in assessing the pros and cons of the automobile (or of some other technology)? Given the complexity of its impact, the choice would not be clear-cut but highly subjective, and would inevitably reflect individual values and judgments. The moral and ethical considerations are not necessarily relevant to the assessment of technological impact and do not provide an answer, and even the criteria of direct functional or economic logic and rationality may be misleading.

The case of nuclear energy, whether in military or civilian applications, illustrates well this difficulty. More than any other, nuclear technology has been the object of public scrutiny and controversy, and extensive governmental regulation.

The reliance of the West on the enormous destructive power of nuclear weapons for maintenance of peace and security in the cold war era following World War II was seen by many as a highly immoral policy which must inevitably lead to destruction on a scale never experienced before. To equate security and peace with the capacity to destroy was seen as a contradiction, a "logic of madness." And yet, as argued in Chapter 7, it is precisely what seemed an illogical, irrational, and immoral strategy that was effective in averting a third world war and maintaining peace until the collapse of the Soviet Union.

The use of nuclear fuel for generation of electricity has been highly controversial: the safety of nuclear power plants and the feasibility of safe disposal of spent radioactive fuel have been questioned. In some countries, as in the United States, Sweden, and Poland, construction of nuclear power plants has been virtually arrested in the 1980s and 1990s in the face of opposition by environmentalists and the public. Other countries, such as France,[6] continue to rely increasingly on nuclear-generated electricity. The choice is not clear-cut and is a matter of opinion rather than objective evidence.

To predict the occurrence of invention and to forecast the impacts of innovation are not the options available to industrial civilization. As pointed out by Sinsheimer (1978, 26), to be able to determine and guide its future evolution would be analogous to "the mind seeking to understand itself"—as noted earlier, a goal that is not attainable.

But there is yet another equally fundamental difficulty that must be mentioned: it concerns the inherent contradiction between the feasibility of predicting the future and controlling it.

Clearly, if the future can be influenced, it cannot be predicted, since it is shaped by all of us who are constantly engaged in changing it in unpredictable ways. Conversely, it is only a preordained and inexorably determined future that could be predicted but, of course, it could not be influenced or controlled. Herein lies the basic paradox: the objectives of forecasting the future and influencing or controlling it are mutually exclusive.

Engineering forecasts

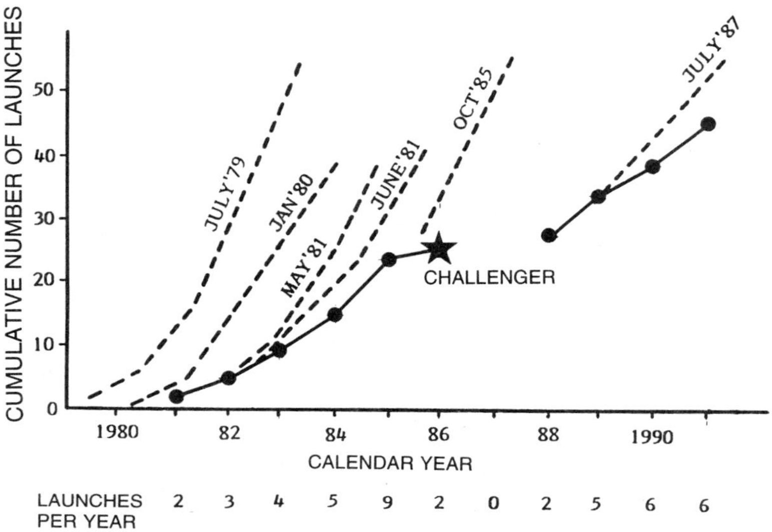

Planning the progress of an engineering project belongs among the least difficult forecasting tasks. But even here overoptimism may interfere with sound judgment, and unforeseen events may completely disrupt the schedule. NASA's predictions of Space Shuttle flights (broken lines with the date of forecast) bore no relation to the actual performance, and the explosion of *Challenger* on 28 January 1986 brought the program to a halt for 32 months.

However, because the future is the only domain in which we can act and, in the world of industrial civilization, change is the only constant, we are continually engaged in trying to accommodate both of these tasks, even though the chances of succeeding are minimal.

No forecasting techniques or methodologies can be of much help. Indeed, all that we know about the future is that it is unknown and uncertain. Nevertheless, with the advent of electronic computers, attempts have been made to develop national and global mathematical models and to examine their behaviour as a function of time.

Probably the best known endeavour on these lines has been *The Limits to Growth* model devised by an international team led by Meadows of M.I.T. (Meadows et al. 1972). This valiant, if naïve, effort to forecast the development of the whole planet considered interaction of five basic factors:

population, food, capital, pollution and non-renewable resources, and several scenarios which all predicted that human life could not be sustained for long. The publicity which the study attracted served a useful purpose in indicating the constraints an unlimited growth must encounter, but its results could not provide specific guidance for action.

This is also true of visions of the distant future created by novelists and science fiction writers and based on imaginative extrapolations of the present. The more significant among such prophecies are considered in Chapter 9.

Faced with the intractable and unpredictable development of industrial civilization, and with the evidence that more knowledge is not a solution to human problems and not necessarily a "social benefit," many have considered the desirability and feasibility of restraining science and technology and controlling their thrust.[7] While it is certainly possible to manage publicly supported scientific and engineering efforts through funding policies, the idea of broad long-range planning contradicts the very nature of research and invention as activities which probe the unknown and therefore follow unpredictable directions and lead to unpredictable results.

One may be able to "invent to order,"[8] but one may not know what to order.

In any event, it seems unlikely that in the environment of industrial civilization, creativity could be censored, or that to do so would be desirable. Rather, deployment of a specific technology can be controlled or selective support can be provided for objectives judged beneficial.

In the second half of this century, as industrialization and consumerism continued to accelerate, as their detrimental effects were becoming increasingly apparent and as governments sponsored many major projects, the management of science and technology along these lines has been expanding.

Before new projects can proceed, they must pass comprehensive assessments of environmental and social impacts. The performance of older technologies has to be upgraded often to meet more stringent standards. Not all that is technically feasible is being pursued. Development of technology in the West is subjected to numerous constraints.

Public technologies, in such fields as transportation, defence, energy, and communications, have traditionally involved government participation, control and regulation. The tunnel under the English Channel is an interesting example of a technically feasible project which for over one hundred years remained dormant for political reasons.

A design was first proposed in 1751 and there were several attempts in the nineteenth century to build the tunnel. In 1881 air-driven boring machines drilled a mile through chalk from both the English and the French coasts. But it was not until 1986 that France and England agreed to construct a railway Chunnel. On 30 October 1990 the French and British tunnelling crews made contact 40 metres below the sea bottom; the Chunnel is to be inaugurated in 1994.

From the earliest days of railroading the governments, the legislatures and the politicians played a key role in the construction of railways. They were often built to satisfy political (national or parochial) rather than economic goals and were financed by all levels of government; indeed, the development of railways was very much the business of a railway-government complex (Lukasiewicz 1976).

When in the 1960s and 1970s the automobile and the airplane — the newer transportation modes — caused the railway share of intercity passenger traffic in the United States and Canada to shrink to a negligible 1 or 2 percent, it was again the federal governments who stepped in to finance, take over, and maintain the money losing passenger trains. But in this case, government intervention, again politically motivated, has served only to preserve — at enormous cost to the taxpayer — a traditional obsolete technology and to delay a highly desirable innovation.

A quantum advance in passenger rail came with the introduction of the 210 km/h (max.) *Shinkansen* bullet trains in Japan in 1964, and the 260 km/h *TGV* (*train à grande vitesse*) in 1981 in France. The exclusive high speed lines and services have since been greatly expanded in Japan and France, the train speeds have continued to increase (in May 1990 a record speed of 515 km/h or 0.4 *Mach Number*[9] was attained by a special *TGV* train), a whole network of high speed rail has been planned for Western Europe. The *TGV* and *Shinkansen* trains have been highly profitable (the capital cost of the first Paris-Lyon *TGV* line was recouped in ten years), have attracted air and road traffic, and have generated new traffic. Over distances up to about 500 km between large population centres high speed rail offers today the most attractive travel in terms of cost, speed, comfort, reliability, safety, energy efficiency, and environmental impact.

This has yet to be recognized by the North American public and politicians who continue to finance the traditional trains, a mode which has become totally uncompetitive and prohibitively expensive. The Washington–New York–Boston route is possibly the world's most suitable one for application of high speed trains. And yet, instead of constructing a *TGV*-type line linking these cities, only marginal improvements were made to the existing tracks at a cost of $2.5 billion (the 1976 North-East Corridor project). In Canada, since VIA Rail was established to operate passenger trains, from 1977 to 1992 $7 billion (!) of taxpayers' money was spent to maintain them; nevertheless, the traffic decreased by over 50 percent. It has been an expensive way to get rid of the passengers who, while paying only a small fraction of the actual travel cost, have opted anyway for the other modes. Instead, public funds should have been used to construct a high speed line between Toronto, Ottawa, and Montreal (the only viable passenger rail route in Canada, with possible extensions to Windsor and Quebec City), which would offer superior transportation, relieve congestion at the Toronto airport, save energy and oil, provide fast access to Montreal's Mirabel airport, and generate considerable industrial activity (Lukasiewicz 1984, 1989, 1990).

As is evident from the case of passenger rail in North America, a government can certainly achieve total control of a technology, but this does not guarantee that the society will benefit from it. Indeed, the record of successful government initiatives in promoting technology and industrial development, at least in Canada, is not good. Philip Mathias (1971) analyzed monumental failures of five major projects which included hydroelectric plants, pulp and paper mills, heavy water plants, and fish works. To this list one could add (cost in $-million and year of cancellation are shown in brackets) the supersonic Avro *Arrow* fighter (400, 1959), the *Bras d'Or* hydrofoil for the Canadian Navy (54, 1971), Ontario's magnetically levitated urban transit (25, 1974), New Brunswick's *Bricklin* car (20, 1975), Newfoundland's cucumber greenhouse (3, 1989), and many other ventures.

The final collapse of ground fish stocks off the shores of Atlantic Canada exposed a monumental mismanagement of this vital resource by federal and provincial governments. Over the past two decades, in spite of warnings by scientists, fish catches were allowed to increase by 60 percent and the number of fish plants doubled to more than one thousand. Even as actual catches declined by a factor of three, between 1986 and 1993 historically high quotas were maintained. And for decades, the government has subsidized boats, processing plants and workers: about one third of their earnings came from unemployment insurance. By December 1993 it was realized that Atlantic Canada had run out of fish: virtually all Atlantic and St. Lawrence cod fisheries were closed and quotas on other groundfish were slashed, putting some 40,000 people out of work. The fish stocks may not recover for a decade and may never reach the levels of the 1980s. The viability of traditional society in the Atlantic provinces of Canada has been put in jeopardy.

A case of political control which would be judged to have benefited society involved the American supersonic transport (SST) aircraft project.

There is no doubt that American industry was the most experienced in design and production of supersonic aircraft and passenger jets, and therefore best qualified to develop a supersonic transport. And yet, in 1971, because of environmental and economic concerns, the United States decided not to proceed with the SST, even though Britain and France were already developing the supersonic *Concorde*. The Anglo-French project featured an earlier design than the proposed American SST and therefore was even less viable. Nevertheless, Britain and France supported it for reasons of national pride and prestige. Introduced into service in 1976, the *Concorde* proved an economic disaster but, heavily subsidized, continued in service. The U.S. decision reflected a mature judgment not swayed by partisan pressures; Britain and France could not resist the temptation of being the first to develop what became technically feasible. A similar attempt by Soviet Russia was unsuccessful: *TU-144* never entered regular service, and was permanently grounded in 1984.

The Blessings and Curses of Industrial Civilization

Material affluence is possibly the most conspicuous manifestation of industrialization. The industry produces all sorts of essential as well as superfluous goods and trivial gadgets and, through advertising, encourages consumption.[10] Indeed, consumption is often seen as the main function of industrial society whose goal of economic growth, as measured by the gross national product per capita, has become an end in itself. This, of course, is only a part of the picture. As Robert Kennedy observed, the GNP takes into account "neither wit nor courage, neither our wisdom nor our learning, neither our compassion nor our duty to our country . . . It measures everything, in short, except that which makes life worthwhile" (Muller 1970, 12).

It could be questioned to what extent the GNP is a measure of society's wisdom and level of learning, and it is probably more correct to state that a certain level of material standard of living must be attained to make life worthwhile. But the converse is not necessarily true: a high GNP does not guarantee a happy and satisfying existence.

Modern technology is the most efficient means yet devised to fulfil the basic physical requirements of a "good life," from "bread man needs before he can realize that he cannot live by bread alone" (Muller 1970, 9) to health and satisfaction of other physiological needs.

With the physical requirements of life efficiently met and with wealth being created on an unprecedented scale, industrial society has also been engaged in vast production of cultural goods. Entire populations have become literate and educated and, given shorter work and longer leisure hours, more people than ever before have been enjoying literature, music, visual arts, travel, and all kinds of entertainment. The materialistic industrial people, "though always inclined to ask where does it get you, . . . do all kinds of things that get them nowhere—except in a pleasurable state of mind" (Muller 1970, 6). Paradoxically, the materialistic industrial civilization has been the source of distinctively non-materialistic values.

It has emphasized personal freedom and respect for individuality, and has provided opportunities for self-realization and fulfilment of natural curiosity, creative impulse and aesthetic sense, a wide range of choices, and power to choose.

The abundance of material and cultural goods as well as abolition of war in favour of peaceful co-operation by western democracies (see p. 85) can be counted among the blessings of industrial civilization; crime, unemployment, recurring economic crises, and undesirable physical effects of massive industrialization and consumption, among others, are its curse. As argued in the next chapter, it is unlikely that industrial society will ever be able to cope adequately with its socio-economic ills, and although such physical evils of industrialization as exhaustion of natural resources and pollution are amenable to some degree of control, their long term effects are uncertain. But in order to gain a balanced perspective on the impact of science and technology, the role of man as the inventor and user of technology needs to be recognized. Since science and technology are uniquely a human domain, and because of our species unique proclivity towards inhuman, or harmful to our kind, behaviour, our use of science and technology for inhuman ends must be viewed as possible and highly probable, if not inevitable. As noted by Muller (1970), "all 'inhuman' behaviour is always human."

Technology: a Domain Unique to the Human Species

If there is one characteristic that distinguishes humans from the rest of the living world, it is creativity. Our ability to reach beyond the sensual experience of the world around us and to imagine, our curiosity which motivates us to understand the functioning of our environment and to construct mental models of it, our drive to build new environments and to develop new lifestyles — are all expressions of creativity. There is no counterpart to it in the animal world, which exhibits instinctive behaviour and where change occurs through natural evolution, a process which goes on outside of the consciousness of the living organisms — and whose time scale is large in relation to the duration of human civilizations.

The manifestations and products of human creativity are infinitely numerous and varied, and necessarily unpredictable. They range from abstract ideas, arts, and systems of knowledge to artifacts and whole new social and physical environments. Physical theories of matter, space technologies, and different systems of government are as much expressions of human creativity as are artistic works of all kinds. As technology developed, invention became no longer a matter of practical ingenuity and know-how but frequently the result of rigorous and imaginative application of science, requiring an intellectual sophistication of the highest order.

In the early era of industrialization, technology and science had little in common. Technology was being developed by practical and clever mechanics and entrepreneurs, away from academia. This was true of textile machinery in eighteenth-century England, or of steam power, or of steel manufacture. The mechanization of spinning and weaving called for novel and imaginative designs incorporating already available, basic machine elements. The development of steam engines, culminating with James Watt's efficient design of 1776, was accomplished before thermodynamic theory was worked out by Carnot, Kelvin, Rankine, Clausius, and others in the nineteenth century.[11] The techniques of making various kinds of iron alloys (pig iron, wrought iron, steel) were arrived at by trial and error well before the fundamentals of iron-carbon chemistry were understood.

As time went by, empiricism gave way to science anchored in theory. In the nineteenth century science had already provided the basis for development of much of the chemical and electrical industry. Fundamental principles and theories, often emanating from university laboratories, were being applied to design new machines, new processes and products. Today, technology is heavily dependent on science. This is particularly evident in such fields as nuclear energy, aerospace, telecommunications, informatics, bioengineering, plastics, and composite materials. Much of technology has become scientific: it takes only a few years for the discoveries of "pure science" to find practical applications. The boundaries between science, which seeks to establish the "truth" about our physical environment, and technology, which provides man with new capabilities and opportunities, have been effectively eroded. Pure scientists, applied scientists, and engineers are all closely involved in the technological enterprise.

Extension of Human Capabilities

Technology, just as science, is clearly and naturally a domain accessible only to our species and is therefore supremely human. Because it is intimately linked to people, it exerts a particularly strong influence on them. The direct people—technology linkage is the consequence of the most fundamental function of technology: the amplification and expansion of human capabilities beyond the limits imposed by nature.[12] Technology has enabled us to overcome the physical limitations of our bodies (as noted by McLuhan (1964), clothing and housing are extensions of our skin; machines are amplifications of our muscular strength) and the constraints of space and time (through fast transportation and instant telecommunications, the ability to go back in time, "stop" time and observe phenomena of extremely short duration), to expand information storage beyond our memory[13] (through all types of records, from written to electromagnetic, electrooptical and chemical, of all kinds of phenomena and events — our thoughts and feelings, visual, aural and other observations), to gain access to radiation frequencies well beyond the narrow band our natural senses register (through electrical, optical and chemical techniques), to measure the elusive time — to mention only a few examples. Moreover, it is through technology that we can quantify our observations and evaluate their accuracy; our senses provide us only, in most cases, with a qualitative assessment.[14]

The man and the machine

Physiologically, man in the normal use of technology (or his variously extended body) is perpetually modified by it and in turn finds ever new ways of modifying his technology. Man becomes, as it were, the sex organs of the machine world, as the bee of the plant world, enabling it to fecundate and to evolve ever new forms. The machine world reciprocates man's love by expediting his wishes and desires, namely, in providing him with wealth.

(McLuhan 1964, 46)

The case of Hank Dekker, a blind man who in 1983 sailed alone in a 7.6 metre sloop from San Francisco to Hawaii is an excellent illustration of technology as extension of man's senses. Braille charts and talking navigational instruments provided the blind sailor with information normally acquired through vision.

(*The Globe and Mail*, 27 August 1983)

Beyond the physical and the biological, the extension of our artistic genius and the development of arts are governed by technology — a connection that is not always appreciated by humanists and others who are not comfortable in the regimented environment of industrial society.

Almost every artistic endeavour relies, critically depends on, and is shaped by exploitation of a particular technology. Classical music did not develop until a few centuries ago because the instruments were not available. Modern rock music had to wait on the development of the electric guitar; rock concerts could not be without electronic amplification of sound and electric lights. Synthetic music (sound) can be composed and produced with no concern for the biological constraints that limit a human performer, equipped only with two legs, two hands, and ten fingers. Picture painting flourished with the invention of oil paint; it superseded mosaic and fresco work. Paper, ink, and the printing press allowed literature to develop. Still and movie (film and television) photography required cameras or devices which could record images.

Technology as an extension of human beings is inseparable from them and is bound to affect them profoundly. To treat technology as a phenomenon independent of humans, which has an existence of its own, is to ignore the very essence of the nature of technology.

People: the Inhumane Users of Technology

The deployment of technology, as well as its creation, depends uniquely on people. If we were satisfied with producing but not applying scientific knowledge and with making and describing the prototypes of our inventions, technology would fill libraries and museums but would not directly affect our lives: it would remain neutral. It is only when technology is applied that it appears to lose its neutrality and may be seen subjectively as good or bad. Rather than technology, it is the use it has been frequently put to by us that should be judged as inhuman, the cause of human misery, alienation, depravation and abandonment of human values.

The confusion arises partly through assuming that people—as opposed to technology—are the embodiment of humane behaviour and humane values. But this is not so: on the contrary, what is human is not necessarily humane and, as already noted, only humans are capable of inhuman, or more precisely, inhumane behaviour.

"... mankind is not quite human"

High profile enemies of the Nazi regime met their grisly deaths in the Plotzensee execution house, now in West Berlin. They died by guillotine if they were lucky; by hanging from meat hooks if they were not. This is where 87 participants of the unsuccessful plot to kill the Führer on July 20, 1944 were themselves killed. The executions were filmed so that Hitler could watch them in comfort.

Julius Fucik, an anti-Nazi journalist, was beheaded in Plotzensee on September 9, 1943. Shortly before he died, he was able to record his thoughts. This is what he wrote:

> "You who survive these times must not forget. Forget neither the good nor the bad. . . . I want this to be known: that there were no nameless heroes here; that they were people with names, faces, longings and hopes, and that the pain of the very last of them was no less than the pain of the very first. . . . Man's duty does not end with this fight, for to be a man will continue to demand a heroic heart as long as mankind is not quite human."

(John Fraser, "Prayers, parades in Berlin," *The Globe and Mail*, 8 May 1985)

▲

As individuals or societies, people could never refrain from taking advantage of each other, irrespective of costs. They have been developing and using technology to augment their capability for mutual exploitation and have found that practically every invention can assist them greatly in this sinister task. Mankind's creative effort in the development of weapons has been stupendous as has been its ingenuity in devising ways to use any technology for gain at the expense of others. A few examples will serve to illustrate this point.

- It was not the textile machinery developed during the Industrial Revolution that was responsible for the exploitation of child labour, but the greed of men who were determined to extract maximum profits from their efficient mills.
- If the automobile or the telephone has been an essential accessory to virtually every crime committed today in any industrialized country, this does not reflect the "badness" of these inventions but only of the people who use them.
- If computers, instead of assisting us in acquiring and analyzing information also facilitate theft and spread of hatred, or if facsimile transmitting equipment is used to send obscene pictures and messages to unsuspecting victims — this is because the world is full of highly educated and ingenious crooks and bigots, clever enough to exploit innovation for their own immoral ends.

  Many professional criminals now rely on computers to carry out crimes including embezzlement, credit card fraud, and theft of services and data. In 1989 computer crime was estimated to cost the

United States $555 million each year. In 1986, a West German computer hacker attempted to gain access to about 450 U.S. computers and succeeded in accessing about 30 military, research, and contractor systems.

- Computer virus epidemics are a recent manifestation of abuse of technology by perverse and ingenious vandals. Viruses are computer programs designed to conceal their presence on a disc and to repeatedly replicate themselves onto other discs and into the memory banks of computers. Viruses often lie dormant and then explode on a certain day or on contact with a specific computer program. By 1988 over 40 computer viruses had been identified in the United States.

  The result can be a trivial message distributed to hundreds of thousands of computer users, or alteration of programs, falsification of data, erasure of entire files of information, or even destruction of equipment.

  To fight computer virus epidemics, scores of "vaccines" and "inoculation programs" have been developed to identify infestations and quarantine them. Anti-virus diskettes are being sold as computer condoms.

- The discovery of bacteria has enabled us to eliminate much suffering and to save many lives, but conversely, it has also provided us with new means to inflict disease and death. The choice to develop bacteriological weapons has been ours alone.

- The airplane — a fast means of transport — has unexpectedly popularized blackmail and has enabled highjackers to extract exceptionally large ransoms. But if we find blackmail objectionable on moral grounds, we should influence human behaviour rather than abolish air transportation.

- Breast milk substitutes, when properly used, can contribute to infant health and welfare. Instead, bottle feeding in less developed countries has been highly lethal: it has been responsible for an estimated one million infant deaths in 1981. Aggressive marketing and sales promotion by infant formula companies competing for a billion dollar market, lack of hygiene, and decline in breast feeding due to increased employment of women have been the culprits. It is only since 1982 that the United Nation's "International Code of Marketing of Breastmilk" is being adopted — a long overdue measure necessary to counteract greed and ignorance and to ensure that society benefits from a new life-sustaining product.

- In the context of scientific progress, the discovery of nuclear energy—as of any physical phenomenon—can be viewed as a long term certainty. But the use of nuclear energy for weapons of war has not been inevitable; in this, as in all such cases, the choice has been ours. We could have foregone the military applications and stayed with uniquely peaceful uses had we not been bent on acquiring supremacy over each other. (Paradoxically, as outlined in Chapter 7, nuclear weapons have been, in fact, most effective in maintaining peace).
- Underground garages provide convenient parking for those who live or work in highrise apartment or office towers. Such garages are also the best location for effective use of high explosives. In the hands of terrorists, underground parking becomes an instrument of great destruction, as demonstrated on 26 February 1993 in the bombing of New York's World Trade Center, which killed seven people, injured hundreds and caused extensive damage to the 110-storey twin tower complex.
- Spray cans make painting easy and fast. But in the hands of vandals they become superb tools for defacing buildings, sculptures, signs, subway cars, and almost anything.
- Misguided transplants of Western technology in the form of huge foreign aid projects may often result in social, economic, and environmental disasters (see p. 90).

Countless other examples of misguided and inhumane uses of technology could be cited. They would all show that the use we make of technology is no better and no worse than we are: it faithfully mirrors our character, our values, and limitations.

Abuses of technology know no bounds

Masturbation and vacuum cleaners

Penis injury, brought about by vacuum cleaners, is in the news again (*Urology*, January 1985, p. 41). Dr. Ralph Benson of the Mayo Clinic in Minnesota described five cases of significant injury to the penis all of which were caused by vacuum cleaners. He blames sexually orientated magazines for the increase in the number of penile injuries—their pages giving what he regards as dangerous testimonials to the practice of masturbation using vacuum cleaners. One injury was so severe that the glans was destroyed.

(*New Scientist*, 28 March 1985, 24)

Robbery with instant glue

Manchester, England. Ambulance men, a policeman and a nurse worked for two hours to free a shopkeeper whose hands had been stuck to the counter with instant glue by an armed robber.

Derek Ryan was left glued to the spot and yelling for help Monday after the gunmen shouted "This is a stickup," then spread glue over the counter and ordered, "Stick your hands down in that," police said.

A passer-by fetched a policeman, but he could not free Mr. Ryan. An ambulance crew failed as well. Finally, a call to a hospital brought a nurse with a bottle of special solvent to dissolve the glue.

The robber fled with the equivalent of $1,530 (Canadian).

(*The Globe and Mail*, 14 January 1987)

Snowplowing the protesters

To mark the 35th anniversary of the death of Stalin, a demonstration was organized on March 6, 1988, in Moscow by Perestroyka-88, an independent discussion group. Police roughed up the demonstrators and took them away in vans. "Snowplows lumbered around the sidewalks although there was no snow, dispersing protesters who remained" reported the *Reuters News Agency.*

Herein lies the tragic aspect of industrial civilization. As Muller (1970) observed, man is "the only animal that steadily, systematically has been exterminating fellow creatures of his own species" and has applied his creativity to develop increasingly lethal weapons for this purpose. With the creation of nuclear explosives man has achieved the power "to blast the entire Earth, destroy civilization overnight, conceivably put an end to the human race. He has achieved the ultimate in biological absurdity, making preposterous his distinction from all other animals, who he still calls beasts and brutes."

When technology is blamed for modern society's malaise, it is necessarily viewed as an autonomous force out of people's control. Nevertheless, the creators of technology — the scientists and engineers — are not absolved, like the rest of us, from the responsibility for the misuses to which society puts their creations. They are often portrayed as insensitive individuals, narrowly interested in pursuing their professional objectives, fascinated with academic problems and useless gadgets, concerned with promoting material wealth as the determinant of quality of life, oblivious to emotional needs and higher aspirations of people. It is the humanists — as opposed to scientists and engineers — who have our true welfare at heart.

Or do they?

Science and technology furnish us with the understanding of the physical world and create the means through which we can — if we so choose — augment and expand our natural capabilities and modify our environment. It is the humanists — the politicians, the bureaucrats, the lawyers, the administrators — who decide, on our behalf, how technology is used and controlled (in a democratic system, their actions reflect the wisdom or ignorance of the majority). Theirs is the responsibility for abuses, excesses, and inadequate controls as well as for the beneficial and humane applications of science and technology. This is not to imply that the moral standards of scientists and engineers are any higher or different that those of the humanists, but only to point out that it is the latter who ultimately control the uses to which technology is put.

Scientists and engineers are not the ones who determine the role science and technology play in society, but even if they were, the notion that humanists (who are actually in charge) would create a more humane world is naïvely optimistic. It derives from the mistaken identification of humanities with humaneness and results in imputing superior moral standards to those who are considered humanists — as opposed to others, among them physical scientists and engineers.

Regretfully, the evidence does not corroborate such views; even some of the leading humanists appreciate this. The following eloquent assessment comes from Jacques Barzun (1959):

> The humanities will not rout the world's evils and were never meant to cure individual troubles; they are entirely compatible with those evils and troubles. Nor are the humanities a substitute for medicine and psychiatry; they will not heal diseased minds or broken hearts, any more than they will foster political democracy or settle international disputes. All the evidence goes the other way. The so-called humanities have meaning chiefly because of the humanity of life; what they depict and discuss is strife and disaster. The *Iliad* is not about world peace; *King Lear* is not about a well-rounded man; *Madame Bovary* is not about the judicious employment of leisure time.

We could add that it is not the humanities that have increased our chances of survival in the harsh environment of nature, or have eliminated much sweat and toil from our daily chores, or have provided us with time and resources needed to exercise that uniquely human attribute — creativity. All of this we owe to our successful pursuit of science and technology. This and much more: the realization that colonial exploitation and territorial expansion are no longer the keys to prosperity (I will return to this topic later).

In spite of those who view industrial civilization as dehumanizing and destructive of the quality of life, clearly it is precisely in the highly industrialized societies of the West that our opportunities for education and self-expression and for equitable satisfaction of material and spiritual needs have been maximized. As pointed out by Mumford (1964), when technology was lacking (as in Ancient Egypt) the most inhuman of machines — the "human machines" based on massive application of slavery and forced labour — were the substitutes.

The Dehumanizer and Depersonalizer

When the fundamental characteristics of technology are carefully examined, it is found that the deployment of technology unavoidably leads to what could be called dehumanization — or perhaps more accurately — depersonalization, but not for the reasons advanced by Marx or the modern anti-technologists.

As noted before, technology's most fundamental function is the amplification and expansion of our species' natural capabilities. Thus technology is the medium through which we interact with others and with the environment, whether natural or man-made. As our extension, the technological link also constitutes a barrier: it impedes our direct interaction with the outside world. The following typical cases demonstrate this clearly.

Mechanization and automation of any production process involves introduction of some kind of machine, a functional element which separates the worker from the product of his labour and from others engaged in the same enterprise. This need not be and has not been the cause of alienation as postulated by Marx. However, compared to a craft shop where only simple hand tools are used, the process inevitably prevents the worker from having as intimate a contact with the object of his work, and diminishes his contacts with other workers; instead, it enhances the worker's involvement with the machine. The worker's role becomes largely determined by the capability of his "extension," that is the equipment he operates, and is less dependent on the work of others. As mechanization and automation progress, the production process becomes increasingly depersonalized. The number of workers in relation to product output decreases and interactions between people are replaced by interactions between people and machines, and among machines.

The area of telecommunications abounds in many interesting cases of depersonalization through technological extension.

Before speech and image could be recorded and transmitted, communication between people required face-to-face confrontation in which the whole human sensorium was called into action. Sound and body language, expressing the content of the message as well as emotions and feelings of the participants, were both involved in the transfer of information. Communication technologies, from writing to electronic media, have abolished the barriers of space and time, and the limitations of human memory—but in doing so they have inevitably depersonalized the process of communication and robbed it of the human touch. They have also affected relations between people. As pointed out by McLuhan, introduction of print ("phonetic culture") has enabled us to "act without reacting," i.e., to control our feelings and emotions when engaged in action. Although the electronic media have tended to restore some of the directness and immediacy of communication between people (as, for example, through telephone), they have not been a substitute for personal encounters and, in some cases, they have curtailed direct personal contacts. For example, earphones have eliminated conversation between air passengers. With the home video, going together to the movies is no longer the habitual way of seeing films.

Thanks to electronic audio-visual technology, practically all public events can be heard and seen in the privacy of one's home. Music, theatre, and sports can be enjoyed with least effort in maximum comfort and at minimum cost. But the feeling of active participation and emotional involvement that one can experience only as a member of a live audience or crowd has been irrevocably lost.

The medium of television

"Television is a medium of entertainment which permits millions of people to listen to the same joke at the same time and yet remain lonesome."

(American poet T.S. Eliot)

* * *

Professor Postman describes a man eating dinner as he watches television. Pictures of starving Ethiopian children linger on the screen as the man says to his companion, "More mustard please." The man is either mad in his complacency or the gulf between information and the ability to act on it has become so great that inaction is perfectly normal.

If so, the information glut is turning us all into New Yorkers who have learned to ignore the poverty and violence around them because they feel they can do nothing about it. If it does not drive us mad, the gulf between information and the ability to act emphasizes our powerlessness and thereby numbs our sense of moral responsibility.

In this light, the information glut is much more than a material problem that can be addressed by editors who conjure order out of chaos for various paying audiences. The information glut is also an agent of dehumanization. It is not just the amount, but the reach and quality of information that affect us. We learn to be indifferent to the most horrendous human tragedies, a withering of our humanity attributable to the existence of information itself.

The counterargument is obvious. Television pictures of starving Ethiopians are precisely what created the public passion for aid and, ultimately, intervention. Similarly, information about the lives of people living in affluent democracies was a potent agent of change behind the Iron Curtain, and even now is altering such things as the status of women in developing countries and global sensitivity about the environment. The fact that the focus often seems arbitrary—why Ethiopia and not Sudan?—does not detract from the ability of information to cause change and inspire action by millions of people living continents away.

(Neil Postman in conversation with William Thorsell, *The Globe and Mail*, 20 February 1993)

▲

Introduction of automated phone answering systems, also known as voice mail, phone mail, voice messaging or, more accurately and euphemistically, "non-simultaneous conversation," has subverted the original purpose of the telephone: the ability to conduct a simultaneous conversation irrespective of physical separation.

Non-simultaneous conversation systems are being increasingly used by offices, thus eliminating the expense of a receptionist or secretary. The claimed greater efficiency—actually cost reduction—is achieved at the expense of the caller, whose time and money wasted in pressing buttons and listening to unwanted messages, apparently do not enter into the efficiency calculation.

There are, of course, simple routine applications well suited to voice mail, such as information on weather forecasts or selection of a particular department within a company. But most systems are guilty of leading the caller through a telephone labyrinth only to return him to square one. For example, getting to talk to a particular person whose position within an organization is not known, or finding information on a flight which is not listed on the answering machine may be impossible.

Since the caller does not know the options available to him, his ability to select the required one is jeopardized. Clearly, no matter how sophisticated the phone mail system is (incidentally, greater sophistication means more options and more time wasted by the caller), it cannot accommodate all requests for information; only a live human voice may be able to do that.

As technology takes over more and more tasks formerly performed by people, the ability of an individual to influence the course of events and the opportunity for people to interact directly decrease. Typically, a tourist equipped with a camera no longer meets people of a foreign land. He behaves like a voyeur and treats people as mere images in his camera viewfinder. A bank teller or an airline clerk, who interact with computer terminals, are unable to handle an unusual situation, no matter how much they may wish to help their customers (needless to say, they are completely helpless if the electric power fails—as is also the whole society). They are totally constrained by the scope of the program written into the computer and the information available in its memory. These reflect standard operations and only the most frequently experienced non-standard situations. High productivity in routine conditions has been attained by foregoing the ability to cope with unforeseen problems which demand the exercise of judgment through interaction of people.

Computer-printed letters suffer from similar deficiency; when complex problems arise, they are near to useless. With human contact eliminated, the recipient of one or more of such communications does not know how and to whom to respond. Engaging in correspondence with a computer is both frustrating and purposeless. Again, in order to attain routine efficiency, the process has been thoroughly depersonalized.

The above could be viewed as trivial examples of technology taking over and eliminating the opportunity for people to judge and act. But technology may have necessarily the same impact in highly significant and potentially dangerous situations, as in a nuclear warfare scenario from the Cold War[15] period. It envisaged "launch on warning" of nuclear-armed missiles as soon as information has been received that the enemy had initiated war by launching his nuclear-armed intercontinental weapons. Such immediate response to the attack was deemed necessary lest the enemy's missiles destroy one's own weapons still on the ground and thus prevent retaliation. The decision to launch on warning needed to be taken literally within minutes and had to be therefore entirely based on remotely-sensed information processed through an array of instruments and computers. There was no time for human intervention, which had to be essentially limited to actuation of the launch button on instruction from the computer whose "judgment" merely reflected a previously inserted program. Indeed, given the inevitable time constraint and the enormous volume of data which had to be instantly processed to ascertain that the enemy action constituted a genuine threat, the actuation of the launch button could also have been programmed, man being completely eliminated from the decision sequence.

Needless to say, in the launch on warning scenario there was no possibility of consultation among the government and elected representatives of the people, and the prescribed political process which should precede a country's entry into war could not take place; it was pre-empted by a technology whose performance exceeded human information handling capacity.

Modern erotica—whether in the form of superbly illustrated magazines or "blue" movies, videos, and telephone messages—represent another interesting and rather extreme case of depersonalization (or perhaps dehumanization would be more appropriate here) through technological extension. For many, such materials have become a substitute for personal experience of a highly emotional and most intimate nature. "Second-hand love" offers a variety of partners and techniques that would be difficult to match—especially for the money and time invested—in one's bedroom or automobile, but robs the viewer of the real experience: all he or she can do is look, listen, and dream. Intensive examination of printed nudes by teenagers replaces boy-girl exploration, or at least denudes early erotic adventures of mystery and emotion.

(Advertisement 1982)

Second-hand love: The ultimate intimate experience!

Dial-a-romance telephone messages, sexually suggestive and titillating, make profits for sponsors and telephone companies. For $1.99 many Bell customers can hear a man whisper: "Hello, dear princess, my name is Eros. Cast aside your inhibitions. Feel my firm flesh against yours, and my sensitive touch on those precious areas of your body that you find most sensitive."

The joys of CompuSex

One of the more bizarre aspects of America's love affair with the personal computer is the growing popularity of CompuSex. This is a new form of erotic entertainment in which consenting computer owners exchange X-rated messages over the telephone lines ... "Eighteen months ago, it was mostly lighthearted flirting," ... "Now people come out with all sorts of obscene propositions right on-line" ... Sometimes 40 people will be on-line at once, their pseudonymous messages scrolling by on the screen faster than the eye can read. "I'm nibbling your earlobe," begins a typical come-on. Reply: "Not so hard!" ... anyone signing on as "Karen the Nympho" will be besieged with requests to /TALK. This is the command that allows two users to exchange intimacies in private ... Tiresome swains can be cut off with a keystroke ...

Many computer buffs find their pleasures habit forming ... Others have trouble separating computer-mediated fantasy from reality. One 35-year-old woman grew so addicted to CompuSex that her husband walked out, complaining that she was neglecting him for her machine. She then hooked up with a series of on-line lovers who were either disappointing or disappointed when she met them in the flesh. Now, complaining that her life is a mess, she is organizing a support group for women having similar difficulties.

(*Time*, 14 May 1984)

Virtual reality sex is the most recent development. Computer partners equipped with special helmets and gloves meet each other's virtual images to have an extraordinary sexual experience.

Increasingly, voyeurism is becoming a substitute for the real thing. In the age of the dreaded sexually transmitted AIDS disease, "safe sex is voyeurism" has become an advertising slogan for porno shows and movies.

Interactive audio-visual technology has become a substitute for pets and children. A mere $100 will buy a video-dog, video-cat or video-baby, programmed to respond on a video screen to commands of their master or parent. Through technology, sex can be enjoyed without fear of pregnancy; now one can enjoy pets and children when one wants, without caring for them.

Miniature cassette players, while providing the headphone wearers with exquisite stereo sound, also cut them off from communication with the outer world. "I am in my little world and I don't want to be disturbed" is the explicit message the headphones project. The isolating quality of personal tape players has been exploited by young couples who regularly make love as each partner listens to his favourite, private music. "She likes classical music and he likes acid rock, so each listens to a different tape"—noted a 1982 press report from Calgary, Alberta. Also in this case, a most natural and intimate human experience has been thoroughly depersonalized through technology. As observed by McLuhan (1964, 108), "technologies for extending and separating the functions of our physical beings have brought us near a state of disintegration by putting us out of touch with ourselves."

More generally, artificial environments, although often highly beneficial or even indispensable to people, inevitably bar them from experiencing nature directly. "The road became a substitute for the country by the time people began to talk about 'taking a spin in the country'. With superhighways, the road became a wall between man and the country," wrote McLuhan (1964, 94). As noted by Kranzberg and Pursell (1967, 742), technology has been defined as "the knack of so ordering the world that we don't have to experience it."

The substitution of the artificial for the natural as a result of industrial mass-production, creation of an ever-present information environment which is fed instantly and incessantly with inputs from around the world, establishment of fast and accessible transportation systems—all have contributed to depersonalization on another, cultural and national, level. As discussed more extensively in Chapter 5, these developments inevitably tend to erode cultural diversity and political sovereignty; they also reduce dependence on traditional national and family ties, foster individualism, and demand self-reliance. The result is a loss of sense of belonging and sense of place—alienation which may cause anxiety and stress.

Technology the Unforgiving

Depersonalization is not the only aspect of technology which may cause anguish and frustration; the perfection and precision which technology demands from its creators and users may be equally disconcerting.

It is no accident that failures of technology are often blamed on "human error." In fact, broadly interpreted human error is the only possible cause of technological failure. The nature of the error may range from sheer ignorance to incompetence and irresponsibility. Many a surgical procedure did not succeed because not enough was known about its consequences. After the first commercial jetliner, the de Havilland *Comet* was grounded in 1954 following several mysterious crashes (see Note 4 below), it was established through extensive research that its designers ignored the effect of pressurization on stresses in the fuselage structure. A designer's ignorance may also reflect a lack of appreciation of a user's limitations: if a device or a system is too complex, or awkward to operate, the probability of its unsafe and improper use is high. Incompetent operation of technology is a frequent cause of failure, as in the case of railway, marine, and air accidents which result from mishandling of signals, navigation instruments, and air traffic control equipment. Irresponsible operation of technology may be a major cause of loss of life, as in the case of drunken drivers who account for most of road fatalities.

If inanimate artifacts and systems fail, it is only because their designers, or manufacturers, or those responsible for maintenance and operation, have erred. If a vital component of a wing breaks and causes an aircraft to crash, it is because the design has been inadequate, or the material deficient, or the manufacturing process inappropriate, or the maintenance and inspection not carried out as necessary, or the aircraft subjected to conditions more severe or different than those specified for the design.

Trouble-free and safe deployment of technology allows for only a small margin of error and demands from people a high degree of perfection. Technology is inflexible, intolerant, and unforgiving; its operation demands strict adherence to prescribed rules, and therefore constrains the behaviour of its user. In this sense, technology must be seen as lacking humanity: it cannot accommodate human frailty. Indeed, to operate a machine successfully, men and women must behave like a machine and must acquire the skills the machine demands. Some people are more adept at this than others who may lack the patience and precision, and sometimes the ability to interface with machines; they may feel helpless and frustrated when the machines fail to respond to their wishes.

As noted by Muller (1970, 191), "Modern technology, governed by the ideals of efficiency and rationality, rests upon the machine, which has acquired an admirable precision, and upon elaborate organization, which requires clarity in communication . . . " It is impervious to emotions and allows little room for spontaneity and improvisation, but it requires — from both its producers and users — intellectual and organizational sophistication and perfection, and therefore a generally high level of education, a desirable social objective.

A degree of depersonalization and the insistence on mechanical perfection are the inevitable traits of technology generally viewed as undesirable; the imposition of change is the other, equally unavoidable but more apparent consequence, often the cause of anguish and misery.

You can't reason with automatic bank tellers

When automatic bank tellers are obediently pumping out 20-dollar bills they do a fine job but you just can't reason with them. If the customer fails to see eye-to-digital-readout with the machine, he cannot hope to win.

Thomas Morton, a Vietnam war veteran confined to a wheelchair, pulled out a pistol and fired six times at an automatic bank teller in Clearwater, Florida when the machine swallowed his plastic bank card and refused to give him the money he wanted to withdraw.

Mr. Morton said he probably didn't hear the machine beeping at him when he incorrectly entered his identification number. Eventually, the teller flashed a message on its screen saying it was keeping his card.

Unpardonable, of course. Still, somewhere a human teller will be happy that a machine has taken his or her place in the firing line.

(*The Globe and Mail*, 13 and 15 August 1983)

The Agent of Constant Change

"If the only constant is change, the ultimate skill is adaptation." (*The Globe and Mail*, 2 May 1985, 6)

"If it works, it's obsolete." (Marshall McLuhan, *Vogue*, July 1966, 115)

Technology is the basic agent of change in the history of the human condition and a merciless destroyer of status quo: as it generates innovation it creates obsolescence. Its deployment, while favouring one sector of society, may make excessive demands on the adaptation by the rest. The process is irreversible (if one excludes the collapse of a whole civilization) and the need to adapt cannot be avoided since the return to an earlier condition is not possible. The wheel, the phonetic alphabet, and the telephone cannot be uninvented; they can only be rendered obsolete by a newer technology. Moreover, as the pace of the development of technology increases, the required rate of adaptation augments and the resulting stress rises.

Era	From	To	Duration (Years)
Old Stone Age (Pleistocene)	2,000,000 B.C.	10,000 B.C.	≈2,000,000
New Stone Age (Neolithic)	10,000 B.C.	4000 B.C.	6000
Urban Civilizations (Bronze Age)	4000 B.C.	1000 B.C.	3000
Greco-Roman	900 B.C.	400 A.D.	1300
Medieval	500 A.D.	1350 A.D.	850
Renaissance	1350 A.D.	1600 A.D.	250
Industrial Revolution	1750 A.D.	1830 A.D.	80
Nuclear Energy	1905 A.D.	1945 A.D.	40
Space Flight	1932 A.D.	1969 A.D.	37
"Spaceship Earth"	1960 A.D.	1980 A.D.	20

Development of mankind: dates and durations of major eras.

Examination of the duration of major civilization eras shows how the development of mankind has been accelerating over the ages. The generally accepted dates and durations of the main eras are listed above and shown below in a logarithmic graph; the dates are plotted as years counted from each period's mid-point to the year 2000 A.D. Nuclear energy, space flight and "Spaceship Earth" are included as characteristic of developments in the present century.

The nuclear energy period is taken as extending from the publication of Einstein's special theory of relativity in 1905 to the first deployment of atomic bombs in 1945 over Hiroshima and Nagasaki. The space flight era covers the years 1932 to 1969, the dates which mark the start of development of large rockets in Germany and the first landing of man on the Moon. "Spaceship Earth" denotes emergence of concern with the exhaustion of natural resources and the quality of the environment in the period 1960 to 1980.

Along the dashed line in the graph the duration of a period is equal to the number of years from the period's mid-point to the year 2000. The actual correlation, given by the full line, shows an even greater decrease in the duration of each era as time progresses, and illustrates how the change in the human condition has been accelerating. Extrapolation of the graph to the present time produces an arbitrarily short duration and therefore breaks down. Indeed, as would be expected, developments which belong to the current century correlate along a flatter slope which gives a longer duration than the full line.

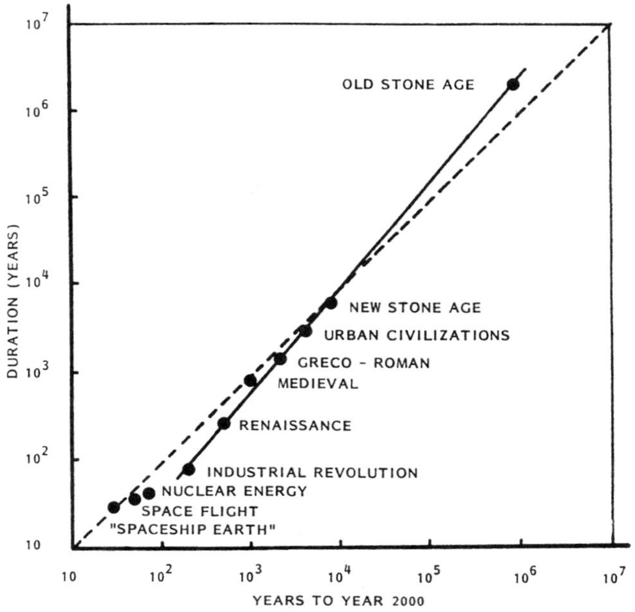

Acceleration of the development of mankind.

Since adaptation to change requires new psychic and material resources to be mobilized, technology—as the cause of change—is often regarded as man's adversary, responsible for the destruction of his well being. Today, at least in the industrialized West, the social costs of technological progress are controlled and kept at levels generally acceptable to society. Nevertheless, adaptation to change—even if slow and facilitated—is a challenge that necessarily generates stress. The latter must be recognized as yet another unavoidable byproduct of industrial civilization. It has given rise to stress management consultants, courses and manuals, and stress avoidance techniques of organizing and managing. One suspects that for persons who know how to cope, stress may enhance their performance, and that the only way to learn to manage stress is to be exposed to it.

The relentless development of science and technology and commercial competition result in a flood of new or improved products and services which render obsolete the ones in current use. Information about innovation must be widely diffused so that the public can learn about it and benefit from its use. How else could one learn about a new and better safety razor, sound reproduction system, ski boot, or lower mortgage rates? Advertising, as a vehicle for disseminating information about new products and services, performs this important role and must be therefore viewed as a necessary adjunct of innovation and a service to the consumer. Regretfully, it is often misleading and abused, and sometimes objectionable on moral grounds, as, for example, when used to promote consumption of cigarettes, known to cause lung cancer.

Curiously, even in the most progressive and industrialized societies, stubborn resistance to change may go hand in hand with dynamic innovation.

As noted elsewhere, the British did not adopt the efficient decimal monetary system until 1971 (see Chapter 6, Note 5), the military have resisted the impact of new weapons on warfare (see Chapter 7), and obsolete passenger trains continue to be operated in North America (see p. 54). Other such cases have been described by Lukasiewicz (1976) and Morison (1966).

The great difficulty of breaking with tradition is well illustrated by the arrangement of seats in airliners. Clearly, by far the safest way is to seat passengers facing the rear, the backs of the seats providing maximum support in case of an accident. Moreover, except at take off and landing, flying at a steady speed at 30,000 feet leaves the passengers totally devoid of any sense of direction of motion. And yet, forward facing seating, which dates to the horse and buggy era, is still the rule. Surprisingly, rearward facing seating is quite common in traditional trains.

Automobile controls are another interesting example of conservative design. Cars equipped with radios have been around for over fifty years. Clearly, radio controls should be easily accessible to the driver: the steering wheel is obviously the most suitable location, the dashboard is not. And yet it is only recently that a few car manufacturers have introduced this innovation.

Since the massive introduction of the automatic transmission after World War II, only three elements have been required to drive, i.e., to control the speed and the direction of a car: the gas and brake pedals and the steering wheel. They could be easily integrated into a one-hand operated joy-stick (similar to classic aircraft control), with displacement to the left and right for steering, fore and aft for speed (gas and brake). Although stick-controls could be more convenient, making co-ordination easier and freeing a hand for other tasks, such as operation of radio, tape and disc players, telephone or other gadgets, so far only one car manufacturer (Sweden's SAAB) has experimented with them (Simanaitis 1992).

Perhaps even more startling is the steadfast adherence by the automobile manufacturers to the dipstick for determination of engine oil level. Although reliable oil-volume gauges have been available for years, the most primitive and dirty device is still universally used.

Population, Environment and Resources

Among the many "faces of technology" must also be included the most obvious and visible among the undesirable ones: fast population growth, pollution of the environment, and depletion of natural resources. Although in many cases their present magnitudes can be relatively well determined, it is their long-term impact that matters.[16]

Is industrialization sustainable? Can industrial civilization survive on Spaceship Earth?

These most fundamental questions cannot be answered with any certainty: the answers depend on assumptions whose correctness cannot be established.

To predict the future of industrial civilization is not the objective of this study. Indeed, such forecasting belongs to the field of futurology, of suspect credentials but fashionable in the 1960s and 1970s. The following brief comments serve only to provide a historical perspective on some of the issues involved.

The 1960s and 1970s saw predictions of an impending environmental crisis of catastrophic proportions. In the highly industrialized and democratic countries, where the impact of industrialization was large and pervasive, and where such concerns could be freely expressed, numerous scientists, intellectuals, and young activists proclaimed the "ecological crisis" to be the most critical issue confronting mankind. Their assessment and dire forecasts often reflected emotional disenchantment rather than objective evaluation.

In the late 1980s, environmental issues came again to the fore. They were extensively discussed in *Our Common Future*, a 1987 report prepared by the United Nations World Commission on Environment and Development, headed by Gro Harlem Brundtland, who was at that time the prime minister of Norway. The study listed pollution, toxic wastes, deforestation, desertification, and depletion of natural resources among the challenges which threaten the survival of life on earth.

The environmental movement, while generally exaggerating the seriousness of the "crisis," has played a highly constructive role in promoting environmental quality through adoption of adequate standards and controls, and reduction of waste (through, for example, recycling) or adoption of more efficient designs (such as smaller automobiles). More importantly, it has sensitized and helped to educate the politicians, industry, and the general public about the social costs of industrialization and the need for truly comprehensive assessments of the impact of technology.

Within a relatively short period of time the situation was significantly improved on many fronts. In North America and later elsewhere, air pollution caused by automobiles was reduced several fold through imposition of mandatory limits on emissions, bans on leaded gasoline, and development of "cleaner" engines. In London, England, the quality of the air was radically improved with the passage in 1956 of the *Clean Air Act*, which prohibited the use of coal in fireplaces. The detrimental impact of aircraft operations was contained and reduced through imposition of restrictions on engine exhaust and noise. Car travel was made safer through attention to car design and introduction of safety devices (seat belts). The use of pesticides and herbicides came under control; application of some particularly dangerous chemicals was prohibited. Progress was achieved in reducing water pollution through restrictions on industrial effluents and untreated sewage.

The imposition of controls is a matter of trade-offs between societal benefits and direct economic costs, and is therefore inevitably opposed by those who see their interests threatened or whose priorities differ; the adoption of compromise measures is often the result. Nevertheless, the examples mentioned above and many others demonstrate convincingly that, at least in local or regional, rather than global dimensions, the physical impacts of industrialization are relatively well understood or amenable to investigation and explanation, and that a democratic society — if it so wishes — can achieve significant control over the impact of industrialization on nature. However, as already noted (see pp. 5, 6), evaluation of the global impacts of industrialization in the far-off future is a matter of uncertainty and speculation. This is true, for example, of such consequences of atmospheric pollution as acid rain, the greenhouse effect and destruction of the ozone layer.

Ecology crusaders

Concern for life on Earth has led many zealous ecologists to engage in propaganda which sometimes borders on intellectual terrorism. The basic elements of their crusades include:

- chronic scepticism (scientists know nothing and the ecosystem is mysteriously unknowable, although somehow with computer programs we can predict the weather 10 years into the future);
- nihilism (human values such as technology are evil);
- emotionalism (the attempt to bypass reason and appeal to people's emotions);
- economic ignorance (evasion of the complete economic impact of their policies);
- statism (an ecological dictatorship making decisions on every proposed business action);

- dishonesty (manipulation of facts and people under the principle that the end justifies the means).

Not everyone sympathetic to the ecology crusade accepts all the above principles, but that has not stopped similar crusades in the past. The ecology crusade is well funded and well organized and has had considerable impact on peoples' lives, particularly loss of productive jobs and the overall deterioration of economy. Hopefully it is not too late [to stop it].

(Glen Woiceshyn, *The Globe and Mail*, 29 March 1991)

* * *

Fish in Sweden's Lake Vänern are dying. Scientists say the body of water, which provides a third of the country's drinking water, has been made ultra-clean by environmentalists and the fish cannot survive the sterility.

(*The Globe and Mail*, 18 November 1992)

In the resource sector, predictions of shortages of oil and other strategic minerals, and of an impending food crisis, popular in the 1970s, have failed to materialize. They were essentially based on the assumption of an exponential growth of consumption coupled with a slowly growing or finite resource base — the same model which provided T.R. Malthus in 1798 with a conclusive argument "against the perfectibility of mankind" and led him to envisage a future of inevitable misery and hardship, devoid of all social happiness. This was also the model which caused W. Stanley Jevons in 1865, an eminent English geologist, to predict the exhaustion of Britain's coal by 1966 (actually, as consumption of coal declined after 1913, by 1966 less than a quarter of the available coal as estimated by Jevons in 1865 was mined).

A century later, the oil, which replaced coal as the main source of energy, was forecast to run out in a few decades. But by 1992 the proven reserves[17] increased to a record one trillion barrels from 640 billion in 1977 and the so-called reserve-to-production ratio — a measure of how long the world's known oil reserves will last — was a third greater than it was in 1979, when oil consumption peaked; it stood at 40 years (at current level of demand), virtually higher than at any time since such records began to be kept in the 1930s (Stone 1993).

Ever since Malthus, the food supply, which could not keep up with a fast growing population, was seen as a cause of impending crisis. "The battle to feed all of humanity is over. In the 1970s the world will undergo famines — hundreds of millions of people are going to starve to death" —

announced a 1968 bestseller (Ehrlich 1968). And yet the record of food production shows that, at least since 1950, there has been an increase in the food produced per capita, and the world food supply has been improving. The data also show that there have been many fewer famine-caused deaths in the third quarter of this century than in the 1875–1900 period (Simon 1981, 61). It is now generally realized that food shortages and famines are as yet not the result of a worldwide shortfall of food but of the politics and economics of the production and distribution of food. This is why some countries, which should be net food exporters (as, for example, Russia, Ukraine and Poland, and before 1992, Soviet Russia), must import food while other countries suffer acute shortages. Incompetent governments, ethnic and religious strife, policies which reflect unjust and unrealistic priorities, corrupt bureaucracies, and transportation and communication difficulties are in the main responsible for present-day famines.

While the early prophesies of doom have failed to materialize, the problems of increase of population and economic growth remain among the most critical that industrial civilization and all travellers on Spaceship Earth have to face. Clearly, it is absurd to suggest that indiscriminate growth can continue indefinitely in a finite world.

Economic growth — that is, production and consumption — continue to be seen in the West and in the less developed countries as a solution to social problems and essential to well-being. Can the growth be gradually slowed down and constrained or, if not, will it be arrested and collapse through catastrophic crises? Will Malthus eventually be proven right, or will the transition to sustainable growth in a dynamic equilibrium be achieved? Opinions vary but the urgent need to address the issue is undeniable.[18]

When considering a less abundant future, one should not ignore the extreme adaptability of people, when circumstances demand it and motivation is there. Those who experienced World War II can attest to the success and even relative ease with which people in Britain and Germany, as well as in the occupied countries of Europe, adjusted — almost overnight, under high stress — to oppressive scarcity of food and other mundane necessities of everyday life, and restrictions of personal freedom.

Adaptability of human society should not be underestimated; without it the deployment of technology could not succeed. Technological innovation is itself the adaptive response of man to new conditions and requirements. And so, innovation provides in a large measure the answers to problems created by older technologies.

The Causes of Suffering

Alarmist warnings from dedicated anti-technologists and environmentalists notwithstanding, today, as in the past, the main causes of suffering and misery in the world are not the alienation of labour, disenchantment with the industrial civilization, fouling of the environment, or exhaustion of the Earth's resources. So far, none of these have had much effect on the well-being of mankind. This has been obvious to the less developed countries, who seek industrialization and consider the Western criteria for environmental quality as inappropriate luxuries that only the wealthy can afford. Clean air and water are much less important in the Second and Third Worlds than the standard of living measured in terms of availability of food, shelter, health services, basic consumer goods, and personal freedom.

The true causes of suffering, misery, and cruel death are buried deeply in human nature. Greed, desire for power over others, self-interest, and the belief that ends justify the means are the forces that drive individuals, societies, and nations and that are responsible for humanity's plight. Over the ages, uncounted millions have been killed and maimed, have perished in prisons and concentration camps, have lived as slaves, or have died from hunger in the name of a "superior" or more "moral, just and humane" socio-economic order, or to satisfy the ambitions of a leader, of his followers, or a nation. People have fought for control over others and their territories since time immemorial, irrespective of the cost in human life and suffering. In this century, military conflict reached global proportions in the First and Second World Wars, and inflicted casualties and devastation on a scale never before experienced. Given the truly overwhelming overkill power of nuclear weapons, a Third World War may appear unlikely; nevertheless, during half a century of the Cold War which followed World War II, enormous resources were being spent to deter war or to prepare for a confrontation that would be wished for only by those who are desperate to cling to power and see military conquest as the only way to maintain and expand their rule.

In 1988, twenty-five major wars were being fought around the globe (see map below). Between 1945 and 1992 more than 20 million people were killed in more than 150 wars. Almost all conflicts have taken place among countries of the Third World. They spend four times as much on defence as on health. Their military expenditures match the value of aid received from the West.

But war has not been the only, nor necessarily the most evil, cause of suffering and death. In the twentieth century, totalitarian rule, whether of the left, right, or religious persuasion, has destroyed and continues to

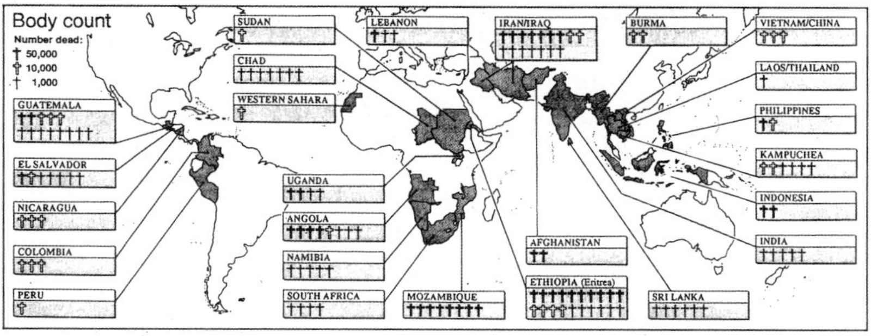

(*The Economist*, March 12, 1988. ©1993 The Economist Newspaper Group, Inc.)

The world's wars in March, 1988.

destroy, both morally and physically, many more people than has armed conflict.

In Hitler's Germany, political opponents and unwanted populations were imprisoned, tortured and killed. As part of the Nazi plan to develop the "master race," the majority of Jews in Central and Western Europe were exterminated; some six million perished in the gas chambers of Oswiecim (Auschwitz), in other death camps, and in the Warsaw ghetto. Thousands from the countries occupied by Germany were summarily executed or interned in concentration camps and used as forced labour for the German war effort.

The human costs of the Chinese revolution — not likely to be ever known with any precision — were immense and continue to mount. The Cultural Revolution of the 1960s — an abberation of China's leadership — has destroyed some of the human resources China is so desperately short of. Ideological and political strife in Latin America, Africa, and Asia take their toll in oppression and human life. Since 1992, an ethnic and religious conflict of extreme cruelty has been raging among the peoples of former Yugoslavia, close to the heart of Europe. Even industrialized Western Europe is not completely free from brutal conflict rooted in religious and political beliefs, as in Northern Ireland.

The communist experiment in the Soviet Union and other countries that belonged to the red empire is perhaps the most tragic demonstration of how a system, which is supposed to benefit the working class, has been used by a determined minority to oppress and exploit it on a larger scale than ever attempted before. An ideology that ignored human aspirations and values, and a disastrous economic system were imposed and maintained through physical and mental coercion. From the very beginning of the Soviet Union, all-powerful secret police, concentration camps, forced labour, rigged justice, and bloody purges have been the norm in the "workers' paradise." For over seventy years, tens of millions have populated the gulags; millions of peasants have died of hunger as they resisted collectivization of agriculture, an article of faith with the communist rulers; others were summarily executed and buried in mass graves (one such grave, estimated to contain over 200,000 bodies, was discovered in 1987 in Bykovnia near Kiev, AP 1989); Stalin's great purge from 1936 to 1938 sent some 8 million to prisons and labour camps (Weissberg-Cybulski 1951). In an attempt to destroy the souls as well as the bodies of those who did not conform, the opponents of the system who were not killed or imprisoned, were exiled or confined to psychiatric institutions. In 1988, historian Roy Medvedev published a detailed account of Stalin's victims, indicating that about 20 million died during his rule (Keller 1989).

An ideology which had as its origin the concern for the worker has led to the establishment of the most cruel, oppressive, and inhuman system in which the supposed beneficiary was impoverished, exploited, and defenceless. It is precisely in the Soviet bloc countries that workers and peasants have lost all control over the conditions of work and wages, where free and independent labour unions have been banned, where strikes were forbidden and any opposition was brutally crushed, with bullets if necessary. The oppression of the soul was matched by oppression of the body. The centrally planned economy has not been able to provide adequately for the elementary needs of population, such as food, housing, and clothing. Interminable line-ups, the black market, and dependence on the West for commodities that could be in abundant supply domestically have been the established features of the Soviet bloc countries. So have been the corruption and creation of a most highly privileged ruling class.

The total failure of red totalitarianism was exposed by Poland's Solidarity movement in 1980–81, the collapse of the communist governments in Central and Eastern Europe in 1989, and finally, in 1991, the disintegration of the Soviet Union itself. Some of the most oppressive and ignominious regimes ever headed into oblivion.

The Benefits of Democratic Industrialization

The doctrinaire views of Marx and his followers have not passed the test of time. Capitalist technology and industrialization or, more significantly, industrialization within a free democratic society, have been the benefactors of the working class; the communist "classless society" has been its worst enemy. Paradoxically — in the context of Marxism — it is in the highly industrialized countries of the West that application of technology has led to the creation of conditions more humane than exist elsewhere. Thanks to high productivity of mass manufacturing and a climate conducive to innovation, a relatively uniformly high standard of material wealth has been attained, coupled with the largest extent of personal freedom (which, incidentally, has allowed the freedom of Marxist expression denied in the countries that purported, and some still purport, to be Marxist).

These gains of democratic industrialization, as important as they are for members of Western societies, have had an even more significant and profound impact on relations between nation states. After two world wars and decades of industrialization, constructive applications of science and technology have proven to be more beneficial to man than territorial expansion and imposition of political control. Conquering ignorance, not territories, has become the key to success. It was Winston Churchill who said that "the empires of the future are the empires of the mind."

In the wake of increased wealth, states' and nations' perceptions of their mission and of the ways to achieve it have changed from conquest, subjugation, and exploitation to peaceful coexistence, interdependence, and competition. For centuries, the countries of Western Europe fought each other to enhance their or their leaders' stature, secure control over foreign territories, populations and markets, or at least preserve or restore the "balance of power." But as World War II drew to a close, the futility of armed conflict as a means of settling issues among states became recognized. Instead, in the West, closer co-operation took over with such structures as the European Economic Community and the establishment of many other international organizations. Since the end of World War II it has been inconceivable to imagine that Great Britain, France, West Germany, Italy, Spain or the Scandinavian countries could ever be at war with each other.[19] In North America, where the United States developed as the first continentally integrated democratic industrial society, for more than a century armed conflict has not been an option in resolving international issues. Technology and industrialization — as argued in some detail in Chapter 5 — are powerful agents of international co-operation and integration. In an industrial civilization, competition of skills has replaced competition of ideologies and physical subjugation.

Physical assets are no longer the determinants of wealth and international stature; superior education, inventiveness and organization, dynamic innovation, and high productivity are. How else could such countries as Switzerland, Sweden, and Israel which have few, if any, natural resources attain a standard of living among the highest in the world? How else could Japan overtake America and Western Europe in many important sectors of technology and industry?

Science and technology determine national power

At the conclusion of World War II, there were only 40 people trained in science and engineering in South Korea. The Korean War that ended in 1953 was devastating. Even with some recovery, the gross national product of Korea in 1962 was only $2.3 billion (1980 dollars), and the GNP per capita was $87. In 1986 the GNP was $94 billion [and the GNP per capita $2,350].

More than 40,000 professional people are now employed in research and development. Many electronic devices are being produced and exported, including computers and 256K random-access memory chips. Shipbuilding is sophisticated and computer-controlled. Steel-making facilities are among the most modern and competitive in the world today. Seven nuclear power reactors are in operation, two are under construction, and two are being designed and will be built by a Korean company.

One recent study showed that 10-year-old Koreans were tied for first place with Japanese children in knowledge of science, whereas 10-year-old U.S. children ranked 8 in a field of 15.

In 1966, the then Korean President Park Chung Hee said, "In modern times development of science and technology is one of the most important factors in determining national power. Science and technology which are driving forces in the cultural development of mankind have greatly contributed toward rapid economic growth and human welfare."

(P.H. Abelson, *Science* 240 (1 April 1988): 9 ©AAAS)

Although armed aggression appears to have lost its utility in the industrialized West, it has not been abandoned by the less developed countries. As would be expected, they continue—as did Western Europe for centuries—to rely on war to attain their objectives or satisfy the ambitions of their leaders.[20] This may require a military response from the West when its interests are or are deemed to be threatened. However, the ability of the West to intervene militarily on short notice anywhere, the tremendous superiority of all components of its war machine (weapons, communications, logistics, intelligence, strategic and tactical planning), the overall operational sophistication of its armed forces—so convincingly demonstrated in the 1991 Iraq war—may limit and eventually eliminate armed conflict as an option in resolving conflicts between the West and the less developed countries. Also in this case, the availability of sophisticated weapons may render war obsolete.

For the first time in human history, peaceful co-operation and competition have replaced armed confrontation and rule of force as the only avenues available to nation states to pursue their political objectives. Democratic industrialization has been instrumental in resolving critical problems of international relations; this has been by far its most significant contribution to human relations.

As already noted, alienation and damage to the environment have been seen in the West as major threats to society. In a global view, the exploitation of man by man appears to be a much more significant issue, an issue which will not be resolved until man's view of himself and society changes in the wake of modernization — a slow process that has yet to run its course in the countries of the Third World and the former Soviet empire. It is the lack of social innovation — as opposed to the abundance of technological innovation — that has been and continues to be responsible for much of human misery and suffering.

Social innovation has usually followed — rather than preceded — technological innovation. In Great Britain, it was decades after the start of the Industrial Revolution that labour legislation was enacted and left-wing political movements gained momentum and representation in parliament; it was not until 1900 that the British Labour Party was founded. Given the rate of technological progress and the unpredictability of the social impact of technology, the precedence of technology over social change is inevitable. Can the time lag between the technological and the social innovation be reduced so that progress toward a more humane society, particularly in the Third World countries,[21] would be accelerated? This is a task that must reckon with the human psyche and is therefore infinitely more difficult than the relatively straightforward and rational process of technology transfer and industrialization.

The Third World and the West: the precarious gap

"SO, BY A VOTE OF 8 TO 2 WE HAVE DECIDED TO SKIP THE INDUSTRIAL REVOLUTION COMPLETELY, AND GO RIGHT INTO THE ELECTRONIC AGE."

(©1981 by Sidney Harris. *American Scientist*, September–October 1981)

The rapid development of industrial civilization has widened the cultural and economic gap between the developed West and the so-called developing countries, which represent the majority of the human race. Unless the First and the Third Worlds[22] find the means to peacefully and gradually reduce the gulf which now separates them, their coexistence may become precarious and the clock of Western development may be pushed back. This is a critical issue not just for the West or the Third World, but for the future of all humanity. The Darwinian survival of the fittest, which has governed international relations, is not the mechanism which could narrow the gap and promote a harmonious relationship between the West and the Third World, the rich and the poor. But because their interests — at least in the short term — are incompatible, the emergence of an alternative effective mode of coexistence (which has been referred to as the New International Economic Order) is fraught with difficulties and uncertainties. The process of industrialization which started in the West with the Industrial Revolution can never be replicated and has little relevance to the development of the Third World. Western development was self-sustained and organic. It was carried out by a force of workers, technologists, and entrepreneurs who became increasingly literate, well educated, and trained in the skills required by industry and commerce.

A vast educational enterprise was established with schools, vocational training institutes, and centres of higher learning; professional societies and journals provided effective means for exchange of information on the latest "state-of-the-art."

The growth of manufacturing was matched by the growth of markets and urbanization was a response to the growth of the industrial plant. An infrastructure of financial institutions, communication and transportation, and a social structure suited to industrial activities were developed. Western industries suffered no competition from the rest of the world. Industrial production was the monopoly of the West; the world was its market.

The situation of the Third World countries, who gained political independence mostly after World War II, has been radically different. In their efforts to industrialize and modernize, they have to compete with highly sophisticated, capital intensive industries of the rich Western societies. The production of the latter is designed to serve Western markets and is ill suited to the needs of the Third World; so are the innovations which emerge from Western laboratories. The objective of Western industry is economic gain and growth; it exploits cheap labour in the Third World to gain competitive advantage.

In the 1970s, E.F. Schumacher in his bestselling *Small is Beautiful: Economics as if People Mattered* (1973) pointed out the inappropriateness of

Western technology to the needs of the Third World and advocated development of better suited "intermediate" technology, "vastly superior to primitive technology but simpler, cheaper and freer than the super-technology of the rich."

Promotion of development and modernization in the Third World by Western governments and industries and by such international agencies as the World Bank and the International Monetary Fund, frequently with the support of elites of their less developed clients, often involved construction of totally unsuitable mega-projects. Giant dams, which were supposed to "modernize" traditional irrigation and agriculture, and produce electricity, caused ecological disasters, uprooted native communities, and generated debt instead of wealth; some were never completed. Giant steel works were built by foreign aid not because they were needed but in order to support Western industries; economic and environmental disasters were the result. Capital intensive, fully automated manufacturing plants were exported from the West only to bring unemployment and increased dependence on foreign expert help and supplies of spare parts.[23]

Clearly, evolution rather than massive transplantation of Western technology is the proper approach to development of the Third World.

The Third World needs a mix of simple and sophisticated technologies. But relatively simple, labour intensive technologies, appropriate for the Third World at its present stage of development, no longer exist and are of no interest to the West. In some sectors, such as health, agricultural genetic engineering and satellite monitoring of crops, the most advanced Western technologies are required but their successful deployment may be constrained by a lack of financial resources and the generally primitive conditions in the Third World.

A holy water fire engine

Some Buddhist monks believe that holy water protects against bad spirits and brings good luck.

Phra Koon, 71, a monk in Nakorn Ratchasima, 260 km north of Bangkok, Thailand used a borrowed fire engine to spray 2500 litres of holy water on thousands of followers to bless them for the New Year.

(*Reuters News Agency*, 3 January 1994)

A non-Western culture inhibits transfer of Western technology and puts it to unintended and unorthodox use (see illustrations on p. 92). During the Mexican civil war in the middle of the nineteenth century, slain Catholic rebels were strung from telegraph poles. Under the regime of Shah Pahlavi, Iran underwent superficial modernization through extensive acquisition of Western products and technology but the society remained untouched and committed to the past. In 1979, Iran reverted to its traditional Islamic culture under the fanatical leadership of Ayatollah Khomeini, and in 1980, engaged in an eight-year religious war against Iraq. In 1982, huge cranes of the most modern design served in Iran as scaffolds for public hanging of the Iraqi unfaithful. A traditional culture imposed its own values on the application of modern technology.

In nineteenth-century India a culturally more appropriate technology was used to execute people. The head of the condemned was placed on a stone and crushed by an elephant underneath his enormous foot.

The mismatch in the technological and economic development between the West and the Third World is a serious and the most obvious obstacle in the path of modernization. But there are other much more significant and profound impediments. Foremost among them are a generally low level of education of Third World populations and radical differences between theirs and Western cultures.

Condoms: Third World and Western applications

Population explosion is a major problem in the Third World but a primitive society is not capable of using birth control technology effectively. According to a 1982 UPI dispatch from the United Nations:

> UN workers felt sure they had stemmed the Asian population explosion after giving birth control lessons in remote villages, using bamboo poles to show how condoms were worn.
>
> But when workers returned several months later, a UN report said yesterday, "they were confronted by a group of irate pregnant women."
>
> They found some husbands had been faithfully keeping their condoms on the bamboo poles, while others had been wearing them on their fingers.
>
> As for contraceptive pills, these were gallantly taken by husbands to save their wives the trouble.
>
> (The Canadian Press, *The Gazette* [Montreal], 16 December 1982)

In the West condoms have been used effectively not only as birth and disease prophylactics. During the Iraq war in 1991, British troops used condoms to protect their armaments from sand. A condom can fit over a 20 mm canon and, in action, a round can be shot straight through.

(*The Globe and Mail*, 29 January 1991)

(Casasola, *Time*, 30 December 1991)

Slain Catholic rebels strung from telegraph poles in 19th century Mexico

(Blackstar, N.Y.; *Newsweek*, 29 November 1982) **Public execution in Iran in 1982**

(Culver Pictures, N.Y.; *Time*, 24 January 1983) **Execution by elephant in nineteenth century India**

Industrialization and deployment of technology demand literacy and specialized skills, efficient organization, unambiguous precise information, and the ability to handle it effectively. As noted before, technology does not tolerate ignorance and incompetence, and requires its users to follow strict rules. Such skills and attitudes are not possessed by Third World societies and cannot be instantly transplanted from the West. On the contrary, the acquisition process is necessarily long, measured in decades rather than years; it cannot be drastically accelerated.

Information: a yardstick of development

The range of topics and issues on which information is available and its accuracy are infallible indicators of the degree of development—in terms of industrial civilization—of society. This is immediately apparent to a visitor whose quest for all sorts of commonplace intelligence ends in frustration and failure.

It may be difficult to obtain maps and plans of cities, roads and railways, of bus, tram and subway routes, of timetables and prices for any mode of transportation; if available, such data may be out of date and inaccurate. For example, an "official" map may show a road crossing a river, but the hapless motorist will discover that the bridge, still under construction, is closed to traffic (this was the author's recent experience in Central America). City plans may not include street indexes; road maps may lack mileage.

- Streets and roads may lack name and direction signs, or the signs may point the wrong way. Buildings may lack numbers.

- Air terminals may lack timely information on departure and arrival of flights, on ground transportation (schedule and cost), and confusion may occur concerning allocation of seats in aircraft.

- Traffic lights may give ambiguous or contradictory signals to car drivers. (At a major intersection in Sankt Petersburg, a traffic signal shows simultaneously a red light and two green arrows which point to the left and straight ahead. In Moscow, signs saying STOP hang at intersections equipped with traffic lights.)

- In office buildings, the rooms may not be numbered in any consistent fashion (or not at all), and there may be no indication where to find a given room.

- Telephone directories may be out-of-date, may lack instructions for making out-of-town calls, and may be unobtainable. Postal rates may also be unavailable, and word-of-mouth information on the required postage may be contradictory.

- The time shops, offices, banks, and other businesses are open may not be posted and, in any event, may not be adhered to. Often a sign on the door will read "Back in ten minutes," but will not indicate when it was posted.

- In general, to obtain any specific information from government or other offices may be difficult and again, such information may vary depending on the source. Securing reliable information may be most difficult.

Even in highly industrialized countries, handling of information continues to present a problem, as evident from the illustrations on the following pages.

Information Highway or Information Mess?

Which way?

The sign at a major U.S. airport gives contradictory directions to "Gates" with both the arrow pointing to the left and the arrow-like aircraft pointing to the right.

In contrast, the efficient aircraft symbol on the road sign indicates both direction and destination.

Confusion in the New York subway . . .

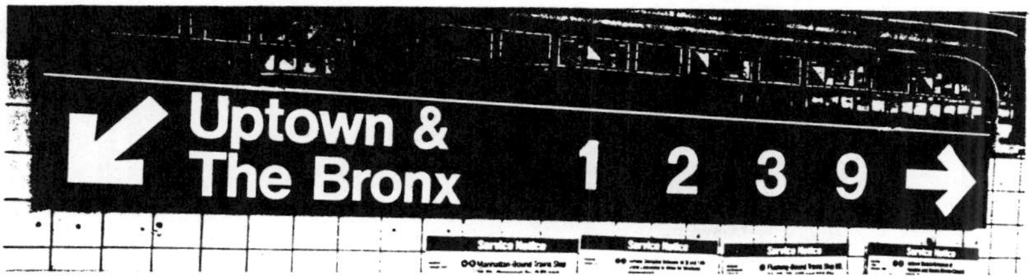

Trains 1, 2, 3, and 9 go to "Uptown & The Bronx," but not according to this sign.

. . . and on Campus

You can't tell that before you reach Athletics, Administration and Residences, you'll find Engineering and Architecture. Or that by turning right you'll reach Chemistry and Physics.

Information Highway or Information Mess? (contd.)

Superfluous and confusing

As you enter the building, you are warned not to smoke inside; when you leave, the same translucent sign also forbids smoking outside!

The "Do Not Enter" symbol is all that is required; the Arrow is both superfluous and confusing.

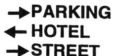

→PARKING
← HOTEL
→STREET

Poor Design: Arrows pointing right are located on the left.

Good Design: After you locate your destination, to find the arrow your eyes must turn in the direction you'll be going.

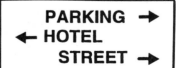

PARKING →
← HOTEL
STREET →

Information Highway or Information Mess? *(contd.)*

What number?

no number

two numbers (210A and 3152)

old number

new number

three numbers (204, 3133, 3149)

You'd think that engineers would know how to handle information, but introduction of an improved, consistent system of room designation in one Faculty of Engineering building resulted in complete chaos. Two years after the change, some rooms have no numbers, some have only the old ones, some have two (the old and the new), some have three. In other places electric clocks which hang from corridor ceilings don't work, each face showing a different and wrong time.

(All photos: Julius Lukasiewicz)

As noted by Schumacher (1973), "Development does not start with goods; it starts with people and their education, organization and discipline. Without these three, all resources remain latent, untapped, potential. Here lies the reason why development cannot be an act of creation, why it cannot be ordered, bought, comprehensibly planned: why it requires a process of evolution. Education does not 'jump'."

It is no wonder that modernization of less developed societies often results in quick adoption of superficial trappings of Western modernity with little impact on the life and behaviour of traditional society. Such symbols of Western affluence as airports and airlines, office towers, large scale industrial complexes, sophisticated weapons and telecommunications are popular with Third World countries but may only marginally influence their industrialization and economic development. Over-impressed with technical possibilities, Third World governments excel in extravagant, excessive, or inappropriate applications of technology, or deployment of technologies which their societies are not ready or capable of adopting.

A Boeing 747 jumbo jet for the ruler of Saudi Arabia, equipped as a flying palace complete with a tub and elevator, at a cost of $150 million, is a typical recent example of extravagance.

The procurement by Third World countries of large arsenals of modern weapons from the West is a more tragic case of misuse of scarce hard currency resources. Encouraged by the West, the Third World spends on armaments sums comparable to the value of the foreign aid it receives. This in spite of the fact that it lacks the know-how and the personnel needed to maintain and operate the sophisticated weaponry, and has no prospects of acquiring either for decades.

Inappropriate uses of technology by societies not familiar with it are a common occurrence. The following examples, albeit trivial, are typical and serve to illustrate the point well.

When an international conference was held a few years ago in a large capital city of a developing country, closed circuit television was used to show the opening ceremonies to the overflow of participants assembled in another, vast auditorium. Lacking large screen television projection facilities, the organizers set up instead on the stage a four-by-six array of 24 small television sets. The twenty-inch television images were of course too small to be recognizable by the viewers.[24] However, as all 24 televisions were continually getting out of tune, the audience was highly amused to watch throughout the ceremony the antics of two technicians moving quickly from one set to another in frantic attempts to stabilize the images. In the same large and congested city recently installed traffic lights were completely ignored by drivers and pedestrians alike. As one native explained, the lights were there to illuminate rather than to control the traffic.

To uneducated members of traditional societies the demands of technology on its operators and users are incomprehensible and cannot be explained in rational terms; they have to be justified by reference to more familiar concepts, as in a case described by Joseph Conrad. In *Heart of Darkness*, first published in 1902, Joseph Conrad tells of the partially educated savage whose job it was to fire up the boiler of a steamer going down the Congo.

> He was useful because he had been instructed; and what he knew was this — that should the water in that transparent thing disappear, the evil spirit inside the boiler would get angry through the greatness of his thirst, and take a terrible vengeance.

Another typical and interesting example comes from Mao Tse-tung's China. In an article which appeared in 1971 in *China Pictorial*, Hou Shu-shan, head of the ground crew of an aviation group of the General Administration of Civil Aviation of China, discussed maintenance of aircraft engines. When he discovered that a broken piston ring caused oil consumption to increase abruptly, he turned to Chairman Mao's writings for an explanation.

> I studied Chairman Mao's teaching and came to understand the relation between normality and abnormality more clearly. Chairman Mao teaches us: "In given conditions, every contradictory aspect transforms itself into its opposite." The normality and abnormality of a plane, too, are constantly transforming into their opposites. A plane in good condition might get out of order after a period of use, while a plane in disrepair can be restored to good condition by overhauling. Only when one is mentally prepared for "transformation" will he look out, under normal conditions, for factors of abnormality, trying by every means to detect faults, forestalling any breakdown and guaranteeing normal flight. . . .
>
> Over the past 15 years no serious mishap has occurred in any of the planes under my care. I have never let a plane take off with an uncorrected fault. I was able to do this because I have studied and applied the "good old three" articles of Chairman Mao and his philosophical thinking in a living way, and on the basis of ideological revolutionization, tried to make my thinking more scientific.
>
> I realize deeply that to do revolutionary work well, we must study and apply Mao Tse-tung. Think conscientiously and in a living way and act at all times as Chairman Mao teaches. So long as one follows Chairman Mao's teachings, the plane will follow his bidding. (Shu-shan 1971)

Whether Shu-shan's views reflect a naïvely genuine faith in the application of Mao's teachings or a desire to prove to the ruling party his political correctness, is unimportant. In either case they demonstrate a primitive, albeit possibly necessary, motivation in dealing with a technical problem.

In her wonderfully informative autobiographical history of Communist China, Jung Chang (1991, 466) records a ridiculously naïve case of party propaganda at the time of the Cultural Revolution. One chapter in a textbook "was about a model youth hero who had drowned after jumping into a flood to save a telegraph pole because the pole carried chairman Mao's voice."

Traffic lights are a technology intended to regulate and facilitate traffic; however, in China in 1966, as the Cultural Revolution was gathering momentum, traffic lights acquired a political and symbolic dimension, as recorded by Jung Chang (1991, 288). She writes:

> Traffic was in confusion for several days. For red to mean "stop" was considered impossibly counterrevolutionary. It should of course mean "go." And traffic should not keep to the right, as was the practice, it should be on the left. For a few days we [the Red Guard] ordered the traffic policemen aside and controlled the traffic ourselves. I was stationed at a street corner telling cyclists to ride on the left. In Chengdu there were not many cars or traffic lights, but at the few big crossroads there was chaos. In the end, the old rules reasserted themselves, owing to Zhou Enlai, who managed to convince the Peking Red Guard leaders. But the youngsters found justifications for this: I was told by a Red Guard in my school that in Britain traffic kept to the left, so ours had to keep to the right to show our anti-imperialist spirit. She did not mention America.

A fire and a car wash in China

[Fire hydrants are rare in China.] Firemen here rely instead on tank trucks. Last February, 80 people died in a department-store fire in Tangshan, a city in northern China. It took 18 minutes for someone to report the fire, partly because the store's only telephone was locked in a box, and the man with the key was out. When the fire truck finally arrived, it used up its water supply in one minute.

* * *

After arriving back in Beijing, I noticed that the headlong dash to capitalism had infected our local fire station. A big sign now announced: Car Wash.

To wash our car, a fireman blasted away at our Jeep with a high-powered fire hose. When it was time to go, the car wouldn't start. The water had shorted out the ignition. Out came a red hairdryer. For 40 minutes, the fireman stood there blow-drying our engine. The whistle blew for lunch, and the other firemen drifted away, returning with chopsticks and bowls full of food.

> With lots of time on our hands, we chatted. In their first two months of operation, they have made about 5,000 yuan ($1,100). What do they do with the money? A fireman paused between mouthfuls. "We get to eat better," he said.
>
> (Jan Wong, "Secrets and a car wash: a bargain at $10." *The Globe and Mail,* 10 May 1993)

The cultural differences between non-Western and Western societies represent perhaps the most fundamental difficulty in the achievement of modernization by Third World countries.

Objectivity and rationality are the cornerstones of Western culture, as is the belief in man's superiority over nature. These notions are incompatible with a subjective view of reality and the idea of oneness of man and nature, the notions found in non-Western cultures. To impose Western culture on a traditional society is to force it to live with two different sets of world views and values, a situation which may lead to destruction of the internal coherence and fabric of society.

The cultural conflict which modernization brings about has been of great concern to the Third World. The following statement by an Indian author illustrates such concern well.

> As an aggressively high-consumption oriented culture intensifies amongst a well-to-do minority across the world, it is creating a rat race amongst the rest, both within and between nations, to become a part of it. The desire to join this growing, multinational culture is so strong that for most people it has left no freedom to choose. The individual has no alternative.
>
> Our growing capabilities in science and technology have helped us to acquire a technological literacy that allows us to converse with the rest of the world as equals and has rightly earned us international prestige amongst the community of nations. But science and technology cannot be allowed to impose their own value system on society. On the contrary, the use of science and technology in society has to be governed by a human, socially appropriate value system. Otherwise we will get a rampant materialism, the extreme symbol of which is the young man amongst us who does not even mind burning his bride if he does not get the promised scooter and refrigerator in dowry.
>
> The culture exported from the so-called developed countries, which we are adopting unthinkingly is at the heart of the crisis. We never ask the question: developing toward what? This growing multinational culture must be destroyed because it leads to economic chaos, increased social disparities, mass poverty and filthy affluence in coexistence, environmental degradation, and ultimately civil strife and war.

> To get a balanced, rational development and to preserve the environment, a new development process is needed. The biggest intellectual and political challenge of our times is to articulate and demonstrate this new kind of development.
>
> It is a reflection of our prevalent culture that development has come to mean a mere increase in consumption of material goods and services. Development is not a product that can be obtained with economic growth. On the contrary it is a process which enables all levels of society — individual, community and nation — to become more self-reliant and more independent in choosing and deciding their own future." (*The State of Environment*, Centre for Science and Technology: New Delhi, 1982, 4)

In the context of the Third World, the "multinational culture," i.e., Western industrial civilization, is seen as a totally negative force, a "rampant materialism" which must be destroyed, and the development process as leading to increased self-sufficiency and independence. This is contrary to the experience in the West: industrialization inevitably leads to greater interdependence and integration (as argued in Chapter 5). Similarly, if a society opts for science and technology, it opts also for the values they impose; no other choice is possible.

The Indian author's view of the cultural impact of the West reveals a desire to achieve "a new kind of development" so that a balance is maintained between the traditional and the modern "multinational" cultures. But the prescription for such a balanced and rational development is not offered. Given the contradictory objectives of industrialization and independence, the conflict between a value system influenced by science and technology and a "socially appropriate" traditional value system, it is not likely that a prescription could be devised.

Difficulties in the West

As for the West — so far the main beneficiary of technology — it is also likely to experience difficulties more serious than any it has encountered in its industrial past. Population growth, degradation of the environment, and depletion of natural resources are the most visible issues, but it is the impact of economic growth and affluence on man's values and expectations, and the complexity of the socio-economic system of an industrialized society that could be the underlying causes of Western civilization's difficulties.

After World War II, material wealth has been on a steep increase in the West. Through innovation and gains in productivity, the standard of living of North Americans, West Germans, Swiss, Scandinavians, and others has continued to rise. Perhaps not unnaturally, Western society became much more conscious of the effects than of the cause of economic growth. An automatic annual increase in earnings (given low level of inflation, this meant also a real increase in purchasing power) was being taken for granted by blue and white collar workers alike, in all sectors of the economy. When in the late 1970s and in the 1980s the economy of the West slowed down and eventually started to contract, the expectations didn't change: demands for high wages, longer holidays and extra benefits continued to escalate and strikes proliferated. Governments, seeking irresponsible popularity rather than responding to objective needs, have been reluctant to resist such demands and have themselves lived beyond the means of the governed, running up huge deficits.[25] "The revolution of rising expectations" — a term often used to describe the impatience of Third World societies in matching Western affluence — also depicts accurately the unrealistic hopes of the industrialized West.

For the economic growth to continue, such excessive hopes must be abandoned and a sound relationship between expectations of growing affluence and economic performance re-established. The notion that the passage of time alone is a guarantee of increased real income must give way to the understanding that the latter can occur only as a result of gains in productivity.

To seek a higher standard of living through a more uniform distribution of wealth is equally unrealistic, at least in the West. Over thirty years of experience of the Soviet bloc centrally planned economies have clearly demonstrated that it is not the way the pie is divided but its size that is crucial to the achievement of material well-being. Inevitably, no matter how it is cut, too small a pie must mean a relatively low standard of living for the great majority. Moreover, the insistence on income uniformity necessarily weakens the dependence of income on effort, ability, and entrepreneurship and removes the very incentives needed to make the pie grow.

A belief in the automaticity of economic growth is not the only unrealistic and damaging expectation characteristic of contemporary Western civilization; belief in the unbounded power and effectiveness of research is another. This is hardly surprising: for decades, the spectacular successes of science and technology have been the daily diet of politicians, intellectuals and ordinary people in the West. Nuclear energy, space travel and exploration, satellite communications, and computers have all furnished incontrovertible evidence of the effectiveness of research. In the 1950s and 1960s, as the funding for research and development continued to grow quickly in the West,[26] organizations of expert consultants, called think-tanks, multiplied. In these circumstances it was natural to believe that the same methodologies that got man to walk and ride an electric vehicle on the Moon would be equally successful in tackling socio-economic problems on the Earth. The fact that in the former case we were merely concerned with the physical properties of mostly inanimate matter (as, for example, described by Newton's, Faraday's and Einstein's laws) and their exploitation through technology was conveniently neglected. In the socio-economic sphere there were no immutable laws to be discovered and applied; the behaviour of individuals and societies continued to be highly unpredictable. Although the results of socio-economic research were highly disappointing, the activity did not diminish. It became routine for all levels of government, and even for private enterprise to seek expensive help of "expert" consultants; many a government economist, engineer, or scientist was turned into a mere administrator of outside contracts and interpreter of consultants' reports which were supposed to provide the 'decision makers' with information needed to arrive at rational and optimal policies. But, more often than not, volumes of sometimes contradictory and often trivial data have failed to indicate the specific practical measures to be taken. In fact, studies and research have become increasingly a substitute for action and a cause of unnecessary delay. Instead of leading to a more sophisticated decision making, they have often prevented the making of a timely, if any, decision, to the detriment of society.[27] The attempts to substitute data and information for judgment have not been successful and have been diverting valuable resources into unproductive use. If continued, this trend will further erode the ability of industrial society to maintain economic growth and to manage itself.

The excessive emphasis and reliance on research in addressing socio-economic problems reflects a more fundamental characteristic of industrial society: its high degree of complexity in relation to man's intellectual capacity. As suggested in the next chapter, this is the basic factor which ultimately constrains the successful management of industrial society.

Notes

1. Indeed, the terms which we use to define the progress of civilization — Stone Age, Bronze Age, Iron Age — refer to development of technologies by man. Man the Thinker (*Homo Sapiens*) was also Man the Maker (*Homo Faber*). Man made tools; but tools made man as well.
2. While highly similar in many respects, such societies may nevertheless exhibit significant differences. For example, although the lifestyles and the standard of living of Americans and Canadians differ little (in 1991, the GDP per head was $22,130 in the United States and $19,230 in Canada), in 1990 an American man was 5.3 times more likely to be murdered than his counterpart in Canada (*The Globe and Mail*, 1 January 1994).
3. Unless otherwise indicated, the examples of inventions, innovations and forecasts given here have been described in one or more of the following: Ayres 1969, Jantsch 1967, Jewkes et al. 1969, Livesay 1979.

4. Curiously, the killer smog in London was not forecast by health officials, city engineers, or scientists, but was most accurately predicted by Robert Barr, an imaginative journalist and author of detective novels. In *The Doom of London*, published in 1877 (reprinted in Lodge 1969), he described a week in November 1899 when coal smoke prevented the sun from lifting the fog and, coincidentally, the air remained totally still. The whole population of London, except for a handful of people, perished; the author of the story was saved by an oxygen machine left in his office by an American who hoped to market his invention in London.

   At least two other remarkable cases of precognition which involved technology are on record.

   Futility, published in 1898 by Morgan Andrew Robertson, foretold the 1912 *Titanic* disaster. Just as the *Titanic*, Robertson's *Titan* was considered unsinkable, had a comparable displacement, had too few lifeboats, and sunk after hitting an iceberg at 25 knots (*Titanic*'s speed was 22.5 knots; Gardner 1986).

   In *No Highway*, published in 1948, Nevil Shute (N.S. Norway) predicted with uncanny accuracy the fate of the de Havilland *Comet*, the world's first jetliner introduced into service by the British Overseas Airways Co. in 1952 and withdrawn in 1954 after a series of mysterious crashes. Shute's BOAC Rutland (read de Havilland) *Reindeer* (read *Comet*), the first jetliner to go into service, crashes in Labrador (read off Elba). Just as in the case of the *Comet*, parts of the *Reindeer* are salvaged and brought to the Royal Aircraft Establishment in Farnborough, England, for examination. At the same time an experimental investigation is carried out at the RAE on components of another *Reindeer* (read *Comet*) jetliner and it is determined that the disaster was due to a fatigue failure of the aircraft's structure, precisely the cause of the *Comet* crashes (Lukasiewicz 1955).

   The precognitions of the killer smog in London, and of the *Titanic* and *Comet* disasters can be viewed as entirely understandable creative projections from contemporary knowledge. But the probability of such startling coincidences must be truly negligible.

5. The Little White Chapel in Las Vegas offers drive-through wedding services. Owner Charlotte Richardson marries about 500 couples on Valentine's Day, the busiest day of the year (*The Globe and Mail*, 7 June 1993).

6. In 1992, nuclear reactors accounted for 73 percent of electrical energy generated in France.

7. Schumacher (1973) advocated "wisdom [which] demands a new orientation of science and technology towards the organic, the gentle, the non-violent, the elegant and beautiful." Rubinoff (1977) hoped that "so long as technology is under firm control of moral wisdom its employment can be trusted and respected." But such wisdom eludes us: the orientation of science and technology is necessarily towards the unknown, rather than towards some ethical, moral, or aesthetic goals.

   Rubinoff (1977) also felt that in our culture "dominated by functional rationality," research is driven by the desire and satisfaction of achieving a goal rather than by the goal's desirability, and that therefore "if it is possible to achieve a given goal, then the goal itself must be rational and we are obliged to achieve it." Here again, since the business of research is to seek the unknown, there can be no certainty that the goal can be achieved.

   The history of research into controlled fusion reaction illustrates this case well. Following the first uncontrolled release of fusion energy in 1952, it was thought possible to achieve this goal within a few years; it has yet to be attained 40 years later.

8. "Inventing to order" has been highly successful in straightforward applications, as in some cases in the military and aerospace fields. Among the remarkable achievements stand out the atomic bomb, developed by the U.S. Army Manhattan District between 1942 and 1945 (in time to be used in World War II), the Apollo "Man on the Moon" project (completed ahead of schedule in July 1969, in eight years and within a budget of $25-billion), the ballistic missile (A4 or V2) first deployed by Germany in 1944, and many other sophisticated weapons.

9. *Mach Number* is defined as the ratio of the velocity of motion to the velocity of sound in the medium in which the motion takes place; for example, the *Mach Number* of an aircraft in flight is the ratio of the aircraft's speed (relative to the atmosphere) to the velocity of sound in the atmosphere; modern jetliners reach a *Mach Number* of 0.9 in cruising flight.
10. Mass production which serves global markets renders sophisticated and complex products affordable but it also necessarily imposes standardization and excludes custom design. Although consumers' choice of products is not nearly as severely limited as in the times of Henry Ford (who is believed to have remarked that "The customer can have the car any color he wants as long as he wants it black"; Kranzberg and Pursell 1967, 2, 47), nevertheless it is restricted to a large but finite number of standardized options (which may involve, for example, several standard colours of cars).
11. James Watt, whose invention of an improved steam engine resulted in widespread application of steam power, was employed as an instrument maker at Glasgow University and benefited from his contacts with the faculty. However, his invention reflected his own practical considerations.
12. Except for the relatively new, computer based technologies of robotics and artificial intelligence, which do not fit this definition. Rather than to amplify and extend human capabilities, they seek to imitate and emulate our intellect and copy our behaviour. As already noted (Chapter 2, pp. 21, 22; also Chapter 4, p. 137), this would require "man to lift himself by his own bootstraps," a feat impossible to perform.
13. Access to huge computer memories has not been necessarily beneficial. Designers of some software (i.e., computer programs) have exploited the enormously large memory of computers but have ignored the very limited capacity of human memory. For example, a word processing manual (such as for the popular *WordPerfect* program) may run to over 800 pages of explanations and instructions (and thousands of specific "moves"), presumably all needed to take advantage of most of the features of word and text manipulation offered. The manual, of course, reflects the capability of the program and not of its user who can't remember but a small fraction of the material. To wordprocess efficiently, one must remember one's moves, and one can remember them only if one makes them frequently. Looking up in the manual other infrequently used options is time consuming and inefficient: indeed, such options, which comprise the majority, will never be used.

    Highly automated photographic cameras suffer from a similar deficiency. They offer dozens of "programs" of exposure (supposedly suitable for a variety of different situations as to light, subject, contrast, etc.) to be chosen by the photographer, who is not likely to remember when to use which alternative. Here automation has merely substituted choosing the program for setting the camera controls as required — a perfectly easy task given through-the-lens light metering.
14. The performance of technology should match the requirements of its application; it has been used on occasion to extend our senses beyond useful range. For example, a traditional analog watch, which translates time into position of the hour and minute hands in relation to the dial, allows one to estimate time to within a minute (a generally sufficient accuracy) but, moreover, makes it possible to "see" at a glance the time interval between "now" and some other past or future instant (such as the time available to catch a plane). With a digital (i.e., numerical) watch, such time interval cannot be "seen" and a much less convenient mental calculation must be made to determine it. Also, a digital watch shows time to within a second or a fraction thereof and may allow events to be "timed" — an application of no use to most people. And, when the battery runs out, it stops without warning, a deficiency the mechanical self-winding watches do not suffer from.
15. The name given to the period of confrontation and armed stand-off between the North Atlantic Treaty Allies and the Soviet Union, which lasted from the end of World War II to the dissolution of the Soviet Union in 1991.

16. See Stone (1993), Gee (1994), Homer-Dixon (1994) and Kaplan (1994) for a critical discussion of these issues.
17. Defined as an estimate of the total amount of oil in areas that have been well prospected.
18. See, for example, Lamontagne (1976) and Simon (1981).
19. In 1991, France and Germany established a 50,000 strong joint army corps, and invited all EEC members to contribute to a supranational Euro-army.
20. The U.S. realpolitik in the Middle East played a part in precipitating the 1991 Iraq war, see below.
21. These issues have been addressed by Adams (1991), Adams and Solomon (1991), and Hancock (1989), among others.
22. These designations refer to the division of the world in the post-World War II period into three distinct categories: the First World of the western, capitalist bloc, the Second World of the communist bloc and the Third World of the less developed countries.
23. Analysis of large foreign aid projects which resulted in monumental failures will be found in Hancock (1989), Adams (1991), and Adams and Solomon (1991). It should be noted that similar blunders were committed in the Soviet Union and Soviet bloc countries when the ruling communist party insisted on construction of huge industries without any concern for the need and environmental impact.
24. To succeed, this would have required precise apportioning of 24 segments of the image among different TV sets to produce a single, composite large video screen. A similar technique is now being developed to create out of an assembly of computer-controlled monitor screens huge "adwalls" or electronic billboards.
25. This has been certainly true of Canada, whose national debt exceeds 50 percent of the country's gross domestic product and whose foreign debt is the largest per capita in the world. In 1992 it stood at 270 billion USD or 47 percent of GDP, equivalent to 168 percent of the value of exports. The U.S. foreign debt amounted to only 7 percent of the GDP and, on a per capita basis, was almost six times smaller than for Canada. Except for Luxembourg, the debt of all members of the European Economic Community exceeded 60 percent of the GDP.
26. See pp. 130, 131 for U.S. expenditures on R&D. Relative to the gross national product (GNP), R&D expenditures levelled-off in about 1959.
27. In Canada, more often than elsewhere, the mechanism of a commission (sometimes called "royal"; the first royal commission was formed in 1783 to inquire into the losses, services, and claims of Loyalists who had fled the American Revolution) has been also frequently used whenever a need was felt to tackle a socio-economic problem. Such commissions, supposedly consisting of experts but not lacking political appointments by governments or other bodies, have usually relied on extensive and expensive questioning of the public. It has been assumed that public hearings would result in valuable insights and wisdom needed to institute effective reforms. A democratic polling of a generally and necessarily uninformed public would somehow lead to solutions which even the people knowledgeable in the field could not discover. (We must be thankful that a royal commission and public hearings were not needed to allow Canadian air carriers to switch from propeller to jet engines. But fast passenger trains, which have been operating in other countries since the 1960s, have been under incessant investigation by scores of commissions and committees; to date, voluminous studies and $7 billion of public funds spent on the maintenance of an obsolete technology, have been the only result; see p. 54). Over the years, innumerable commissions have studied science policy, transportation, education, law, competitiveness, environment, reproductive technologies (i.e., how to make babies), etc. Shelved reports rather than action have often been the only outcome.

References

Adams, P. 1991. *Odious Debts: Loose Lending, Corruption and the Third World's Environmental Legacy*. Toronto: Earthcan.

Adams, P., and Solomon, L. 1991. *In the Name of Progress: The Underside of Foreign Aid*. 2d ed. Toronto: Earthcan.

AP. 1989. "Stalin Blamed for Slaughter of Thousands," *Associated Press*, March 1989.

Ayres, Robert U. 1969. *Technological Forecasting and Long-Range Planning*. New York: McGraw-Hill.

Baier, K., and Rescher, N., eds. 1969. *Values and the Future*. London: Macmillan. p. 3.

Barzun, J. 1959. "The Misbehavioural Sciences." In *Adventures of the Mind*, ed. R. Thruelsen and J. Kobler. New York: Knopf. p. 20 (cited in Florman, 1976, 39, 156).

Brooks, John. 1967. "Profiles: Xerox, Xerox, Xerox," *New Yorker*, 1 April 1967, 46–90.

Capra, F. 1981. *The Turning Point*. New York: Simon & Schuster.

Chang, Jung. 1991. *Wild Swans: Three Daughters of China*. New York: Simon & Schuster. p. 466.

Conrad, Joseph. 1910. *Heart of Darkness*. New York: Bantam Books. p. 61.

Dessauer, J.H. 1971. *My Years with Xerox: The Billions Nobody Wanted*. New York: Manor Books.

Dubos, R. 1968. *So Human an Animal*. New York: Charles Scribner's Sons.

Economist. 1988. "The World's Wars," *The Economist*, 12 March 1988, 13–14, 19–22.

Ehrlich, P.R. 1968. *The Population Bomb*. New York: Ballantine Books.

Ellul, Jacques. 1964. *The Technological Society*. New York: Vintage Books. 1967 edition.

———. 1980. *The Technological System*. New York: Continuum Publishing.

Florman, Samuel C. 1976. *The Existential Pleasures of Engineering*. New York: St. Martin's Press.

Forrester, J.W. 1971. "Counterintuitive Behaviour of Social Systems," *Technology Review* 73 (January 1971): 52–68.

G&M. 1993. "Hindsight," *The Globe and Mail*, 8 February 1993, A13.

Gardner, M. 1986. *The Wreck of the Titanic Foretold?*. Buffalo, N.Y.: Prometheus.

Gee, M. 1994. "Apocalypse Deferred," *The Globe and Mail*, 9 April 1994.

Hancock, G. 1989. *The Lords of Poverty*. London: Macmillan.

Homer-Dixon, T. 1994. "Is Anarchy Coming? A Response to the Optimists," *The Globe and Mail*, 10 May 1994.

Jantsch, Erich. 1967. *Technological Forecasting in Perspective*. Paris: O.E.C.D.

Jevons, W.S. 1865. *The Coal Question*. London and Cambridge: MacMillan.

Jewkes, John; Sawers, David; and Stillerman, Richard. 1969. *The Sources of Invention*, 2d ed. New York: W.W. Norton.

Kaplan, R.D. 1994. "The Coming Anarchy," *The Atlantic Monthly* 273(2) (February): 44–76.

Keller, B. 1989. "Soviet Paper Details Victims of Stalin Era," *New York Times Service*, 4 February 1989.
Klemm, F. 1964. *A History of Western Technology*. Cambridge, Mass.: MIT Press.
Kranzberg, M., and Pursell, C.W. 1967. *Technology in Western Civilization*, Vol. 1. Oxford: Oxford University Press.
Lamontagne, M. 1976. "The Loss of the Steady State." In *Beyond Industrial Growth*, ed. A. Rotstein. Toronto: University of Toronto Press.
Life. 1972. *Life*, 5 May 1972.
Livesay, Harold C. 1979. *American Made: Men Who Shaped the American Economy*. Boston & Toronto: Little, Brown and Co.
Lodge, J.P. 1969. *The Doom of London: Two Prophecies*. Elsmford, New York: Maxwell Reprint Co.
Lukasiewicz, J. 1955. "Messing about with Aeroplanes," *CAI LOG*, Canadian Aeronautical Institute, 1, no. 6 (February 1955): 16–17.
———. 1976. *The Railway Game: A Study in Socio-technological Obsolescence*. Toronto: McClelland and Stewart.
———. 1984. "High Speed Rail Projects in North America." In *Proceedings, 19th Annual Meeting, Transportation Research Forum*. pp. 327–41.
———. 1989. "Via Rail's Future: Scrap the Trains and Take the Bus," *The Globe and Mail*, 7 December 1989.
———. 1990. "The Little Engines That Conk Out—Repeatedly (and so Do the Brakes, Lights and Heating)," *The Globe and Mail*, 12 January 1990.
Malthus, T.R. 1798. *An Essay on the Principle of Population as it Affects the Future Improvement of Society, with Remarks on the Speculations of Mr. Godwin, M. Condorcet, and Other Writers*. London.
Marx, K. 1867. *Das Kapital*, Hamburg. Trans. Eden & Cedar Paul, London 1930.
Mathias, P. 1971. *Forced Growth: Five Studies of Government Involvement in the Development of Canada*. Toronto: Lewis and Samuel.
McLuhan, Marshall. 1964. *Understanding Media: The Extensions of Man*. New York: McGraw-Hill.
Meadows, D.H.; Meadows, D.L.; Raders, J.; and Behrens III, W.W. 1973. *The Limits to Growth*. New York: Universe Books.
Morison, E.E. 1966. *Men, Machines and Modern Times*. Cambridge, Mass.: MIT Press.
Muller, H.J. 1970. *The Children of Frankenstein: A Primer on Modern Technology and Human Values*. Bloomington and London: Indiana University Press.
Mumford, L. 1964. "Authoritarian and Democratic Technics," *Technology and Culture* 5(1): 1–8.
———. 1967. *The Myth of the Machine*, vol. 1, *Technics and Human Development*. New York: Harcourt Brace Jovanovich.
———. 1970. *The Myth of the Machine*, vol. 2, *Pentagon of Power*. New York: Harcourt Brace Jovanovich.
Newman, O. 1972. *Defensible Space: Crime Prevention*. New York: Macmillan.
NYT. 1972. "Housing Study: High Rise—High Crime," *The New York Times*, 26 October 1972.
Reich, A. 1970. *The Greening of America*. New York: Random House.
Robertson, M.A. 1898. *Futility*. New York: M.F. Mansfield.

Roszak, T. 1972. *Where the Wasteland Ends*. New York: Doubleday.

Rubinoff, L. 1977. "Technology and the Crisis of Rationality: Reflection on the Death and Rebirth of Dialogue," *Philosophy Forum* 15: 261–87.

Schafer, A. 1988. "A Desperate Need for Scientific Literacy," *The Globe and Mail*, 16 July 1988.

Schumacher, E.F. 1973. *Small is Beautiful: Economics as if People Mattered*. New York: Harper & Row.

Schwartz, H. 1971. "Forester's law," *The New York Times*, 14 June 1971.

Shu-shan, Hou. 1971. "The 'Thoughts of Mao' Applied to Aircraft Maintenance," *China Pictorial*, reprinted in *AIAA Student Journal* 9, no. 4 (December 1971): 13.

Shute, N. (N.S. Norway). 1948. *No Highway*. New York: William Morrow.

Simanaitis, D. 1992. "Saab 9000 CS". *Road & Track*, January 1992, 82–83.

Simon, Julian L. 1981. *The Ultimate Resource*. Princeton: Princeton University Press.

Sinsheimer, R.L. 1978. "The Presumptions of Science," *Daedalus* 107, no. 2 (Spring): 23–35.

Snow, C.P. 1969. *The Two Cultures and a Second Look*. Cambridge: Cambridge University Press.

Stone, C.D. 1993. *The Gnat is Older Than Man: Global Environment and Human Agenda*. Princeton: Princeton University Press.

Thoreau, H.D. 1948. *Walden; or, Life in the woods. On the duty of civil disobedience*. New York: Rinehart.

Time. 1966. "Blackout fallout," *Time*, 14 August 1966.

Weissberg-Cybulski, Alexander. 1951. *Hexensabbat*. Verlag der Frankfurter Hefte. Also: *Conspiracy of Silence*, London: H. Hamilton, London 1952; *Wielka Czystka*, Paryż: Instytut Literacki, 1967.

Winner, L. 1977. *Autonomous Technology: Technics-out-of-Control as a Theme in Political Thought*. Cambridge, Mass.: MIT Press.

4

The Ignorance Explosion[1]

"The art is getting longer and longer, the brain of the student not bigger and bigger."

(Hippocratic aphorism, ca. 400 B.C.)

IN "The Paradox of Human Progress" (Chapter 1), I suggested that the complexity of the industrial environment exceeded our capability to manage and control it and I pointed out that in this respect we did not differ fundamentally from our primitive, non-industrial ancestors who did not comprehend the workings of nature. I have further argued (in Chapter 3) that the impact of affluence on peoples' values and expectations, and the complexity of the socio-economic system were probably the most serious problems facing industrial civilization.

Examination of the limits of human intellectual capacity as compared to the complexity of the industrial environment supports this latter assertion. It also indicates—perhaps unexpectedly—the inevitability of industrial man's predicament, irrespective of his intellectual prowess.

As a result of two centuries of industrialization, the industrial environment comprises today a plethora of ever-changing technologies and a multitude of local, regional, national, international, and global activities of all kinds. This is a highly complex and unpredictable environment; it is conditioned by a myriad of technologies which interact with each other and with the natural environment and, as noted before, it is subject to the vagaries of human conduct. But, even if the human element of unpredictability were not present, the environment's complexity alone would tax our ability to manage and control it. In this task we are limited by our finite and biologically fixed intellectual capacity, a situation noted already in 1929 in an essay on the future of mankind by Bernal (published in 1969, 33, 42), who wrote:

> The increasing complexity of man's existence, particularly the mental capacity required to deal with its mechanical and physical complications, gives rise to the need for a much more complex sensory and motor organization, and even more fundamentally for a better organized cerebral mechanism.
>
> Normal man is an evolutionary dead end; mechanical man, apparently a break in organic evolution, is actually more in the true tradition of a further evolution.

Human Intellectual Capacity

It appears reasonable to postulate that our intellectual capacity has been substantially constant and finite. On the time-scale of development of civilized society, biological evolution of homo sapiens has been at a standstill. Although we lack a definition and measure of intellectual capacity, several symptoms of our intellectual limitations have been identified (Miller 1967). For example, the span of our immediate memory is known to extend over no more than about seven or eight items. This short-term storage can be identified with consciousness and with the working memory — that is, with the system in which problems are solved, decisions are made, and information flow is directed. It thus follows that we cannot think simultaneously about everything we know and our ability to reason and to perceive complex relationships is restricted. Overabstraction, oversimplification, analogies, and coding are effective methods of overcoming this limitation. By the use of informationally rich symbols, such as words, abbreviations, images, or laws, complex material can be translated into a few units that can be grasped at one time. Such terms as Oedipus Complex, Law of Supply and Demand, Second Law of Thermodynamics, Socialism, or such symbolic statements as $F = ma$ (classical, Newtonian dynamics) or $E = mc^2$ (relativistic, Einstein dynamics) are shorthand for large volumes of complex concepts and information. This might suggest that our memory is limited by the number of symbols that we can master rather than by the amount of information that they contain. That is not so; the inherent limitation lies in our ability to perform efficient coding — that is, to identify significant variables or to perceive laws governing complex phenomena, this ability itself being subject to our limited information handling capacity.

Another aspect of human limitations, extensively studied by psychologists, concerns the so-called channel capacity. As we are subjected to an increasing number of stimuli (which may be directed at any of our senses) or to an increasing amount of input information, our ability to discriminate and to transmit information reaches an asymptotic, maximum value. Although its magnitude varies with the type of stimulus, we find that on the average we can identify and transmit no more than about seven from among the stimuli received. Such small channel capacity presents a severe limitation on the amount of information we are able to receive and process. Again, through proper organizing or coding of the input information, this limitation can be stretched — but it cannot be altogether removed.

The speed with which the human nervous system can process information represents another constraint. The biological brain operates on a millisecond or longer time scale — orders of magnitude larger than that of electronic computers.

Some have suggested that, although the intellectual capacity of *one* person is limited, the capacity of *many* has no known limit (Darlington 1975). This view appears to assume that a population of individual intellects is equivalent to a single, superior intellect of a much larger capacity. This is not so: although the contributions made by individual intellects add up to augment the total volume of information, it still requires one brain to integrate it, analyze, and draw conclusions, tasks in which we are limited by our finite intellectual capacity.

In the course of evolution, the development of the brain provided homo sapiens with a capability adequate to assure his survival in the competitive environment of nature. Evidently, this required some capacity for abstract thinking; we are apparently the first creatures to acquire it. We are also endowed with a sensorium which, while relatively extensive, is in many respects limited, for example, in terms of response to electromagnetic and acoustical spectra, or to passage of time. Our bodies do not respond to radio, radar, and ultrasonic frequencies; we do not see infra-red, ultraviolet and smaller wave length radiation. We need special devices to sense them and special instruments to measure time. Neither have we been genetically provided with built-in skills and packets of knowledge, such as mathematical operations, properties of elements, or laws of physics; every generation must learn them anew.

The mismatch between the capability we acquired through natural evolution and the demands our intellect is increasingly subjected to, is well illustrated through the following example quoted by Sinsheimer (1971):

> A physicist friend of mine frequently remarks on how much more difficult it seems to be to teach a 17-year-old a few laws of physics than it is to teach him to drive a car. He is always struck by the fact that he could program a computer to apply these laws of physics with great ease but to program a computer to drive a car in traffic would be an awesome task. It is quite the reverse for the 17-year-old, which is precisely the point. To drive a car, a 17-year-old makes use, with adaptation, of a set of routines long since programmed into the primate brain. To gauge the speed of an approaching car and manoeuvre accordingly is not that different from the need to gauge the speed of an approaching branch and react accordingly as one swings through the trees. And so on. Whereas to solve a problem in diffraction imposes an intricate and entirely unfamiliar task upon a set of neurons.

The Growth of Science

A quantitative description of the complexity of the industrial environment and society would require consideration of many factors, from production of food, raw materials, consumer goods, energy, and waste to provision of information, communication, government, and other services (on a *per capita* basis). If one recognizes that science has been at the base of the development of modern industry and technology, it appears that scientific development alone may be used as an indirect but single gauge of environmental complexity. Taking this approach, I shall consider the growth rate, specialization, complexity, immediacy, and obsolescence as those properties of science that indicate the limitations of our grasp of scientific information and, by analogy, of our ability to cope with the science-based environment. I shall also inquire into the future limitations of scientific growth and mention the possibilities of biological manipulation of humans and development of superior intelligence machines. The data used in this essay pertain mostly to U.S. society, as the one most advanced technologically and for which information is readily available, but the results could be considered applicable to any society at a similar stage of industrial development.

A number of indirect indicators, such as quantities of publications, numbers of scientists, funds spent on research and development (R&D), or changes in academic curricula, can be used as measures of the growth of science.

In 1665 the first two scientific journals were founded: *The Philosophical Transactions* of the Royal Society of London and the *Journal des sçavans*, started by Denis de Sallo in Paris. As pointed out by Price (1961), it is remarkable that, except for the first 100 years, the number of scientific journals has been increasing at a constant exponential rate since about 1760, doubling every 15 years (or increasing tenfold every 50 years), until over 100,000 journals have been founded. The estimate of the journals appearing in the 1960s (as opposed to the count of all founded journals) varies between 30,000 and 100,000 (E.B. 1968); as early as 1938, Bernal (1939) estimated that some 33,000 scientific journals were being published; a 1968 estimate (Zelikoff 1968) puts the number at 50,000. The world total of scientific papers was estimated in 1963 (Price 1963) at six million, doubling every 15 years; a yearly count of one million was quoted in 1968 (Zelikoff 1968).[2]

It appears that our ability to handle scientific information was exceeded early in the development of modern science (E.B. 1968). One of the first periodicals devoted exclusively to extracting parts of other publications appeared in 1714 in Germany (*Aufrichtige und unpartheyische Gedanken*, or *Science and Unbiased Thought*), when less than 10 scientific journals had been founded. When their number attained about 300, the abstract journals started to multiply at the same exponential rate as their predecessors, doubling in number every 15 years and attaining the figure of 1,855 (including indexing services) in 1963. With the multiplicity of the abstracting aids, the information pressure has not been relieved. At a time when the count of journals was measured in thousands, and when about ten abstracting publications already existed, the German physicist Hermann von Helmholtz (1821–1894) wrote:

> I have already noticed the enormous mass of materials accumulated by science. It is obvious that the organization and arrangement of them must be proportionately perfect, if we are not to be hopelessly lost in the maze of erudition.

It is noteworthy that proposals for a comprehensive, worldwide system for the dissemination of scientific information were made as early as 1933 (Davis 1933; Bernal 1939). A World Science Information System (Unisist) was being developed in the 1970s by the United Nations. It envisaged computer storage of all scientific information machine translated into a common metalanguage and its retrieval in any desired language (Sullivan 1971).

Von Helmholtz's fears have not been dispelled but are shared by scientists and engineers today. In spite of tremendous progress, data-processing technology has a difficult time keeping pace with the accumulation of scientific and technical information. The printed journal, still the main—albeit inadequate—medium of dissemination of current information, is likely to be superseded by electronic publications. With information stored in a central computer and accessible via telephone lines to scientists equipped with computer terminals and printers, on-line retrieval of individually selected papers and reports becomes feasible as a more economical and faster technique of information distribution than the traditional journal.

The estimates of the growth of science based on scientific publications are confirmed by the count of scientists and engineers active in the United States (assuming that the American scientific literature paralleled the growth of the world's scientific literature). Since about 1930 their total number has been doubling every 12 to 14 years, indicating, not surprisingly, a direct relationship to the growth of publications.

Another confirmation of these growth rates comes from a different quarter. Zelikoff's (1968) investigation of engineering curricula (referred to in more detail below; see also Lukasiewicz 1971a, 1971b, 1971c, 1971d) between 1935 and 1965, covering five departments in each of five typical U.S. universities for a total of 7,000 undergraduate and graduate courses, showed that, if no courses were eliminated, the number of courses offered would have been growing exponentially, doubling every 17 years, i.e., at a rate only slightly smaller than indicated for the populations of journals and scientists. The close adherence to the exponential law is remarkable.

In light of the growth rates reviewed above, the volume of scientific information appears to have been doubling every 15 years; the volume of general information has probably been increasing much faster as a result of spectacular development of computers and their widespread application in all walks of life. Since 1944 computer performance[3] has been increasing tenfold every four years and sales have been doubling every four to five years. The compounded effect of these factors could be estimated to result in doubling of computer-processed information every year.

In relation to human intellectual prowess, both static and dynamic aspects of this situation (sometimes referred to as "knowledge" or "information explosion") are significant. The static effects are those of specialization and complexity; the dynamic ones, those of immediacy and obsolescence.

Specialization

On the assumption that the total quantity of scientific information is proportional to the number of journals published, its rate of growth was found approximately equal to the rate of expansion of the scientific population, each doubling every 15 years. By extrapolation into early times, it follows that over the past 200 or more years the volume of scientific literature per living scientist remained substantially constant. This may be in fact a good confirmation of the assumption that human intellectual ability may be regarded as a biologically fixed quantity. Had it been increasing over the years, the gain would have been reflected in the augmentation of the above ratio. With the volume of scientific information per scientist being a constant quantity and defining specialization as the ratio (total quantity of information)/(quantity of information per scientist), the growth of specialization is found to equal the growth of science, with a doubling period of 15 years or less.

With the quantity of information being equated to the number of scientific journals, the specialization of journals must be assumed to grow at the same exponential rate and to reflect directly—as would be expected—the specialization of scientists. Indeed, it is likely that a modern scientist does not read more papers than did his predecessors and—while perhaps resenting it—becomes inevitably more specialized.

An independent measure of the specialization of journals may be obtained from examination of dispersion of the literature on a given subject among a number of journals (Goffman and Warren 1969). It has been shown, for example, that of 10,000 papers published over a period of 110 years on a specific subject, half of the contributions were to be found in less than 50 journals (out of a total of 1,700).

Another indication of mounting specialization comes from a count of the authorship of papers over the years. Whereas in 1870 it was very rare for a paper to be co-authored, the solo paper has now almost completely disappeared (Price 1967). Specialization is among several reasons to which this may be attributed.

The figures given above define in no uncertain terms the irresistible progress of specialization. An equally clear impression of it is gained from the descriptions of specific skills possessed by individuals in the earlier phases of the development of modern science and at present. For example, von Helmholtz (1821–1894), who through his career held the chairs of physiology, pathology, anatomy, and physics, made basic contributions to optics, acoustics, thermodynamics, electrodynamics, physiology, and medicine; in fact, it was suggested (Fung 1967) that the title "Father of Bioengineering" may be given to him.

To the nonprofessional, the rise of specialization since von Helmholtz's days has been particularly apparent in the field of medicine: it has left the poor patient searching for the right doctor, his body and ailments fragmented among a multiplicity of specialists. It has been reported that currently only two percent of doctors become general practitioners (i.e., multidisciplinary doctors). The consequences of the rising specialization of medicine may lead to a situation described by Moss (1968):

> The day may not be far off when the specialist of the right coronary artery will meet with the specialist of the left coronary artery and in greeting each other will encounter the specialist on the collateral circulation at the interventricular separatum.

The Complexity of Science and the Environment

The total quantity of scientific information and the specialization, which can be thought of as the inverse of our ability to comprehend the whole of the information available, have been shown to increase at a high exponential rate (doubling every 15 or less years). Consideration of the complexity of information, as opposed to mere quantity, indicates that it may be increasing much faster. This is due to the inherent interdependence of the "units of information," which are all tied together to a higher or lower degree by a closely knit mesh of interactive relationships: they exhibit a high degree of feedback. With the volume of information growing exponentially, the complexity would be increasing in a doubly exponential fashion and creating a degradation of our relative intellectual ability even faster than indicated by the growth of the information volume alone (see the Appendix to this chapter for estimating the magnitude of complexity).

Although more difficult to measure, the analogous complexity of the environment is easily appreciated. From the standpoint of an individual member of modern society, the environmental complexity is apparent in terms of his complete dependence on goods and services that have to be provided by others and by a faultless technology. The manufacturing, distribution, and communication activities form a closely coupled, interactive network in which a failure of one link may affect the whole system and may result in undesirable and unforeseen consequences. Also, it is interesting to note that the inherent complexity of the natural environment has been much in evidence in recent times, as a result of detrimental changes caused by industrialized society. It is now recognized that both natural and artificial environments are characterized by a high degree of interdependence, with environmental changes feeding back their influence to modify the original causes. This high degree of feedback is a major symptom of the complexity of the environment.

The issue of the complexity of industrial society was addressed from another perspective by Polanyi (1951). He argued that, because industrial production and consumption involve a very large number of interdependent and concurrent activities, central planning of an industrial economy is strictly impossible. The number of adjustments per unit time required for efficient functioning of such an economic system cannot be achieved through a necessarily hierarchic system of central direction. A deliberate ordering agency cannot replace the operations of a system of spontaneous order in society, such as the competitive order of a market. This was evident, as discussed by Polanyi (see p. 129), from the failure of central planning in Soviet Russia, a consequence of the complexity of industrial society.

The Immediacy and Obsolescence of Information

For exponential growth, such as that exhibited by science, the "coefficient of immediacy" (introduced by Price 1963) is a convenient measure of the dynamic effect. It is defined as the ratio of the increment of a function over a specified time period to its total value at the end of that period.[4] For a given exponential growth rate the coefficient of immediacy, unlike the specialization, is invariable with time.

To determine the immediacy of information, with its doubling period of 15 years, consider the incremental amount over a human productive life span of 45 years. The corresponding coefficient of immediacy equals 7/8, or 87.5 percent, and indicates that this fraction of all information existing at the end of a person's life would have been produced during his/her life. With the number of scientists and engineers also doubling about every 15 years, the same figure gives the number of scientists who have been productive during a human life span in terms of the total number of scientists who have ever lived. In some specialized fields (e.g., computer sciences) even higher values must be attained by the coefficient of immediacy. For example, with a doubling period of four years, the coefficient of immediacy attains a value of 98 percent in a lifetime of only 24 years.

The immediacy of scientific information can be also determined on the basis of more specific data. Price (1965) has studied the distribution of citations in papers dealing with a specific field and found the formation of a "research front" comprising about 50 of the most recent papers that are much more frequently cited than the older contributions. When expressed as a time interval for a paper count doubling every 15 years, the time-width of the research front decreases from 15 years at the time the 100th paper is published to less than three years when the field contains 300 papers.

In general, the immediacy of science is indicated by more frequent citation of recent literature. A study of Garfield's *Science Citation Index*, which covers all papers cited in over 1,000 journals published in 1961 (see Price 1965), shows that 20 percent of cited papers had been published in the preceding two years, 41 percent in the preceding five years, and 57 percent during the 10 years preceding the year of survey. In the fastest-advancing fields, as many as 70 percent of citations may cover the preceding five years (Price 1967).

Still more specific information relating to the dynamics of the growth of science can be derived from the already mentioned survey of changes in the engineering curricula (Zelikoff 1968; Lukasiewicz 1971a, 1971b, 1971c, 1971d). The significance of these changes can be measured by "potential obsolescence," defined as the ratio of the number of new courses offered at the end of a specified period (equated with "new knowledge") to the number of courses available at the start of the period (representing information at the time of graduation). The qualification "potential" is necessary since in the estimate of obsolescence the additional knowledge that could be acquired after the start of the period (after graduation) is neglected. The time to reach 50 percent potential obsolescence has been decreasing from about ten years for the 1945 graduates to five years for those graduating 20 years later. Extrapolating into the next century, we find the class of the year 2056 reaching 100 percent potential obsolescence in only one year.

As in many other cases, as in this one, extrapolation of exponential growth too far into the future leads to an absurd result but, nevertheless, it indicates the seriousness of the present situation and the drastic changes to be expected in the near future.

The Vanishing Grasp

As a consequence of the exponential growth of science and, with it, of the informational content and complexity of the artificial environment, we face a serious crisis. As a measure of it, we may consider the rate of erosion of our "intellectual power," relating our inherent intellectual ability — which we regard as a biologically fixed quantity — to the environment with which we must cope. We may thus define our "degree of grasp" as the ratio of information the human intellect is capable of retaining and handling to the volume of information available, and the "degree of ignorance" as the analogous ratio involving all the remaining information (beyond our grasp). In these admittedly very loose definitions, the denominator stands for the total volume of knowledge in all fields, and, therefore, refers to total, completely unspecialized "grasp" that could be possessed at any time by a "super intellect."

As noted before, the volume of information is growing exponentially and doubling every 15 years or less while its complexity increases much faster: one faces the prospect of "instant antiquity." In these circumstances, one's grasp is quickly diminishing while one's ignorance is on a fast rise. (Customarily, and more flatteringly, this is referred to as a rise in specialization, the latter being the inverse of the degree of grasp. The ultimate specialist has been defined as the one who knows everything about nothing. Paraphrasing Winston Churchill it has been said that "never so many knew so much about so little.") Indeed, it is the "ignorance explosion," rather than the "information explosion," that is the significant cause of the difficulties that industrial societies face. A specialist can handle effectively only specialized problems but lacks the overall grasp required to overcome the environmental and societal difficulties, for which specialized approaches are highly inadequate.

The immediacy of information, resulting from its fast growth (in volume and complexity), demands of human intellect a high rate of absorption of the new knowledge (which, to some extent, replaces the old) or the ability to maintain a high rate of transfer. Thus, new knowledge to be assimilated per unit time becomes an increasingly large fraction of the total human information-storage volume. Moreover, under these conditions the assimilation of new knowledge occupies an increasingly large fraction of available time and creates a continually mounting "information pressure."

The relationships between the degree of grasp (or specialization), the total volume, and the immediacy and obsolescence of information can be illustrated by means of a simple graph shown below. Let the areas bounded by the three circles represent the total volume of information available at time intervals equal to the doubling time D (thus, the largest circle has twice the area of the middle one and four times the area of the smallest). The areas of the segments in each circle are equal and correspond to the human intellect's capacity. The angle of the segments γ is a measure of the degree of grasp ($1/\gamma$ is a measure of specialization), which is seen to diminish by a factor of two over the doubling period. The area of the annulus marked in the second and third circles represents the new information added over the doubling period; its ratio to the circle area (= 1/2) equals the coefficient of immediacy based on the same doubling period. The shaded areas of segments γ_2 and γ_3 represent new information (within a particular specialty) that has been added over the doubling period, and which has eliminated an equal amount of obsolete information.

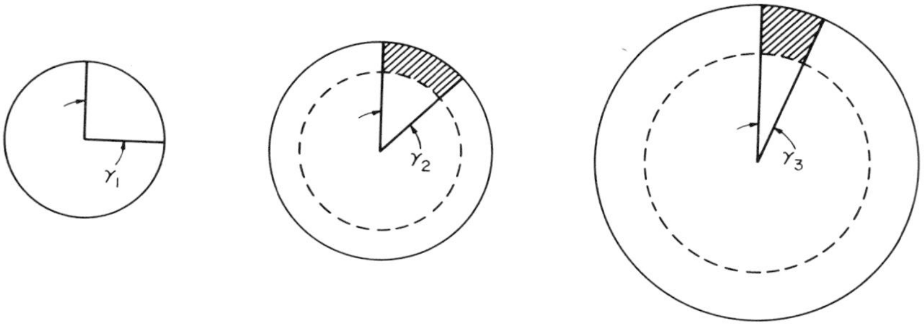

The total volume, specialization, immediacy, and obsolescence of information.

Comparison of angles γ_1, γ_2, and γ_3 (= 1/4 γ_1), spanning two doubling periods, vividly indicates the fast decrease of the degree of grasp.

Another factor that contributes to our relative ignorance in the understanding of the artificial environment and society concerns verifiability. Unlike the situation in the natural physical world, the experimental verification of the laws and relationships that apply to this class of phenomena presents inherent difficulties. With people the essential driving force, and time the essential variable governing the development of the artificial environment, such verification can be accomplished with respect to past events only, and its generality or its significance for the future must be necessarily limited. These are the very difficulties which beset the social—as opposed to the physical—sciences, an issue already addressed in Chapter 2.

New Tools and Techniques

The difficulties in guiding and controlling the environment of an industrialized society have now been widely recognized but the notion of the human intellect's limitations as the underlying cause has seldom been acknowledged.[5] And yet this is the basic reason that some of the new tools and techniques being developed to overcome environmental and societal problems prove less effective than expected.

In the educational field, the problems of specialization and obsolescence, almost as old as modern science itself, never cease to be discussed and experimented with. In view of the rate of growth of specialization and obsolescence, only relatively insignificant gains may be expected from the prolongation of studies. In the long-term, perhaps the only answer to educational obsolescence is a complete integration of work with education—a lifelong education. The two would be hard to tell apart when that stage had been reached.

To combat specialization, numerous attempts have been made to devise "inter-," "trans-" or "multidisciplinary" programs and organize teams of specialists to carry them out. New disciplines, such as ekistics or bioengineering, emerge as umbrellas under which segments of traditional disciplines are to be found. The success of interdisciplinary programs as a means of breaking down the rigid divisions of specialization has been limited. In the context of our finite intellectual ability, this should have been expected. To be truly successful, a multidisciplinary scientist would have to encompass, in the same measure as an ordinary specialist, a much larger segment of knowledge — and it is his intellectual capacity that limits his success in this endeavour; no amount of enthusiasm or exhortation can alter this fact. It is likely that the main benefits from development of new multidisciplinary disciplines will be the production of scientists just as specialized as their more traditionally trained colleagues have been but in the fields currently more relevant, particularly as regards environmental and societal problems.

In the area of government (on all levels), the "systems approach," a methodology originally designed for the handling of complex technical tasks (such as telephone communications or intercontinental ballistic missile weapons), is being increasingly applied to tackle such problems as administration of criminal justice, operation of hospitals, and development of integrated government information systems. However, so far, little success has been achieved in its application in the broader and more complex areas of poverty, transportation, energy resources, etc. In these cases, the complexity of industrial society is reflected in the very large number of highly interdependent units of authority and ever growing volume of regulations. Typically, the problem is how to ensure co-operation and effectiveness of some 100,000 governments in the United States (excluding school boards), or over 90 federal regulatory agencies (26 of which were created between 1969 and 1980), or some 40 federal agencies which offer "domestic programs" to "assist the American people in furthering their social and economic progress," or how to devise an efficient transportation system in the Northeast Corridor with its 150 sovereign transportation authorities, or how to keep track of and administer regulations listed in the 87,012 pages of the Federal Register (in 1980; in 1970 it ran to only 20,008 pages). Even in some relatively straightforward situations the systems approach has not been a success. Some of the major weapon systems, such as the F-111 U.S. Air Force — Navy fighter aircraft, or the North American automotive industry in the 1970s and 1980s are typical cases in point.

The disenchantment with the effectiveness of systems studies was voiced in 1968 (WST, 1968) by the U.S. Assistant Secretary of Transportation, when he observed that many systems analysis contracts are late, cost more than expected, or "end up with little more than junk." Commenting on the problems besetting the airports/airways and the post-interstate-highway-system programs, he told the Transportation Research Forum that

> if systems analysis cannot provide some immediate inputs to the decisions and plans which will be made over the next two to three years — starting as of yesterday — it will miss out on probably the most important set of transportation decisions that will ever have been made in the United States. . . . The time is now and models completed and perfected in 1972 will have missed the bus.
>
> It may be that, without the help of highly sophisticated systems analysis, some wrong decisions will be made, but this is an area where some wrong decisions are probably preferable than no decisions at all.

In fact, as already noted, extensive analysis has become a frequent substitute for action.

The effectiveness of any technique of information handling, such as the systems approach, depends entirely on the intellectual ability of those who develop and use it — and this, as we have pointed out, is essentially a limited ability. In our highly complex environment we lack the understanding of the factors involved and of their interdependence: we do not know what priorities to set and how to optimize the attainment of desired goals. A statement by Dr. Daniel P. Moynihan, on his appointment as head of the U.S. Council on Urban Affairs, is typical as an indication of the difficulties (NYT, 1968). Speaking at a news conference on 10 December 1968, Dr. Moynihan emphasized the importance of deciding just what the urban crisis was all about before attempting to devise solutions for such ills as poor education, seemingly ineradicable slums, and racial discrimination. "We have difficulties we don't understand," he said. "It's simply not enough to want to do good. We've outgrown our ability to deliver on our promises."

Thirteen years later, David Stockman, U.S. President Reagan's whiz-kid appointed as the new director of the Office of Management and Budget, was even more outspoken than his former professor at Harvard. Before his first year in office was up, he confessed in a 1981 interview with *The Atlantic Monthly* (Greider 1981):

> None of us really understands what's going on with all these numbers . . . You've got so many different budgets out and so many different baselines and such complexity now in the interactive parts of the budget between policy action and the economic environment and all the internal mysteries of the budget, and there are a lot of them. People are getting from A to B and it's not clear how they are getting there. It's not clear how we got there, and it's not clear how Jones [the Democratic chairman of the House Budget Committee] is going to get there.

When the OMB computer forecasts for the federal budget and the national economy gave frightening and "absolutely shocking" results (including federal deficits without precedent in peacetime), the OMB director discarded predictions which—based on orthodox economic premises—said that "basically . . . the world doesn't work," and had a new model developed which assumed a dramatic surge in the nation's productivity. Stockman himself appeared to deny the validity of such procedure when he said that "it's based on valid economic analysis but it's the inverse of the last four years." He summed up his position by explaining that "the whole thing is premised on faith, on a belief how the world works."

Computer predicament

"To err is human but to really foul things up requires a computer."

(*Farmers' Almanac for 1978*)

Such admission is hardly reassuring and must come as a shock to politicians and to those inside and outside the government who do not appreciate the complexity of the industrial state and believe in rational management of the nation's economy by highly competent experts assisted by the most powerful techniques available.

A $120 billion piñata

> The institution of [Canadian] government has simply grown too big and too complex to be subject to human control: a great, bulging, $120-billion piñata swinging this way and that, spilling its goodies on every interest group or empire-builder that can get close enough to take a whack at it. It is so overgrown that no one can even keep track of spending, let alone try to make some sense of it.
>
> (Editorial, *The Globe and Mail*, 21 January 1994)

Indeed, the complexity of the modern industrial state may seriously affect the effectiveness of the democratic system of government. Paul Valéry, the late poet and philosopher (1871–1945), observed that politics, once "the art of preventing people from minding their own business," was now "the art of forcing people to decide things they do not understand" (as quoted by Muller 1970). Dennis Gabor (1970) emphasized the same difficulties when he asked, "How could the simple man decide with his vote a question, such as was put by Bertrand de Jouvenel: 'How to maintain full employment, not more than 2 per cent inflation per annum, and a good balance of international payments at a steady rate of real growth of not less than 3.5 per cent?' "—a question particularly relevant in the context of the recessions the industrialized West suffered in the 1970s, 1980s, and 1990s, the worst since the crisis of the 1930s.

Economic forecasting has its pitfalls

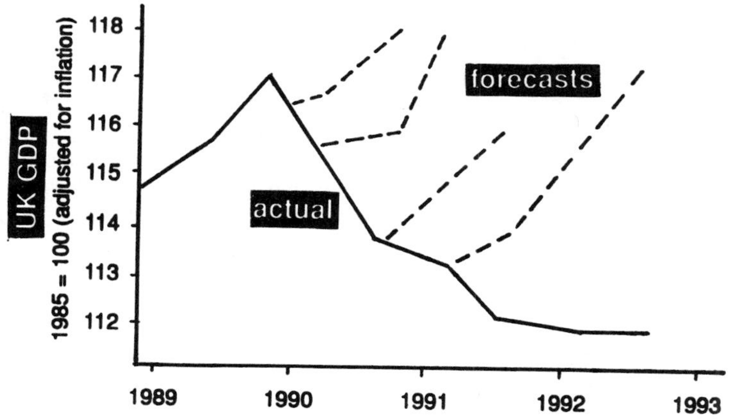

Forecasting of economic performance is the task of over 20 economists employed by Her Majesty's Treasury and an IBM 4381 computer which runs one of the most sophisticated models of Britain's economy. As shown above, the recovery, repeatedly predicted by the Treasury, has failed to materialize as the longest post-war recession persisted into the 1990s. The Bank of England forecasts, based on a different model, also failed. In September 1991 its governor was "confident that we are now coming out of recession." Eleven months later the Bank admitted that "recovery was elusive" (Chote 1992).

Economic forecasting has its pitfalls *(contd.)*

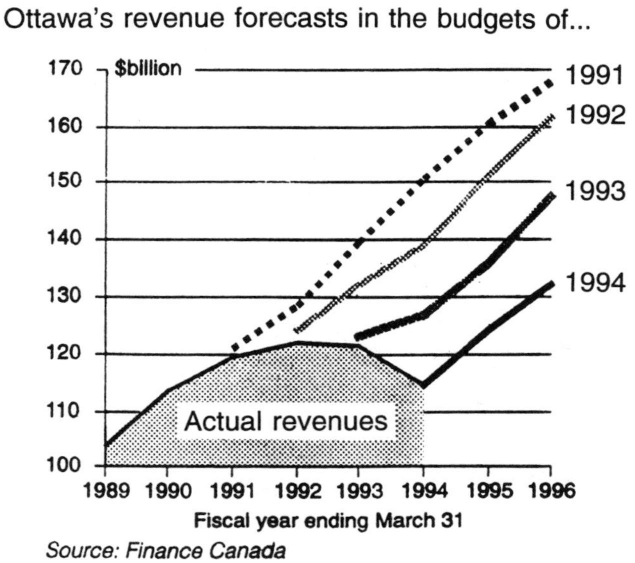

In Canada, the federal Finance Department's forecasts of deficit have a constant record of being wrong. Grossly inaccurate and optimistic estimates of revenues, shown above, are partly to blame (*The Globe and Mail*, 28 February 1994).

Confused with seemingly untractable economic and social problems, governments (national and local) have resorted to appointing numerous commissions, committees, and councils, in the hope that they might identify the causes and prescribe effective cures. These activities amount, in effect, to government sponsorship of multidisciplinary programs—and are presumably subject to the limitations already mentioned. They are symptomatic of the high degree of environmental and social complexity—but they do not guarantee that the desired effective answers will be forthcoming.

It is interesting to note that, paradoxically, the complexity of industrialized society has been least appreciated by the Communist governments that have been attempting—unsuccessfully—to develop a totally planned society and repeatedly finding their ability inadequate for the task, even as Western societies are finding now, as a result of their higher stage of development.

The inevitable failure of a centrally planned economy, in which direct physical controls, consciously applied from one centre, are supposed to replace adjustments spreading automatically through a network of market relations, has been pointed out before by Polanyi (1951). The demonstration came already during the early years of the Bolshevik revolution. The major industries of the country — which had been brought entirely under governmental control — came virtually to a standstill. There was a complete breakdown of the productive apparatus. The towns, unable to feed themselves by offering industrial goods to farmers, were ravaged by famine. Large parts of their population drifted into the countryside. By 1921, the peasants had reduced sowing to less than one-half of the areas sown in 1913. The policy of central planning was paid for by the death of over five million people.

Leo Trotsky, one of the original organizers of the Bolshevik revolution and, in the 1918–1920 period, protagonist of a rigorously centralized system, by 1931 admitted that it would take a "universal mind" as conceived by Laplace to make a success of such a system. But, unable to renounce the dogma of central economic planning as the pivotal ideological principle, communist governments have continued to exert central control of the economy by the party while at the same time attempting to allow the market mechanism to play an increasingly important role in the country.

Such attempts — in the face of disastrous economic performance — culminated with the introduction in 1985 in the Soviet Union of a program of "perestroyka" and "glasnosti" by Mikhail Gorbachev, the general secretary of the Communist Party and the USSR's president.

Gorbachev's initiatives led to more drastic and far reaching reforms in the Soviet satellites, the countries under communist rule imposed by Moscow after 1945. Starting in 1989 the former satellites deposed their communist governments and embraced radical programs of privatization and transition from state controlled to free market economy, reforms without precedent in history. In 1990, communism came to be seen as the longest road from capitalism to capitalism.

In the Soviet Union, the attempt to preserve the system of one-party dictatorship and political integrity of the country while restructuring its economy and opening up its society failed dismally in the wake of the August 1991 unsuccessful coup to depose Gorbachev and turn the clock back. After 74 years of communist totalitarian regime, peoples of the Soviet republics looked to national identity, political independence, democracy, and free market economy as their future.

Some Future Limitations

Faced with such environmental problems as overpopulation, pollution, and exhaustion of natural resources, one now accepts the notion that most growth processes are self-limited, their growth rates stabilizing around a fixed value or diminishing to zero. Is the same true of science which has been growing faster than other sectors and activities of industrial societies? The answer could be yes, for several reasons:

1. In the United States, the growth rate of the scientific population and information has been much higher than that of the total population. If maintained, it would result in a totally scientific population early in the next millennium. Since this is an unlikely event, a reduction in the growth rate of science and scientists may be expected in the future. If the total population remained at a fixed level and the number of scientists at a constant fraction of the population, the growth of science would slow down from an exponential to a linear rate.

2. A similar observation may hold with respect to the relative magnitude of scientific activities in the United States. Some very general impressions may be obtained from consideration of the expenditures on R&D and the magnitude of the gross national product (GNP) over the years; their variation since the 1940s, as well as that of research intensity (defined as the ratio of R&D expenditures to the GNP) is shown in the graph below.

Before 1960, R&D expenditures in the United States were rising three times as fast as the GNP; extrapolation of this trend would show the GNP equal to R&D activity in the mid-1990s and would thus indicate the decline of the R&D growth rate to be imminent. Indeed, contrary to what had been generally perceived at the time, the decline started around 1959, at the dawn of the "space decade." After 1959, the exponential growth rate of R&D expenditures decreased to about one-half of its former value (the doubling period increasing from 4.3 years to 8.5 years) and became about equal to the GNP growth rate. Thus the growth rate of research intensity, which exhibited a doubling period of 6.7 years, has been arrested, with research intensity remaining relatively constant after 1959, at a level of about 2.5 percent.

3. As science grows, the level of specialization may become so high that the productivity of scientists, in terms of discoveries new to science rather than to themselves, may decrease. When it takes more time and effort to find out whether a problem has yet been solved than it

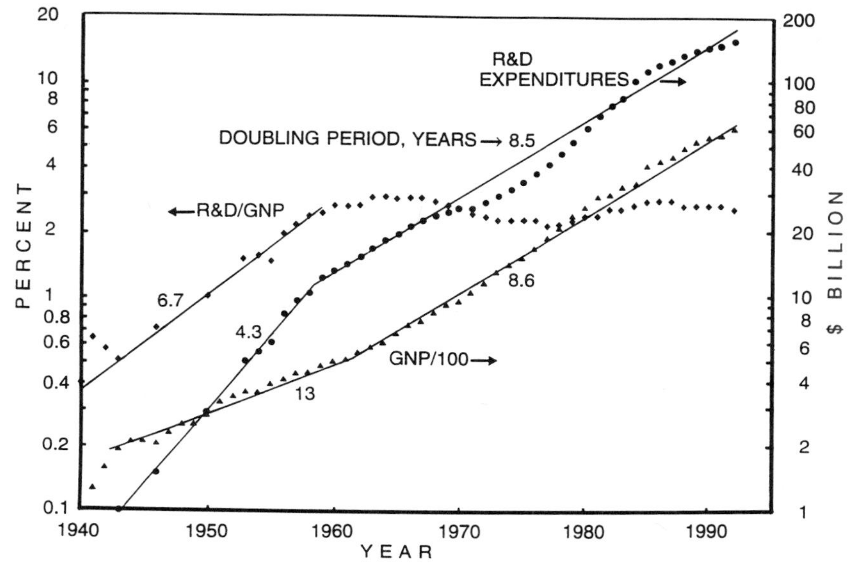

United States' gross national product and expenditures on research and development.

takes to solve it, or when the efficiency of the information retrieval system is inadequate, rediscovery may become a common result of research.

Until now, multiple, simultaneous discovery has been a more frequent occurrence (as, for example, with calculus, developed concurrently by Newton in England and Leibniz in Germany around 1670), but the situation may change in the future. A case recently brought out was that of Graham's law of diffusion, first discovered in 1851 and rediscovered experimentally 122 years later (Mason and Kronstadt 1967).

The history of the logistic function $y = [1 + exp(-x)]^{-1}$, also known as "sigmoid" or "s" function, which models effectively a wide range of physical, biological, technological, and economic phenomena, has been similar. The logistic function was first formulated in France by Verhulst in 1838 (as an alternative to the Malthusian, exponential population growth model) and reinvented 82 years later by Pearl and Reed (1920), who used it to predict the growth of the U.S. population.

Another famous example of rediscovery concerns Mendel's (1822–1884) work which established foundations of genetics. Mendel's laws of heredity were first presented in 1865 and published in 1866. In 1900, three other

European botanists, Correns, von Seysenegg, and de Vries independently obtained results similar to Mendel's, and searching the literature found that both the experimental data and the general theory had been published 34 years previously.

4. Recent developments in what has been called the "publishing game" also reduce the effectiveness of the dissemination of scientific information as well as its quality, and thus affect the rate of growth of science adversely.

In a "publish or perish" climate, the pressure to list in one's biography as many papers as possible has been irresistible. In 1958, when James D. Watson, the co-discoverer of the DNA structure and Nobel laureate was promoted to the rank of associate professor at Harvard, he had on his curriculum vitae 18 papers. Twenty-five years later, it is usual for a candidate facing a similar advancement to list 50 to 100 publications; in biology and medicine, researchers sometimes list 600 to 700 papers (Broad 1981).

An excessive zeal to publish has led to fragmentation of data and its publication in several papers (the length of the "least publishable unit" has been decreasing), multiple submission of manuscripts and simultaneous publication of the same material in two or more journals, repeated publication at intervals of overlapping data or of material that is different in form but not in substance, premature publication of studies still in progress (for fear of being scooped), and an increasing number of papers co-authored by two or more workers. All of these are the common techniques of getting into print as often as possible.

As noted by Philip Abelson, then editor of *Science*:

> Excessive publication hinders effective communication among scientists. It places an unfair burden on those who wish to be informed. It steals the time of conscientious reviewers. It increases the work of editorial offices and slows the processing of meritorious material. It creates excessive costs of publication which are borne by someone else, such as the government, libraries, and members of scientific societies.
>
> (Abelson 1982, ©AAAS)

Moreover, excessive publication inevitably adversely affects the quality of printed information. It makes the process of critical review more difficult and results "in a horde of journals filled with fragmented and redundant research." Multiple authorship, which has been known to include gratuitous listing of authors, adds to the list of one's publications and has been rising, from an average of 1.67 authors per paper in 1960 to 2.58 in 1980 (according to the Institute of Scientific Information in Philadelphia which indexes 2,800 journals; Broad 1981); for some journals it had reached five authors in 1980. The result, in some cases, has been a dilution of the author's responsibility for the published material and therefore a lowering of its quality.

Attempts are being made to control the proliferation of papers and to maintain the quality. Such sanctions as refusal to publish authors who submit the same material to more than one journal, or submit material already published elsewhere, are being introduced or considered. One half-serious suggestion has been to limit the number of papers by each author to five per year, with research funding reduced as a penalty for each paper published above five. Measures designed to constrain paper inflation are certainly desirable but are unlikely to be totally effective.

Can anyone top 193 authors?

An item in the September 1988 issue of *Physical Review Letters* raises the question of whether we need an international Author Non-proliferation Act. The article, "Experimental mass limit for a fourth-generation sequential lepton from e^+e^- annihilations at $\sqrt{s} = 56GeV$," is by G.N. Kim and 103 authors from 19 universities, most of them in Japan. (A companion piece seems a bit skimpy with only 75 authors from 18 universities.) The list of authors was so long it forced the usual two-page table of contents onto a third page.

Scientific value aside, the paper naturally makes one wonder what the record is for number of authors on a published paper. The National Library of Medicine recently turned up a 1986 paper in *Kansenshogaku Zasshi* ("Comparative study of MK-0787/MK-0791 and piperacillin in respiratory tract infections") by R. Soejima and 192 others from 20 institutions.

Can anyone top 193 authors? Send your entries (include a copy of the title page) to "Random Samples," *Science*, 1333 H Street, NW, Washington, D.C. 20005. Submissions must have been published in a peer-reviewed journal.

(*Science* 241, 16 September 1988, ©AAAS)

Superhumans and Superscience

It has been suggested that the intellectual capacity of the human could be regarded as a constant, and biologically limited quantity. The pessimistic assessment of our confrontation with the environment of our own making was based on this assertion. If this were true, could our predicament be alleviated? Could we overcome our biological limitation? If we could, would we be better equipped to handle our environment?

Engineering and bioscience techniques may provide the answer to the second question.

Computing science and technology have been looked upon as the tools with which our intellectual capability could be enhanced. Computers can store much more data than the human brain and can manipulate it much more quickly. Indeed, the "brute force" performance of computers, measured in terms of memory and speed, exceeds natural human capability by many orders of magnitude and therefore can be helpful to us.

As infinitesimal calculus in the 17th century, today computers and computer techniques are the new tools which enable us to solve problems which we could not tackle before.[6]

But it is not the mere volume of information or the slowness of its handling that are at the heart of our difficulties. Rather, it is the complexity or interconnectedness of the environment that are their cause. If we knew what questions to ask, computers might give us the answers; but they will not invent the questions nor tell us where to look for the answers or what the answers mean.

Computers can be made to "think" within constraints of a programmed logic or any other programmed system (such as pattern recognition)— but much more is involved in the human mind. Computers cannot be instructed to be creative, to reach non-obvious conclusions or discover non-obvious associations. How could one instruct a computer to produce a political cartoon or a column based on last week's news fed into its memory?

As noted by Dreyfus (1972), programmed rules do not contain the rules of their own application. They cannot contain all the necessary information about the contexts in which they should be applied, because this would require more rules for the application of these rules, and so on, ad infinitum. Common sense, intelligence, wisdom, imagination, and intuition are among the ill-defined qualities of the human intellect which influence the process of thinking and are needed to gain comprehension of complex phenomena or grasp the meaning of complex data. It is unlikely that human-designed computers will acquire such qualities, much less that they will ever exceed human capabilities in these areas.

Nevertheless, efforts to develop computers that can "think" have been underway for many years under the label of artificial intelligence (AI; Waldrop 1984a, 1984b; Hacker 1984). The difficulties facing this endeavour are obvious if one notes that we have yet to understand and define what natural intelligence is and how it functions. Clearly, until we accomplish this, we will not succeed in creating an artificial counterpart to the natural phenomenon.

The fundamental assumption of AI is that the mind can be modeled as a processor of symbols — in effect, a computer program. This has been the basis of so-called expert systems, one of the more successful products of AI research. Expert systems are programs seeking to apply professional judgment to real-life problems and to give advice like a human specialist.

Paradoxically, mimicking a highly competent human expert is much simpler than imitating an everyday ability such as language; expertise is easier because it is specialized and focuses on narrow classes of problems. Although helpful in routine cases, expert systems inevitably operate within a "closed world" assumption — that nothing outside of the program is relevant. They are shallow, they follow thousands of rules of thumb, they are unable to infer missing knowledge and, most importantly, they are unable to learn: their "expertise" has to be supplied from outside. But most significant of all — in every application of AI, not just expert systems — is the lack of anything that might be called common sense.

AI's focus on logical deduction ignores people's common sense ability to retract a conclusion upon further information. Minsky's "Dead Duck Challenge" illustrates the point: "If all ducks can fly and if Charlie is a duck, then Charlie can fly ... unless Charlie is dead, in which case he cannot fly."

Attempts to make computers play chess illustrate well the obstacles to creation of artificial intelligence (Hapgood 1982). Expert human chess players rely on strategies designed to attain certain goals, a process which reflects the player's experience, judgment, intuition, and feeling, and involves consideration of a limited number of options. According to Waltz (1982), tests have shown that a good human player examines no more than about 100 board options before choosing a move. Australian champion Darryl Johansen sees one position a second (Dayton 1991). Only the most promising lines of attack are considered, but they are exploited in relatively great depth. By comparison, IBM Deep Thought II — the most powerful chess playing computer — examines 10 million positions per second. The criterion of success of computer chess is winning the game, not mimicking human ability. Even if Deep Thought II has achieved grandmaster status, it has done so through a process drastically different from the one used by human players. Clearly, a computer's artificial intelligence amounts merely to its ability to examine an enormous quantity of alternative moves in a very small time interval; brute force rather than intelligence is the basis of its method. Presumably, if a computer could examine all possible moves, it could always win. But this is not likely in a human opponent's lifetime: it has been estimated that there are 10^{120} possible moves in the average game of chess and today's fastest computers would require over 10^{100} years to consider all of them and find the best one.

Attempts are made to bypass the limitations of brute force technique through development of computers which imitate the workings of the human brain and are capable of "learning." However, as noted below, this approach also suffers from fundamental constraints.

The use of language illustrates another limitation of the computer's capability. In human communications, the meaning of words and phrases is governed by the context in which they are spoken or written; new words and new meanings of old words appear as our experience and activities develop and change, and the context is infinitely variable. We could feed a computer an unlimited number of words—but we could not write a program for compilation of a *Roget's Thesaurus* without compiling the *Thesaurus* ourselves. A computer translation of "out of sight, out of mind" may read "a blind fool"; "The spirit is willing but the flesh is weak" could come out as "The vodka is strong but the meat is rotten." Because correct spelling depends on the context in which a word is used, word processors equipped with spell check programs do not guarantee freedom from errors. For example, correctly spelled, *discrete* could be printed instead of the intended *discreet*, *principal* instead of *principle*, or *public archives* could be misspelled as *pubic archives*; a spell check program would not catch such errors. In fact, naïve reliance on such programs often leads to errors which would be corrected through ordinary proofreading. Regretfully, spell check programs encourage sloppy typing and are probably most useful in eliminating only the typographical errors.

The hazards of spell check

Spell check programs and computer set print do not guarantee freedom from errors, which creep into even the most carefully edited and produced magazines. The example below appeared in *TIME* of 14 March 1994.

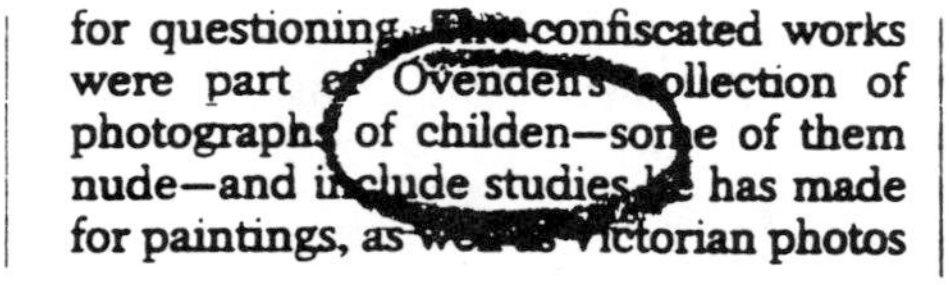

for questioning. The confiscated works
were part of Ovenden's collection of
photographs of childen—some of them
nude—and include studies he has made
for paintings, as well as Victorian photos

In any event (as pointed out by Waltz 1982) computers, no matter how extensively programmed for language understanding, literally can't know what they are talking about: their only contact with the world is through language.

The same applies to visual recognition programs required, for example, by robots. They could easily mistake a three-legged black cow for a grand piano.

A scientific, materialistic formalization of the thought processes would be required in order to construct machines that can think. But it is doubtful that mental processes could be reduced solely to the biochemistry of the brain and thence to the physics of molecules and atoms. Understanding how each of the billions of brain cells works separately would not tell us how the brain works as an agency — notes Marvin Minsky (1986).

> The "laws of thought" depend not only upon the properties of those brain cells, but also on how they are connected. And these connections are established not by the basic, "general" laws of physics, but by the particular arrangement of the millions of bits of information in our inherited genes.

Not knowing what the mind is, we have no reason to believe that we could design a device which could imitate or, even less, transcend it. The human thought processes encompass much more than learning and rational reasoning. As Theodore Roszak (1982) points out, such relatively straightforward operations

> hardly scratch the surface. The mind can dream, hallucinate, tell jokes, make laws, invent fairy tales, goof off, meditate, forget, repress, lie, go crazy, and commune with God. It has spent the greater part of its history fabricating aesthetic, metaphysical, and theological castles in the air.

Moreover, since at any level of development we have only our own intellect with which to comprehend our mind, it is not likely that we can ever succeed. To quote Roszak again, "All we have is a diamond that must cut a diamond."

As noted by Andreski (1974, 18, 25; see Chapter 2):

> the mind might be able to make a perfect model of things simpler than itself," [but] "it is logically impossible that anyone could ever acquire an understanding of his own mind . . . because . . . the mind would have to contain a model as complex as itself as well as an agency which would draw inferences.

We are not conscious of the mental processes involved in even the simplest and most obvious manifestations of intelligence. A two- or three-year-old child has no difficulty in distinguishing on sight between a man and a woman — a feat that no computer program is likely to ever match. We do not know how we do it.

Clearly, the term artificial intelligence, which was introduced in 1956 in anticipation of future capabilities of computers, is highly inappropriate and misleading. Indeed, given the very fundamental and inherent limitations of AI endeavour, they would be more accurately described as "caricatures of intelligence" and AI tools — the computers — as "intelligent morons."

"Accumulation of information" or "animal intelligence" would be more appropriate explanations of the AI acronym. MI for "machine intelligence" would accurately describe what passes today for artificial intelligence.

While we cannot perform the feat of lifting ourselves by our own bootstraps with the help of computer science, bioengineering techniques could allow us to do just that. It is conceivable that the present "biological ceiling" of our intellectual capability could be lifted in the future by exploitation of biosciences and genetic engineering. This would amount, in effect, to artificial and accelerated evolution, the very bootstrap process through which we have improved our capacity "all the way from the jungle."

No system can explain itself

His work with programs like George and Martha had led him to understand that relatively simple computer instructions could produce complex and unpredictable machine behaviour. It was also true that the programmed machine could exceed the capabilities of the programmer; that was clearly demonstrated in 1963 when Arthur Samuel at IBM programmed a machine to play checkers — and the machine eventually became so good that it beat Samuel himself.

Yet all this was done with computers which had no more circuits than the brain of an ant. The human brain far exceeded that complexity, and the programming of the human brain extended over many decades. How could anyone seriously expect to understand it?

There was also a philosophical problem. Goedel's Theorem: that no system could explain itself, and no machine could understand its own workings. At most, Goedel believed that a human brain might, after years of work, decipher a frog brain. But a human brain could never decipher itself in the same detail. For that you would need a superhuman brain.

Gerhard thought that someday a computer would be developed that could untangle the billions of cells and hundreds of billions of interconnections in the human brain. Then at last, man would have the information that he wanted. But man wouldn't have done the work — another order of intelligence would have done it. And man would not know, of course, how the computer worked.

(Michael Crichton, *The Terminal Man*, Bantam, 1973, pp. 124–25, ©Ballantine Books)

But, even if we were successful in such an evolutionary endeavour and gained an intellectual excellence adequate to cope with the problems created by the naturally evolved human, we could not improve his lot.

By analogy to the present situation, it is unlikely that the superhumans would then not engage in the development of a superscience civilization whose complexity would eventually more than match their ability. This possibility was already envisaged in 1929 by Bernal (1969, 68, 77) when he wrote:

> . . . the scientists are not masters of the destiny of science; the changes they bring about may, without their knowing it, force them into positions which they would never have chosen. Their curiosity and its effects may be stronger than their humanity.
>
> The immediate future, which is our own desire, we seek; in achieving it we become different; becoming different we desire something new, so there is no staleness except when development itself has stopped. Moreover, development, even in the most refined stages, will always be a very critical process; the dangers to the whole structure of humanity and its successes will not decrease as their wisdom increases, because, knowing more and wanting more, they will dare more, and in daring will risk their own destruction. But this daring, this experimentation is really the essential quality of life.

Forty years later, the same sentiments were echoed by Chargoff (1969):

> Our modern sciences began — one could say — around the beginning of the seventeenth century. Until that time humanity had been nestling in the hollow of the hand of God. They knew the How because they knew the Why. But then the question "How really?" began to be asked ever more urgently, and this went on for 300 years. Now the light of knowledge — ever bigger and more fragmented — has become so strong that the world threatens to fade before it. We are able not only to register facts of nature, but also to create new ones. We manipulate nature as if we were stuffing an Alsatian goose. We create new forms of energy; we make new elements; we kill the crops; we wash the brains. I can hear them in the dark sharpening their lasers. Soon the hereditary determinants themselves will begin to be manipulated. I am afraid the "dark satanic mills" of which Blake wrote will be no less satanic for being brightly illuminated.

An alternative to the biological "improvement" of humans has been discussed by Good (1965) and others, who have considered creation of an "ultra-intelligent machine," "the last invention that man need ever make," and the cause of an "intelligence explosion." The ultra-intelligent machine has been defined as "a machine that can far surpass all the intellectual activities of any man, however clever." Not surprisingly, the consequences of ultra-intelligent technology appear just as uncertain as those of a biological improvement of humans. The survival of humans may depend on the early construction of an ultra-intelligent machine — or the ultra-intelligent machine may take over and render the human race redundant, or develop another form of life. The prospect that merely intelligent humans could ever attempt to predict the impact of an ultra-intelligent device is of course unlikely, but the temptation to speculate seems irresistible.

Notes

1. Based on a study first published in 1972 under the same title; see Lukasiewicz 1972, also 1970, 1974.
2. It was reported in 1993 that major libraries double in size every 14 years. In 1993 about 1,000 new books were printed in English every day.
3. Measured in terms of memory size (number of "words" or 10-digit numbers in storage) and speed, i.e., the number of additions per second (addition time equal to time to add two "words").
4. Coefficient of immediacy, $C_I = [f(t_2) - f(t_1)]/f(t_2)$, where t = time. For exponential function, $f(t) = a\, exp(\lambda t)$, $C_I = 1 - exp(-\lambda \Delta t)$, where Δt is the specified time period. In terms of doubling time D of $f(t)$, $C_I = 1 - 2^{-\Delta t/D}$.
5. This aspect was mentioned as "number-density-interaction" in *Daedalus* 1967, p. 703.
6. It should be noted that, although computer techniques have been very successful in tackling many physical problems, their success has been limited when dealing with physical phenomena of enormous complexity, such as weather or climate. Computer models failed to predict the worst storm in southern England in memory, which on 16 October 1987 killed at least 13 people and downed an estimated 15 million trees. Much uncertainty is evident in the diverse predictions of climatic and other consequences of the "greenhouse effect."

References

Abelson, P.H. 1982. "Excessive Zeal to Publish," *Science* 218 (3 December): 953.

Andreski, S. 1974. *Social Sciences as Sorcery*. Harmondsworth, England: Penguin Books.

Bagdikian, B.H. 1971. "How Much More Communication Can We Stand?" *The Futurist* (October): 180–83.

Bernal, J.D. 1939. *The Social Function of Science*. England: Routledge and Kegan Paul.

———. 1969. *The World, the Flesh and the Devil*, 2nd ed. England: Routledge and Kegan Paul.

Broad, W.J. 1981. "The Publishing Game: Getting More for Less," *Science* 211 (13 March): 1137–39.

Chargoff, Erwin 1969. "The Paradox of Biochemistry," *Columbia Forum* 12, no. 2 (Summer): 15–18.

Chote, R. 1992. "Why the Chancellor is Always Wrong," *New Scientist* (31 October): 26–31.

Daedalus. 1967. "Toward the Year 2000: Work in Progress," *Daedalus* 96, no. 3 (Summer): 639–994.

Darlington, C. 1975. "The Ignorance Explosion," *New Scientist* (18 September): 670.

Davis, W. 1933. *Project for Scientific Publication and Bibliography*. Science Service, Washington, D.C.

Dayton, L. 1991. "Stalemate in Battle between Man and Machine?" *New Scientist* (7 September): 18.

Dreyfus, H. 1972. *What Computers Can't Do: A Critique of Artificial Reason*. Cambridge: MIT Press.

E.B. 1968. "Information Processing," *Encyclopedia Britannica*, 2: 244A–246B.

Fung, Y.C.B. 1967. "An Approach to Bioengineering." In *Journeys in Science*, ed. D.L. Arn. Albuquerque, N.M.: University of New Mexico Press. 108–30.

Gabor, D. 1970. *Innovations: Scientific, Technological, and Social*. Oxford: Oxford University Press.

Geake, E. 1992. "Playing to Win," *New Scientist* (19 September): 24–25.

Goffman, W., and Warren, K.S. 1969. "Dispersion of Papers among Journals Based on a Mathematical Analysis of Two Diverse Medical Literatures," *Nature* 221: 1205–07.

Good, I.J. 1965. "Speculations Concerning the First Ultraintelligent Machine." In *Advances in Computers*, ed. F.L. Alt and M. Rubinoff, vol. 6. San Diego: Academic Press, 31–88.

Greider, W. 1981. "The Education of David Stockman," *The Atlantic Monthly* (December): 27–54.

Hacker, A. 1984. "Are You a Machine?" *Fortune* (17 September): 199–202.

Hapgood, F. 1982. "Computer Chess Bad — Human Chess Worse," *New Scientist* (23/30 December): 827–30.

Lipetz, Ben-Ami 1965. *The Measurement of Efficiency in Scientific Research*. Carlisle, Mass.: Intermedia, Inc.

Lukasiewicz, J. 1970. "The Ignorance Explosion" (The editor comments: guest editorial), *Impact of Science on Society* 20, no. 4 (October–December): 251–53; also "L'explosion de l'ignorance," *Impact: science et société* 20, no. 4 (octobre–décembre): 269–71.

———. 1971a. "The Dynamics of Science and Engineering Education," *Engineering Education* 61, no. 8 (May–June): 880–82.

———. 1971b. "La dinamica de los cursos de ingenieria en Estados Unidos," *Alta Dirrección* 7, no. 38 (July–August): 89–100.

———. 1971c. "Integrating Engineering Education with Work," *Astronautics & Aeronautics* 9, no. 8 (August): 5.

———. 1971d. "The Dynamics of Engineering Curricula in the U.S.A." In *Proceedings of the Twenty-first International Astronautical Congress*. Amsterdam: North-Holland. 1062–73.

———. 1972. "The Ignorance Explosion: A Contribution to the Study of Confrontation of Man with the Complexity of Science-Based Society and Environment," *Transactions of the New York Academy of Sciences*, Series II, 34, no. 5 (May): 379–91.

———. 1974. "The Ignorance Explosion," *Leonardo* 7, no. 2 (Spring): 159–63.

Mason, E.A., and Kronstadt, B. 1967. "Graham's Laws of Diffusion and Effusion," *J. Chem. Educ.* 44: 740–45.

Miller, G.A. 1967. *The Psychology of Communications.* New York: Basic Books.
Minsky, M.L. 1986. *The Society of Mind.* New York: Simon & Schuster.
Moss, N.H. 1968. "The Pursuit of Knowledge—Synthesis or Fragmentation," *Transactions of the New York Academy of Sciences* 30, no. 3: 393–96.
Muller, H.J. 1970. *The Children of Frankenstein.* Bloomington, Indiana: Indiana University Press.
NYT. 1968. *The New York Times,* 11 December 1968.
Pearl, R., and Reed, L.J. 1920. "On the Rate of Growth of the Population of the United States since 1790 and Its Mathematical Representation," *Proc. Nat. Acad. Sci.* 6: 275–88.
Polanyi, M. 1951. *The Logic of Liberty.* London: Routledge and Kegan Paul.
Price, Derek J. de Solla. 1961. *Science Since Babylon.* New Haven, Conn.: Yale University Press.
———. 1963. *Little Science, Big Science.* New York: Columbia Univeristy Press.
———. 1965. "Networks of Scientific Papers," *Science* 149 (30 July): 510–15.
———. 1967. "Research on Research." In *Journeys in Science,* ed. D.L. Arn. Albuquerque, N.M.: University of New Mexico Press.
Roszak, T. 1982. "Silicon Intelligence and the Self," *New Scientist* (17 June): 782.
Sinsheimer, R.L. 1971. "The Brain of Pooh: An Essay on the Limits of Mind," *American Scientist* 59 (January–February): 20–28.
Sullivan, W. 1971. "Scientific Research Conference Supports a Worldwide System for the Storage and Exchange of Data," *The New York Times,* 11 October 1971.
Verhulst, P.F. 1838. "Notice sur la loi que la population suit dans son accroissement," *Correspondences Mathématiques et Physiques* 10: 113–21.
Waldrop, M. Mitchell. 1984a. "Artificial Intelligence (1): Into the world," *Science* 223 (24 February): 802–05.
———. 1984b. "The Necessity of Knowledge," *Science* 223 (23 March): (1279–82).
Waltz, D.L. 1982. "Artificial Intelligence," *Scientific American* (October): 118–33.
WST. 1968. "Transportation Official Challenges System Analysts," *Washington Science Trends* 23, no. 4: 1.
Zelikoff, S.B. 1968. *The Obsolescence of Engineering Personnel under Conditions of Rapid Technological Change.* Ph.D. diss., University of Pennsylvania, Philadelphia. Also, "The Obsolescing Engineer," *Science and Technology* 88: 46–51.

Appendix to Chapter 4

On estimating the magnitude of complexity

If we were to consider the number of different pair-links as an index of complexity, we would find that the complexity varies as the square of the size of the assembly. For triple-linked combinations, the complexity varies (approximately) as the cube of the whole. In general, the number nCr of different groups of elements, each group containing r elements from among an assembly of n different elements is given by $nCr = n!/[r!(n-r)!] = [n(n-1)(n-2)\dots(n-r+1)]/r!$ and therefore, for $n >> 1, n >> r$, $nCr \approx n^r/r!$

The total number of such interactive relationships (involving from 2 to n different elements) within an assembly of n elements is equal to $2^n - (n+1) \approx 2^n$. Thus, to a good approximation, the complexity doubles with each additional element, or, as the number of elements n increases twofold, the complexity is raised to the second power. In general, we may conclude that the growth of complexity is of a much higher order than the growth of the volume of information.

The fast growth and the large magnitude of complexity are illustrated by the following example: For an exponential function the number of elements increases from 1 to 32 in five doubling periods; the complexity attains a value of $2^{32} \approx 4.3 \times 10^9$.

5

The Brave New World of Globalization

The Origins

As soon as specialized knowledge and skills are acquired by some members of a society, individual self-sufficiency and independence are destroyed, interdependence takes their place, co-operation and integration become necessary in order to benefit from products of specialization. This has been the story of industrial civilization, which in the twentieth century attained a truly global reach.

The post-World War II era has seen a dramatic growth of transnational and global activities in the industrialized West and beyond. The desire of the nations of the world to liberalize and expand international trade led to the conclusion in 1947 by 23 founding countries of the General Agreement on Tariffs and Trade (GATT). The last round of negotiations ended in December 1993 with a wide ranging agreement by 117 states; pending ratification, it will come into force on 1 July 1995.

Efforts to integrate the economies and policies of the European Community member states have continued unabated since the 1950s. The North American continent became a free trade area in 1994, after the United States, Canada, and Mexico ratified the North American Free Trade Agreement. Since 1992, the Association of Southeast Asian Nations has been promoting the establishment of the ASEAN Free Trade Area of 330 million consumers.

A global organization has become necessary to perform all kinds of tasks whose scale exceeds the capacity of even the largest and wealthiest among nation states. This includes manufacturing, research and development, trade, services, communications, transportation, management of the environment, and many other endeavours. Production of sophisticated goods at affordable prices requires extremely large, global-scale markets.[1]

Industrialized nation states have been progressively losing their independence and sovereignty in order to achieve greater economic efficiency and material wealth. Nation state sovereignty was being superseded by consumer sovereignty.

In the West, war ceased to be a means of resolving international issues, achieving power and riches through control of population and territory. Innovation and superior productivity became the new, and the only way. Science and technology — as a basis of industry — played a leading role in the process of transnational integration and globalization.

Moreover, globalization has led to the projection of moral sovereignty by the industrialized states beyond their borders. The global reach of the media, which bring into every home the images of tragic and horrible events, played a significant role in creating a moral impulse to intervene. Under the auspices of the United Nations or on their own, Western countries increasingly assume responsibility — anywhere in the world — for peaceful resolution of conflicts, conduct of democratic process, respect for human rights, national reconstruction, and provision of resources when lives are threatened by famine, disease, or strife.[2]

A Historical Perspective

The phenomenon of technology as an agent of integration is not new; throughout history technology has played an important role in the establishment of effective rule and administration over large territories, and has led to the development of international commerce and industry in a fragmented world of empires, kingdoms, and nation states.

The Roman Empire could be looked upon as the foremost early example of technology in the service of intercontinental integration, a precursor of the United States as the first "republic of technology" (a term coined by Daniel Boorstin 1978).

The rule of ancient Rome extended over provinces on three continents, separated by thousands of miles. The establishment of the efficiently administered, far-flung empire was only possible because Romans developed excellent technologies of communication and transportation. One language, Latin, was universally used by the bureaucracy. (This was also the language which for centuries assured effective communication within the international organization of the Roman Catholic Church.) Uniform laws, standard weights, measures, and currency were enforced. Some 50,000 miles of first class paved and straight highways (together with 200,000 miles of lesser roads) made superior transportation possible. The construction of road pavement, bridges, and tunnels was standardized to take advantage of the economies of scale and to ensure uniformly high quality. Staging posts for horses were maintained at ten mile intervals with lodgings every 25 miles. (The analogy to our modern system of individual transportation is striking: the United States has over 41,000 miles of interstate highways built to uniform standards, equipped with gas stations and motels.) Roman cities were provided with such facilities as baths, arenas, temples and aqueducts. A highly uniform infrastructure of Roman civilization resulted in a standard lifestyle for the Romans.

Following the fall of Rome and the Dark Ages, it was in response to demands of trade and industry that international organizations and transborder operations developed in Western Europe.

In the thirteenth century, the Hanseatic League was organized by the north German towns to protect and monopolize trade in the Baltic and the North Seas. The League's international membership grew to over 80 towns and agencies in Germany, Russia, England, Flanders, and Poland.

As the money economy replaced the barter system (or as handling of information replaced handling of goods), a need arose for the development of a system of international credit. In the Renaissance period, during the fourteenth and fifteenth centuries, such services were provided by the Medicis of Florence and the Fuggers of Augsburg. As international bankers, the Medicis had branches in Italy, France, and England. The Fuggers established an even more extensive financial and industrial network, with centres from Spain to Poland and mining interests in Hungary, Germany, and Spain. Their activities preceded by some 400 years our era of multinational corporations.

In the sixteenth century, extraterritorial operations gained momentum with the creation in Western Europe of chartered companies. Starting with the Muscovy Co., established in 1555 for trading with Russia, ten chartered companies were formed in England by 1631. Between 1599 and 1789, France founded seventy chartered companies; several were established in the Netherlands.

Granted a special charter by the sovereign authority of the state, a chartered company was assured monopoly in its sphere of operations and became the instrument of economic development, foreign trade, and exploration. It was responsible for peaceful extension of sovereignty over foreign territories and their administration, the political functions which were eventually transferred to the state.

The internationalization of trade and manufacturing was accelerated by the Industrial Revolution (1750–1830) which marked the beginning of large scale industrialization and the appearance of cheap goods in large quantities. The pervasiveness of technology and industry had already become apparent during this period. Industrial activity acquired an existence of its own, transcending political and geographical boundaries.

The aristocracy, an early international organization based on family ties, was being replaced by industrialists whose operations and interests reached into many countries. Availability of a free, integrated domestic market facilitated the rapid industrialization of England, a process frustrated in France, which was divided, until 1789, into thirty-two intendancies with different tax levels and trade tariffs. As industrialization gained momentum in England, exports to Europe and the colonies accounted for a significant proportion of industrial output; economies of scale were assured by a large international market.

Continental Integration: The United States

It was in the United States that the integrating pressures of technology reached the highest intensity and encompassed the largest territory and population. In fact, as noted below, the impact of technology became generally identified with America and its results with a peculiarly American culture.

America was not to become a "new Europe" but a transcontinental federated nation of divided sovereignties and near-limitless opportunities. The founders of the new "republic of technology" were interested less in ideology than in "organizing the means for satisfying needs and desires," that is, technology. The U.S. constitution was endowed with anti-doctrinaire spirit and designed to allow territorial expansion through admission of new states by vote of Congress. America became an "international nation," a magnet attracting some of the most capable and original individuals, and millions of other nationals in search of freedom and economic security (Boorstin 1978).

The large size of the domestic market, the availability of resources, the social dynamics, and the democratic and pragmatic politics were extraordinarily favourable to massive industrialization. The United States became the first, and is still the only country to achieve effective integration on a continental scale; after World War II it moved to global scale industrial operations.

Foreign investments and operations by American industry rose dramatically in the 1950s and 1960s. As shown below, between 1950 and 1966 the number of foreign affiliates of U.S. multinational corporations has increased threefold world-wide, and nearly quadrupled in Western Europe.

Year	**1950**	**1957**	**1966**
World	7,417	10,272	23,282
Western Europe	2,236	2,654	8,611

(UN 1973)

Number of foreign affiliates of U.S. multinational corporations

The process of globalization, which was seen in the 1960s as expansion of American power, an economic invasion of Europe by the United States, and a threat to Europe's sovereignty, in the 1980s has turned into a challenge of foreign investment in the United States. From 1983 to 1987, an estimated $800 billion in foreign funds have flowed into the U.S. economy, fuelled by huge trade surpluses with the United States and a weak dollar. Between 1980 and 1986, direct foreign investment in the United

States increased threefold, from $68 billion to $210 billion (according to the U.S. Department of Commerce). Britain, at $51.3 billion, was the largest investor in 1986, followed by The Netherlands ($42.8 billion) and Japan ($23.4 billion). Some of the largest American enterprises in manufacturing, advertising, publishing, merchandising and real estate are now owned by British, Japanese, Dutch, German, and Canadian interests. By 1988, one-third of downtown Houston and Minneapolis, and almost one-half of downtown Los Angeles were foreign-owned. Between 1986 and 1988, foreigners bought over 600 large U.S. companies. In 1986, the United States surpassed Brazil as the world's largest debtor.

The shoe is now on the other foot. The concerns voiced in Europe and Canada in the 1960s and 1970s are now being heard in the United States. Many Americans worry that their country is losing control of its destiny, and advocate stricter foreign investment rules and economic nationalism — the very policies the United States has opposed for decades in an effort to ensure that U.S. firms abroad enjoy the same rights as local firms. Again, the process of globalization that the United States is experiencing within its own borders reflects the need to be global in order to survive and compete successfully. The same requirement that U.S. business recognized and exploited to its advantage since the 1950s is now pursued by the new world players. For them, globalization means direct access and participation in the largest national economy, that of the United States.

Political integration did not encompass the northern half of the continent which evolved, in the wake of the American Revolution and dissolution of the British Empire, into politically independent Canada. The division could be regarded as highly anomalous since there are no two countries in the world whose economies and territories are more closely interwoven and interdependent.[3] A *de facto* extensive integration has been the basis of Canada's wealth by providing a large market for Canada's resource industries and easy access to American technology and manufactured goods. The economic integration of Canada within North America has been further augmented with the conclusion of free trade agreements with the United States and Mexico which came into force in 1989 and 1992 respectively. Nevertheless, many Canadians and Canadian politicians (of liberal and socialist persuasions) have resisted integration and promoted nationalistic and "independent" policies, fearing the cultural impact of the southern neighbour and loss of jobs to the United States and Mexico. Quebec's endeavours to become a fully sovereign state of North America are an extreme example of such tendencies. Moreover, unlike the United States, Canada has not achieved continental integration: parochial provincial interests (including barriers to interprovincial trade) still dominate in Canada and take precedence over federal concerns.

Science: A Precursor of Globalization

Centuries before the demands of industrialization and consumerism led to the development of extensive transnational activities and organizations, science had been a thoroughly international endeavour, a discourse conducted across political, linguistic, and cultural divisions. As members of an international community, scientists anticipated the impact of technological progress long ago.

In October 1914 Albert Einstein co-authored a *Manifesto to Europe*, which condemned the two-month-old war waged "at the very time when progress in technology and communications clearly suggests that we recognize the need for international relations which will necessarily move in the direction of universal, world wide civilization. ... Technology has shrunk the world" (BAS 1979, 22). In the inter-war period, as the League of Nations failed to establish a semblance of world order, Einstein again objected to nation state rivalries. Interviewed in 1931, he believed that "men ... should fight for things worthwhile, not for imaginary geographical lines, racial prejudices and private greed draped in the colours of patriotism. Their arms should be weapons of spirit, not shrapnel and tanks" (BAS 1979, 10).

Thirty-three years after the *Manifesto* and two years into the Cold War which followed the conclusion of the second world conflict, the Emergency Committee of Atomic Scientists, chaired by Einstein, noted that "the developments in science and technology have determined that the peoples of the world are no longer able to live under competing national sovereignties with war as the ultimate arbitrator" (BAS 1979, 13), and advocated the creation of a supranational world government.

Toward a Voluntary Federation of Nations

In the twentieth century the political and economic organization of societies has been evolving in two distinct and opposite directions.

As multinational structures maintained by coercion have been dissolving into ethnic states, the sovereign industrial democracies of the West have been evolving into a voluntary federation of nations. No longer constrained by national borders, their activities have increasingly been seeking global expansion.

In the wake of World Wars I and II, the West European empires disintegrated (in Europe and overseas) and some 80 new nation states were formed. Finally, before the end of the century, the process of national emancipation has reached into the last remaining empire. In 1989 Moscow's European satellites gained political sovereignty, a move completed in

October 1990 with the unification of East and West Germany. At long last, the dissolution of the Russian and, since 1917, the Soviet empire, had started.

In 1990 the Baltic republics, annexed by the USSR in 1940, declared independence, and nationalist movements surfaced and gained ground in several European and Asian Soviet republics (including Russia, Ukraine, Transcaucasian republics, Kazakhstan, and other Central Asia republics).

Ironically, the final *coup de grâce* was delivered by the Soviet hardliners themselves whose failed coup of August 1991 led to the collapse of the Soviet Union and emergence of the former Soviet republics as soverign states, joined in a loosely structured Commonwealth of Independent States.

The Russian Republic became the Russian Federation, a multinational state with about a 20 percent non-Russian population. Inhabited by more than a hundred major and minor ethnic groups it includes (as of January 1991) 31 autonomous republics, oblasts, and okrugs; Russians are a minority in many of them. The Federation continues to be the legacy of Imperial Russia; it is not a voluntary union of peoples and it may yet see its minorities seek and gain independence.

Since 1945, the United Nations' membership has grown from 51 to 180 countries in 1993.

Secessionist nationalists have been active in Asia, as in Kashmir and Iraq. Ethnic movements broke up Yugoslavia. Even in North America a nationalist movement has been gaining ground. Some forces in Quebec, no longer satisfied to be in a confederation arranged by a colonial power, have been demanding independence from Canada and sovereignty.

In Central and Western Europe the process of national emancipation has been completed through World War I; World War II has demonstrated the futility of military conflict. It became apparent that to realize the benefits of industrialization and establish credible defence required resources and markets larger than any one country could provide. Thus, starting in 1952, the politically sovereign and independent states of Western Europe embarked on entering into a voluntary federation, the European Economic Community. The now again independent countries of Central and Eastern Europe have been seeking closer ties with the EEC. International groups have been formed outside the EEC, such as the 7-member European Free Trade Association (EFTA).

The lesson of the European Community and, much earlier, of the emergence of the United States — the Civil War notwithstanding — is clear. The integration of diverse peoples, often with a long history of mutual hostility, into a supranational organization can only succeed through open and absolute consent. People are not likely to appreciate the benefits of confederation unless and until they can choose them freely. Federation works only under the condition of freedom.

This is why — as noted by Krauthammer (1990) — "the only way to turn . . . empires held by coercion into real federations is to allow them to break up into their constituent parts and hope that in their wisdom they will see fit to knit themselves back together again." Such empires "require divorce before reconciliation."

Freedom of choice is one of the conditions that must be satisfied for a federation of nation states to be viable. Perception of benefits that such federation brings about is the other indispensable element.

It is no accident that, in spite of political obstacles, the first voluntary multinational federation — the EEC — has emerged among the world's most highly educated societies and most highly industrialized countries. The evolution towards a federal structure has been preceded by the development of science and technology and driven by industrialization and consumerism. A vast, efficient, and continually growing infrastructure of transportation and instant information handling has enabled transnational and global economic operations to expand in spite of national borders. The demand for new and often sophisticated products became nearly universal. Resources and markets large enough to make possible the manufacture of such products at affordable and competitive prices had to be created through integration of the economies of nation states. This has also been true of weapons and defense which require, except in a few cases, a larger base than a nation state can provide. Moreover, as discussed in some detail in the next chapter, international consumerism, be it in products, services, information, or arts, has been eroding national cultures, traditional values, and lifestyles; indeed, it has been an effective "cultural leveller."

Highly industrialized nation states have found that "the vessel of sovereignty is leaking" (Skolnikoff 1971, 45) and "national independence is national impotence" (Williams 1973, 37). Interdependence has become the price of affluence.

The process of integration and, increasingly, of globalization has been in conflict with the traditional organization of societies which did not progress beyond voluntary consolidation to the nation state level. Inevitably, it has been deterred by efforts to preserve national independence and sovereignty.

In a world of sovereign states, the integrative pressures of technology and industrialization are often seen as economic and cultural domination of the smaller states by one country, or of the less developed societies by the West. In the 1960s and 1970s it was common to talk about Americanization or economic takeover by American multinational corporations and imposition of the American lifestyle and popular culture. The consequences which derive directly from the very nature of technological and industrial development were not attributed to the process itself but were identified with the country where such development had occurred

(LAF Canadian Cartooning Co.)

earlier on a larger scale. In the 1980s and 1990s we could be talking about Japanization as Japanese products flood the Western markets, Japanese industries expand their foreign operations, and Japanese management style is being imitated in the West. Such developments have led many a politician to suggest initiatives which would supposedly maintain political, cultural, and economic sovereignty as well as ensure efficient industrialization—incompatible objectives that are no longer fully attainable and not necessarily desirable.

The contradiction between independence and interdependence has been particularly acute in the less developed countries where it is precisely the awakening of ethnic and cultural identity that provides incentive to achieve modernization.

A Rough Road to European Union

In Western Europe, the two World Wars have been a major factor in the elimination of traditional conflicts (as between France and Germany) and the promotion of co-operation. Continental integration began in the years following the end of World War II, at a time when American industry was already engaged in world-wide expansion. Imperatives of economy, competition and defence have fuelled the process. Although the pace and extent of industrial co-operation have continued to grow, the progress of political consolidation of Western Europe has been much slower.

Attempts to overcome some of the obstacles in the way of economic efficiency led to the formation in 1952 of the European Coal and Steel

Community and its expansion in 1957 into the European Economic Community (EEC or Common Market). In the same year the European Atomic Energy Community (Euratom) was established. Since then, France, West Germany, Italy, and the Benelux countries were joined by the United Kingdom, Ireland, Denmark, Greece, Spain, and Portugal to form a 12-member Common Market. In March 1994 Sweden, Finland, and Austria negotiated to join by 1995, subject to membership referendums to be held later in the year; negotiations with Norway, jealously guarding its fishing rights, continued.

The irreconcilable goals of achieving economic integration while preserving independence and identity, national pride, prestige, and world power status have hindered European consolidation. The global expansion of U.S. industry through direct investment abroad was seen as the result of power politics play by the U.S. government rather than the consequence of rationalizing mass production to achieve economic efficiency and maximize profits. European integration was not to serve economic growth per se; rather, it was necessary to counter the American threat and restore the political supremacy of Europe. This was the view advocated in the 1960s by the French journalist and politician Jean Jacques Schreiber (1967) in his best-seller *The American Challenge.*

The problem of post-war Europe — argued J.J. Schreiber — was to become a great power; to become a Sweden or an overgrown Switzerland was not acceptable; Europe could not be confined to second place. Since the maintenance of a world-order power status was no longer possible on a national scale, "Europeanization" was to be the answer and "European identity" a barrier to the impact of American culture.

Paradoxically, the prescription for meeting the American challenge amounted to "Americanization" of Europe by Europeans rather than Americans. Clearly, political and economic unification would bring about in Europe changes similar to those already accomplished in the United States, would cause erosion of national identities through adoption of common lifestyles and products, and would thus accelerate the process of "Americanization."

The call for re-establishment of Europe's status as a world power has been the European's typical response to foreign economic pressures. However, not all countries have been apprehensive of the economic and cultural impact of industrialization and consumerism. Scandinavian states, Switzerland, West Germany, and Finland have participated in, and taken advantage of, global markets and products without fearing the loss of their cultural identities. Evidently, highly developed and creative societies can maintain significant national characteristics while participating in the process of global industrialization.

The problem of a politically fragmented Western Europe was neatly and amusingly summed up by Professor H.B.G. Casimir, the director of research for Philips, the Dutch electronics multinational giant. He offered in 1968 the following prescription for closing the "technology gap" between the United States and Europe:

> Abolish the Federal Government of the US. Divide the country into its several states and make sure each has a mildly different system of taxation, a different currency, different banking and insurance laws, and different customs regulations. Regroup American minorities into as many distinct language areas as possible and in any case not less than 15, and try to make sure that whenever possible there is at least one competing minority language requiring dual language schools. Oh yes, you will need 40 or 50 distinct patent systems. Do this and the technology gap between the US and Europe will fill up rapidly. (Williams 1973, 37)

The transformation of Western Europe into a truly integrated economy has run into many obstacles, from lack of uniform technical standards to problems with co-ordination of fiscal and monetary policies.

European railways are electrified but voltages differ between some countries, making locomotive switches necessary. Continental freight cars often do not fit British platforms and tunnels. Toll-free telephone numbers do not operate between different countries. And, as anybody who has moved in Europe knows, electrical plugs come in all sorts of shapes and sizes, as shown below. Curiously, the most practical, efficient, and cheapest to make, the flat-blade American plug, has not been adopted in Europe (but is used in Japan), where several two- and three-, round- and square-pin designs are used.

Financial services have been fragmented among national banks and complicated through each country's adherence to its own currency and through currency fluctuations. A uniform market would require some co-ordination of tax rates and consistent application of subsidies. But, inevitably, the governments have been protecting jobs in inefficient industries rather than letting the most efficient and competitive survive and benefit the EEC as a whole. Qualifications of one country's professionals have not been necessarily recognized by other members of the EEC, thus impeding the movement of people.

The nine (!) official languages have hampered the operation of the EEC. As much as a third of the Community's budget has gone into translation and interpretation. One "Eurocrat" in three has been occupied full time in changing one language into another.

Criticizing national governments' concern with their own narrow interests, Lord Cockfield, a commissioner of the EEC, felt that "the lesson which has to be driven home is that the prosperity of every single member

2 flat blades	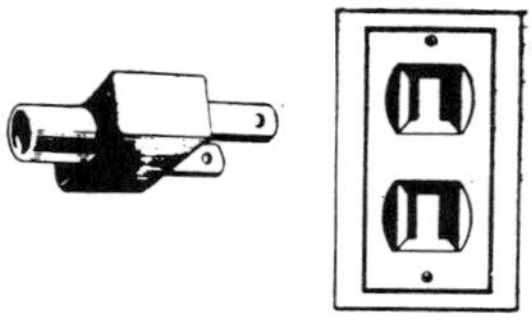	USA Canada Costa Rica Spain Japan
2 round pins	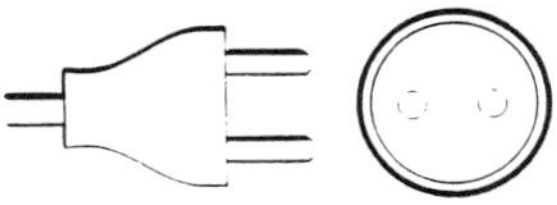	many countries in Western Europe Spain Ireland Iceland
3 round pins		Czech Republic Slovakia Greece Ireland Iceland Malta Switzerland Belgium
3 square pins	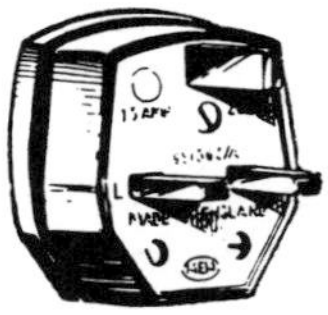	Channel Islands U.K. Iceland Malta

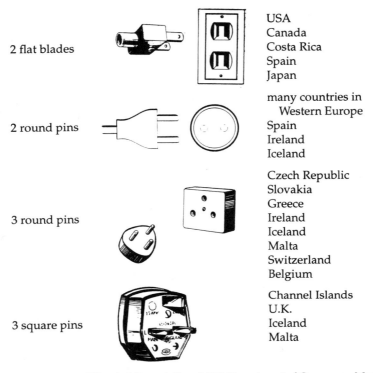

(*Electrical Current Abroad,* U.S. Department of Commerce, May 1975)

Types of electrical plugs in domestic and commercial use

state depends on the prosperity of the community as a whole. Europe stands at the crossroads. We either go ahead or drop into mediocrity" (*The Globe and Mail,* 5 and 8 March 1988). But as George Taucher, a professor of business at the International Management Development Institute in Lausanne, noted, "No European politician ever got elected by being a good European. They get elected by being good local politicians" (*The Globe and Mail,* 5 March 1988). Nevertheless, "Europe has no other choice but to become a third pole of equivalent dimension," stated Alain Madelin, French industry minister. "Otherwise, poor in raw materials, politically fragmented and technologically dependent, it would soon become a subcontractor to the other two [United States and Japan]" (*The Globe and Mail,* 5 March 1988).

The "United States of Europe" remained Winston Churchill's 1946 distant vision.

The heaven and hell of United Europe

> "In heaven," says a T-shirt popular in Europe, "all the policemen are English, all the cooks are French, all the lovers are Italians, and everything is organized by the Germans. In hell, all the policemen are French, all the cooks are English, all the lovers are German, and everything is organized by the Italians." Emblazoned on the chest is the slogan "United Europe."
>
> (*The Globe and Mail*, 19 May 1993)

Nevertheless, efforts towards unity have continued on a wide range of economic and social issues.

Three decades after its creation, all EEC members ratified the 1986 Single European Act, designed to make Western Europe a single economic entity by the end of 1992. The Act was to implement fully "the four freedoms of the single market": the unrestricted movement of goods, services, capital, and people among the EEC member states. Even before it could be consummated, it was followed in December 1991 by the Maastricht treaty on European Union. Although Maastricht stopped short of a political union, this far reaching agreement envisioned commonality of defence and foreign policies,[4] a common European currency and central bank, a package of labour laws called "the social chapter," and joint action in several fields including health and education. The European Parliament will be given authority over the European Commission, the EEC's unelected executive.

The ratification of the Maastricht treaty, which reduces significantly the sovereignty of national governments, has met with strong opposition. Denmark and Britain negotiated "opt-outs" on key elements of the treaty and a referendum in France mustered only 51 percent of the "yes" vote.

The treaty went into force on 1 November 1993 and officially transformed the EEC into European Union (although some governments would prefer to preserve the Community designation). However, a common monetary policy, a single currency, and a central bank appear to be unattainable any time soon. Under the terms of the treaty, a single currency cannot be created until EEC members meet strict economic criteria, which include a ceiling of 3 percent of gross domestic product for the government budget deficit and a ceiling of 60 percent for total government debt. At the time, only Luxembourg fulfilled all the criteria. In the meantime, the European Monetary Institute was established in Frankfurt, which will turn into the European Central Bank once monetary union is complete.

As could be expected, the Maastricht experience demonstrated considerable resistance of member countries to further expansion — at their expense — of the EEC's sovereignty. More significantly, the opposition had no constructive alternative to offer. The European Union may be a matter of "when" rather than "if."

Free trade in Europe is being further expanded through conclusion of a treaty between the EEC and the European Free Trade Association. The treaty creates the European Economic Area (EEA) and comes into force in 1994. The single market and competition rules of the EEC will apply to the six members[5] of the EFTA. With a population of 380 million, the 18 EEA countries will constitute the world's largest common market.[6]

Following the collapse of the Soviet Union, several of the former Soviet bloc countries have been seeking closer ties with Western Europe and admission to the EEC. By 1993 Poland, Hungary, the Czech Republic, Slovakia, Romania, and Bulgaria had signed association agreements with the EEC.

In an address to the Council of Europe in Vienna on 8 October 1993 Vaclav Havel, the president of the Czech Republic, pointed out that the unity of Europe is not a matter of purely technical and administrative measures, new ingenious institutions and regulations, or finding some formula for compromise with which everyone agrees. For European Union to succeed, the old idea of the nation state as the highest expression of national life must be overcome and replaced by a broad civil society created by the supranational community. This means serving the welfare of the community rather than private and partisan interests, a willingness to be guided by its collective voice, and a belief that the sacrifices needed to realize long-term benefits are worth it.

> If various Western states cannot rid themselves of their desire for a dominant position in their own sphere of interests, if they don't stop trying to outwit history by reducing the idea of Europe to a noble backdrop against which they continue to defend their own petty concerns, and if the post-Communist states do not make radical efforts to exorcise the ghosts their newly won freedom has set loose, then Europe will only with great difficulty be able to respond to the challenge of the present and fulfil the opportunities that lie before it. (Havel 1993)

When national sovereignty is not directly threatened and required resources exceed the capability of a single nation, highly successful collaboration has been possible within the EEC and with other countries, particularly in the fields of science, technology, and industry.

Research in physical sciences often requires very large and expensive experimental equipment. International projects in "megascience" have been established in astronomy, high energy physics, and nuclear fusion research. Several countries have teamed-up to construct and operate large astronomical telescopes. CERN, the European Center for Nuclear Research, was established in Geneva, Switzerland, in the 1960s. JET, the Joint European Torus for fusion research, sponsored in England by the EEC, Sweden, and Switzerland, will be followed by International Thermonuclear Experimental Reactor.

Major international research programs have been formally organized by the EEC, often with participation of other countries. They include the $3.2-billion ESPRIT in support of information technology and ERASMUS to assist technology transfer from research institutes to industry and business. Seventeen countries have established EUREKA to develop advanced technologies in a variety of fields. International collaboration has been expanding in molecular biology, geoscience, oceanography and polar studies.

The European Commission of the EEC requires international participation in research projects it funds, and oversees an international peer review system. The European Science Foundation supports scientists from different countries who work in similar fields and co-ordinates international research.

On the government-to-government level, collaboration has been particularly extensive in space exploration and defence. Europe's space activities are coordinated by ESA, the European Space Agency. Several countries participate in the US–NASA space station project. In defence, joint aircraft and missile projects have been frequent among NATO members. In 1990 the European NATO members formed the EUCLID (European Cooperation for the Long Term in Defence) program on research and development in 11 key areas, each to be managed by a "pilot country."

Globalization of Industrial Operations

As would be expected, the basic incompatibility of modern industry and the nation state as an economic unit has been well appreciated by business leaders. They see the world's political structure as highly obsolete, the nation state as an obstacle to world-wide economic development, the political boundaries as too narrow to define the scope of business, the search for global optimization of resources, and the independence of nation states as the critical issues of our time. "For business purposes," noted the president of IBM World Trade Corporation,

> the boundaries that separate one nation from another are no more real than the equator. They are merely convenient demarcations of ethnic, linguistic, and cultural entities. They do not define business requirements or consumer trends. Once management understands and accepts this world

> economy, its view of the marketplace — and its planning — necessarily expand. The world outside the home country is no longer viewed as series of disconnected customers and prospects for its products, but as an extension of a single market. (Barnet and Muller 1974, 14–15)

The global corporation has been seen as "the most powerful agent for the internationalization of human society" (Aurelio Peccei, Club de Rome and FIAT Co., Italy; Barnet and Muller 1974, 13). Its pioneering role has been summarized as follows:

> The global corporation is the first institution in human history dedicated to centralized planning on a world scale. Because its primary purpose is to organize and to integrate economic activity around the world in such as way as to maximize global profit, the global corporation is an organic structure in which each part is expected to serve the whole. Thus in the end it measures its successes and its failures not by the balance sheet of an individual subsidiary, or the suitability of particular products, or its social impact in a particular country, but by the growth in global profits and global market shares. Its fundamental assumption is that the growth of the whole enhances the welfare of all the parts. Its fundamental claim is efficiency. (Barnet and Muller 1974, 14)

The process that led to the development of global industries and markets comprised several distinct phases.

In the early era of industrialization, with production concentrated in only a few countries, economies of scale were realized through international trade: manufactured goods were exported and raw materials imported, as necessary. As latecomers to industrialization wanted to increase their share of the economic gain, they erected tariff barriers to render imports prohibitively expensive and thus encourage foreign suppliers to produce locally. Such policies led to the establishment of foreign subsidiaries (so-called branch plants) by major manufacturers. Since this mode of operation created employment and tax income, helped the balance of foreign payments, and generally upgraded the industrial base, it met to some extent the objectives of the host countries. However, the branch plants as suppliers of essentially domestic, rather than international markets could not benefit from the economies of scale. Moreover, they were usually limited to the manufacturing of products already developed in the base country and therefore did not engage in sophisticated research and development activities and did not provide the highly skilled and creative jobs that go with them.

The branch plant mode of international production was greatly expanded, modified, and diversified in the post World War II period. The traditional system of closed national production and international trade (i.e., exports and imports) has rapidly evolved towards international production by enterprises "designed to accomplish the age-old dream of

McDonald's restaurants in the world

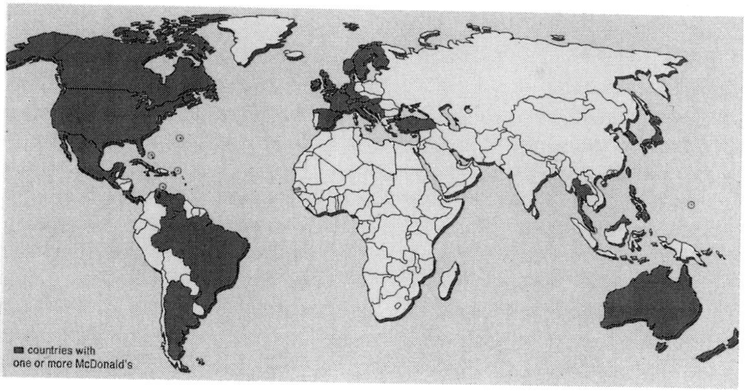

You can eat the very same Big Mac at 10,200 restaurants in 52 countries. Today a quarter of those outlets are outside the United States. Japan has 815 outlets; Canada is third with 541. Nineteen countries have three or fewer. A new McDonald's opens somewhere in the world every 18 hours. (*The Globe and Mail, Report on Business*, August 1988; *The Globe and Mail*, 10 January 1991). Since this map was drawn, McDonald's has expanded into the former Soviet bloc countries and USSR republics.

economists: to minimize the economic significance of national boundaries" (U.S. 1976, 16). The fast growth of operations by the so-called multinational corporations[7] has been the most visible—and the most resented—indication of the integrative pressures exerted by modern industry. The essential characteristics of multinational corporations were well summarized in a 1976 study by the U.S. Library of Congress. The multinational corporation

> does help to alleviate once-potent economic causes of international disputes, and it can be an effective agent of technology transfer, but it also generates new causes of conflict and frustration. Characteristically, the MNC moves capital, materials, credit, managerial expertise, technological skills, intellectual property, and even trained labour from country to country in order to maximize its total overall and long-term profit. In the

> process it erodes the national sovereignty of host countries, diverts capital and labour from nationally planned economic allocations, and competes for economic and even political power, while preserving its own economic and technological power base remote from the countries it penetrates. At the same time, because of the complex and far flung nature of its operations, it tends to elude controls which the base country seeks to impose, or even at times to outpace the base country's perception that certain controls may be needed in its own national interest. In so doing it tends to neglect political, social, and institutional costs of its operations.
>
> As an institution the MNC offers the capability of influencing constructively the evolution of a stable world economy and the development of lagging economies. But as the MNC currently operates, it excites resentment among labour unions as an instrument to cause unemployment at home; it excites resentment in developed countries by superimposing foreign management over domestic labour; and it excites resentment in developing countries by co-opting labour and resources to feed into technologies which are often inappropriate to, and tend to distort, the development process in those countries. (U.S. 1976, 16)

In spite of such negative aspects, MNC operations, driven by the economic imperative, have been rapidly expanding.

To appreciate the significance the MNCs have attained, it is useful to compare their operations with the economies of nation states.

In 1985, the combined sales of the 350 largest MNCs amounted to one-third of the combined gross national products of all industrial countries and exceeded the aggregate GNPs of all less developed countries, including China (Heilbroner 1993).

The enormous scale of operations of some MNCs is evident from a comparison of their sales with the GNPs of several countries in 1990, shown below. The sales of GM, EXXON and Ford rivalled the GNP of Austria, Finland, Denmark, Turkey, and Norway and exceeded by a large margin the GNP of many nations. The sales of IBM and GE were comparable to the GNP of Greece and Portugal.

As a result of direct foreign investment through MNC operations, international production (defined as production by foreign affiliates) has exceeded in many cases the value of exports. It offered important advantages.

It has allowed multinationals to seek cheaper labour, more favourable tax and labour legislation, and lower anti-pollution costs. Production could be rationalized through specialization of plants and standardization of products in the global context. This could be accomplished through division of labour among plants, each being responsible for production of one or more components of the final article (as in the automotive industry,

Country	GNP* or sales** U.S. $ million	Company
USA	5,465	
Japan	2,910	
France	1,188	
U.K.	975	
Canada	558	
Sweden	225	
Austria	158	
Finland	137	
	126	GM
Denmark	124	
Turkey	110	
	106	EXXON
Norway	105	
	98	Ford
	69	IBM
Greece	67	
	59	Mobil
Portugal	58	GE
	44	Philip Morris
New Zealand	42	
	41	Texaco
Ireland	37	

*1993 *U.S. Statistical Abstract*
***Fortune* 22 April 1991

GNP of nation states and sales of industrial companies in 1990.

different plants, sometimes in different countries, making engines, transmissions, bodies, and assembling the cars), or for exclusive production for the global market of only one line of products of the company. This so-called world mandating usually includes the related research, design and development, guarantees participation in the activities at the leading edge of technological progress and therefore the availability of highly skilled and specialized jobs. Indeed, world mandating is the mode of transnational operations most favourable to the host country.

Co-production as another mode of international industrial operations has paralleled the growth of MNCs; it amounts to division of labour among several firms and countries, each participant being responsible for a specific component or phase of a product or project. Co-production arrangements are particularly common where an industry wishes to catch-up with more advanced technology developed elsewhere (as in the case of U.S. and Japanese automotive industries), or where R&D expenses are high (as in the aerospace, electronic, and defense industries in general). Indeed, extremely large research and development costs of many modern products have been a powerful incentive for seeking international participation and global markets. In many cases, these costs couldn't possibly be paid for by a national market, a national government, or one company alone.

For example, the R&D costs of aircraft development have been increasing tenfold every decade (26 percent annually; see table below). It cost only $200,000 to develop the famous DC-3 airliner which entered commercial service in 1936 (and is still operating in many parts of the world); $1 billion, or 5,000 times as much, was spent on development of the first jumbo-jet, the Boeing 747, which started operations in 1969. In terms of unit aircraft price, the development of the DC-3 amounted to less than two aircraft; the development of the B-747 amounted to 50 jumbo-jets. Or, assuming a 10 percent profit margin, a sale of only 18 aircraft would pay for the development of the DC-3, compared to 500 in the case of the Boeing 747.

Year	Aircraft Type	R&D $ million	Unit price $ million	R&D/Unit Price
1935	DC-3	0.2	0.11	2
1960	DC-8	100	5	20
1970	B-747	1,000	20	50
1975	US-SST	3,000 to 5,000	—	—
1976	Concorde	6,800	56	120

(Lukasiewicz and Studnicki-Gizbert 1977)

Aircraft R&D and unit costs.

The *Concorde* supersonic transport project was undertaken jointly by France and England largely because of very large development costs. Similarly, the *Airbus* jetliner development and production have involved a consortium of four countries (France, England, West Germany, and Spain), but products of many more have been used in the construction of *Airbus* jets. The *Airbus Industrie* has suppliers from 27 countries, with about one-third of them from the United States.

Jetliners are probably the most expensive products mass-manufactured for civilian use (a Boeing 747 jumbo-jet costs today about $130 million); to be commercially viable, their constructors must command a significant share of the global demand. The scale of such operations is truly enormous.

In 1990 the Boeing Company of Seattle, Washington, the largest and the most successful developer and constructor of commercial jets, took firm orders for 448 jets worth $40.75 billion (averaging $91 million per aircraft and bringing the backlog to $85 billion) and had sales of $27.6 billion. It employed 265,000 people worldwide; 7,300 Boeing jetliners were flying. Boeing's global market share in commercial jets stood at 55 percent. Boeing 777, the newest wide-bodied jetliner, will cost over $100 million; the investment required to deliver the prototype (rolled out in April, 1994) was estimated at $3 to $4 billion.

High developmental costs have been experienced by the automotive industry as well. The introduction of the front-drive X-cars in 1979 cost General Motors $2.7 billion (equivalent to over 300,000 units). Computer, electronic, communication satellite, and chemical process industries among others all require very large R&D expenditures and correspondingly large markets.

Internationalization of Labour

Just as for nation states, multinational corporations have been a challenge for traditionally structured labour. The operational flexibility of the MNCs and their ability to pursue a single corporate goal cannot be matched by unions organized nationally along trade lines.

Capital and technology are highly mobile; workers are not. This is why, compared to national industries, multinational corporations enjoy many advantages in their dealings with labour.

The power of strikes as labour's bargaining weapon is eroded or lost when companies can close plants and shift production from one country to another, from unprofitable to profitable locations. Overtime in one plant can compensate for a strike in another. The strategy of multiple sourcing, or production of same component by several plants in different countries makes the company largely independent of the labour force in any one plant.[8]

Unlike multinational corporations, whose goal is growth and profit maximization, workers lack a global purpose.

Many unions are nationalistic and labour union leaders cannot afford to risk the jobs of their members in support of workers in other countries. Workers employed by competing industries, such as in the automotive and electronic sectors in the United States and Japan, cannot be expected to represent a common front. Parochial interests often prevail over broader concerns. Unions are reluctant to demand parity of wages (the same wages for the same work) between developing and developed countries,[9] or even between, for example, Western Europe and the United States, fearing that a company may decide to close down its foreign operations completely. Even when the industrial production is completely integrated, as in the case of the American automotive industry in the United States and

Canada, Canadian unions oppose the granting of concessions negotiated with their counterparts, but insist on wage parity if the U.S. contracts are more favourable.

For all of these reasons, to be fully effective, bargaining with multinational corporations would have to be conducted internationally, by a union representing workers in all countries in which the multinational is operating.

Given national and cultural differences among the workers of different countries, formation of cohesive international labour unions has met with many difficulties. Nevertheless, several International Trade Secretariats have been formed as world umbrella bodies for unions in transportation, chemical industries, metals, food processing, and electronics. The Secretariats are the instruments through which union activities, such as strikes and refusals to work overtime can be co-ordinated internationally, and financial assistance provided.

To deal effectively with the multinationals, unions must not only be capable of concerted international actions but need to be organized as equivalents of corporations, representing all workers, preferably in all trades, that a multinational employs. This has been achieved through establishment of Corporation Councils by some International Trade Secretariats. Their goal is to facilitate co-operation among unions in different countries where members work in the plants of one multinational company, and thus prevent the company from using divide-and-rule tactics in the negotiation of contracts. One such organization, the World Michelin Council, which embraces unionized employees of the giant tire manufacturer in twelve countries, has successfully averted shut-down of a French plant through refusal of extra work by plants in Italy and Germany. The World Auto Council has successfully intervened on behalf of General Motors workers in Mexico. Councils have been formed in metal, electronic and electrical industries. The achievement of world-wide contract termination dates could be regarded as one of the ultimate objectives of Corporation Councils.

It is the global development of capitalistic, free market industry that has galvanized labour into overcoming national barriers and has led to the emergence of labour organizations capable of concerted action in the international arena. Paradoxically, workers have not been uniting in response to Marx's call "Workers of the world, unite," but have found that to protect their interests they must match the flexibility and efficiency of modern, capitalist industry whose operations are not constrained by national borders.

Environmental Challenge to Sovereignty

It is not only the socio-economic impacts of massive industrialization and consumption that challenge the sovereignty of nation states. Also the physical consequences of these activities often do not respect political divisions, may affect the whole balance of global ecology, and cannot be controlled and regulated by national governments.

The list of physical problems caused by industrial operations and exploitation of resources, which require international and global control, is inexhaustible. While sources of pollution may be state-specific, the reach of pollutants is usually international and sometimes global. This is particularly true of contamination of the atmosphere, rivers, lakes, and oceans.

Pollutants produced in Britain affect the air in Scandinavia, emissions from U.S. industry affect the atmosphere over Canada. Radiation resulting from nuclear explosions (weapon tests) or accidents (as in Chernobyl in 1986) may contaminate the whole atmosphere.

The quality of water in the Great Lakes depends on the enforcement of controls by both the United States and Canada. Pollution of the Rhine originates in four countries; The Netherlands have no control over contamination which originates in Switzerland, France, and Germany. The North Sea, whose waters wash the coasts of eight countries, has been a convenient midden for the effluent from the rivers that flow through the industrial heartland of Western and Central Europe, and a dump for industrial waste and sewage sludge, for garbage from shipping and the offshore petroleum industry. The Mediterranean is a receptacle of pollutants from some twenty countries, from highly industrialized to underdeveloped. International controls need to be exercised even over the "open seas," where tanker accidents can be the source of pollution of territorial waters and coastlines.

The cumulative effects of pollutants may affect the ecological balance of the globe and lead to drastic changes in the climate or other undesirable consequences. There is concern that augmentation of carbon dioxide content in the atmosphere could cause, through the so-called greenhouse effect, an increase of temperature, melting of the ice caps, a rise in the sea level, and extensive flooding of the inhabited coastal areas. There is evidence that atmospheric pollutants (such as chlorofluorocarbons, or CFCs, used in aerosol sprays, refrigerators, and chemical industry) reduce the ozone layer in the stratosphere and thus allow more ultraviolet radiation to reach the Earth's surface. This could result in an increase in skin cancer, a decrease in crop production, and danger to aquatic life. Emissions of sulphur and nitrogen oxides are the cause of acid rain, which is detrimental to vegetation and aquatic life.

Clearly, a country's ability to control the quality of the environment over its own territory is severely limited. Also in this area the sovereignty of the nation state has been eroded, and international, rather than national, mechanisms must be created.

International criteria for maximum allowable levels of pollution must replace widely varying national standards, and must be uniformly enforced. Global monitoring systems are needed to assess compliance and determine the effects of pollutants and anti-pollution measures. Safety standards concerning the use of drugs, chemicals, and technologies in general should be universal.

Typically, emission standards for automobiles vary from non-existent to highly stringent, as between Third World countries and North America, and so do structural safety requirements for cars, restrictions on gas additives, and maximum highway speed. Even in countries as closely coupled as the United States and Canada, different criteria apply. Each country insists on exercising what it perceives as "sovereignty," in spite of objectively identical environmental and safety consequences and requirements.

The pressure to establish uniform environmental standards has been coming from the international scientific community, rather than from politicians. It led to the signing in 1987 of the Montreal Protocol which, amended in 1992, pledged 87 countries to phase out the manufacture of CFCs by 1995. In 1988 in Toronto, a conference on "The Changing Atmosphere: Implications for Global Security," attended by delegates from 46 countries, called for a 20 percent reduction of carbon dioxide emissions by the year 2005, and drawing-up of a "law of the atmosphere."

Economic considerations often stand in the way of adequate regulation. Since regulation increases the cost of products, countries that are lax enjoy a competitive advantage over those which observe strict controls. In this and in other cases, the exercise of sovereignty is subject to perceived advantage. A country may allow a foreign company to exploit a natural resource, such as timber, and leave impoverished, eroded soil. When foreigners point out that the process may be irreversible and harmful, the complaint is seen as interference with sovereignty.

International global action is also needed to deal with environmental disasters which may be accidental (such as oil spills in coastal waters) or deliberate (such as dumping of oil into the Persian gulf or setting oil wells on fire during the 1991 war with Iraq). Creation of an International Green Cross which, like the Red Cross, would enjoy a protected status from all sides and would work to clean up contamination and rescue whatever creatures are stricken, has been proposed recently (Boyer 1991). Indeed, Green Cross would provide an effective mechanism for coping with ecological calamities across national borders.

In 1972 in Stockholm the nations of the world for the first time stated their concern with the problems of environment at a United Nations conference which led to the founding of the UN Environmental Program.

Twenty years later, in June 1992, the UN Conference on Environment and Development was held in Rio de Janeiro. This Earth Summit — the biggest international meeting in world's history — was attended by 114 heads of state and delegations from over 150 countries.

The results of the Earth Summit were long on rhetoric and short on commitment and action. A declaration of global principles and a document on sustainable development were approved, conventions on biodiversity and climate were signed. But there was no agreement to halt increase in emissions, let alone to reduce them in order to control the warming of the atmosphere. No mechanism was established for global management of forests. The less developed countries, organized as group G77 of over 120 members, refused to accept any international control of their forests and other resources. The industrialized countries made no long-term commitments of aid to the Third World. The conflict between the relative evils of overpopulation and overconsumption was largely ignored. In general it was the short-term economic concerns that prevailed over the environmental ones at the Earth Summit.

The Relentless Progress of Globalization

Globalization has been the direct consequence of large scale industrialization. Global transportation and communication infrastructures make possible the creation of world markets needed to enable mass production of a multitude of artifacts, from simple consumer goods to enormously sophisticated and expensive systems. Driven by demands of efficiency and profits, globalization progresses in spite of traditional barriers to political and economic integration. Its pervasive impact reaches beyond the material and affects the intellectual and the spiritual. These aspects of globalization are explored in the next chapter which examines the issue of language in a world that is quickly turning into a "global village."

Notes

1. The case of jetliners and cars, which belong among the most expensive goods mass produced for civilian market, is considered in some detail above, pp. 166, 167.
2. In 1993, the UN was active in 13 global trouble spots. Military contingents under UN command have been engaged in peacekeeping, peacemaking and humanitarian operations. Economic sanctions and withdrawal of aid have been also used to support democracy and

human rights. Over the past two decades, Canada has applied economic pressure on 21 countries.

3. Introduction of the metric system or, more accurately, the SI units (Système International d'Unités) in Canada independently of the United States shows that this has not always been recognized. Although the metric system of units is self-consistent and rational, nothing is gained if less than one-tenth of the market uses it; on the contrary, considerable inconvenience and extra costs are the result. Since 1977, the use of kilometres, litres and degrees Celsius confuses American tourists, just as Canadian motorists must adjust to miles, gallons and degrees Fahrenheit, south of the border. Not surprisingly, in many cases metrication in Canada has been only nominal: the quantities the products are packaged in have remained the same, but the labelling has been converted to metric units, which no longer represent round numbers. For example, 4 1/2 fl oz jars of baby food have been "converted" to 128 mL, 12 fl oz beer bottles to 241 mL, 7 oz tuna cans to 113 gm. Indeed, it would make more sense to switch in Canada from British gallons and fluid ounces to the American ones. In the construction industry, feet and inches are still the norm. Paper for typing and printing comes in inch sizes, and copiers are designed to fit, but the Post Office specifies letter sizes in millimetres. And so on . . .
4. The need for a common foreign policy has become acutely evident since 1991, when EEC states were unable to agree on effective measures to stop killings and savage atrocities perpetrated by the fragmented Balkan society in the former Yugoslavia.
5. Austria, Finland, Iceland, Lichtenstein, Norway, and Sweden; Switzerland rejected closer ties with the EEC.
6. Interestingly, it is the American rather than the European companies that have been quick to seize and exploit the opportunities of the single market. They have been operating in Europe for decades and have always viewed Europe as a single entity. Nationalist allegiances, financial and other ties to government, lack of enforcement of single market rules continued to intrude in the operations of the European industry.
7. This generally accepted term does not convey accurately the nature of such corporations. Although they conduct operations and own assets in many countries, the corporate control and ownership remain in the "base country." "The multinational is about as 'multinational' as the Indian army was 'Indian' under the British raj. While the troops were Indian, the officers were British" (Gilpin 1975, 15). "Transnational" or "global" reflect more accurately the nature of the multinationals.
8. However, multiple sourcing may prevent rationalization of production and realization of economies of scale.
9. In Mexico, unions feared exploitation of low wages by the United States and Canada under NAFTA and demanded parity of wages.

References

Barnet, R.J., and Muller, R.E. 1974. *Global Reach*. New York: Simon & Schuster.

BAS. 1979. *The Bulletin of Atomic Scientists*. ("Einstein and Peace" issue) March.

Boorstin, Daniel J. 1978. *The Republic of Technology*. New York: Harper & Row.

Boyer, Patrick. 1991. "Three Steps on the Road to a Safer World," *The Globe and Mail*, 6 March 1991, A21.

Gilpin, R. 1975. *US Power and the Multinational Corporation*. New York: Basic Books.

G&M. 1988. "Business without Borders," *The Globe and Mail*, 5, 7, 8 March.

Havel, Vaclav. 1993. "Short-sighted Stumbling toward a New Europe," *The Globe and Mail*, 30 November.

Heilbroner, R. 1993. *Twenty-First Century Capitalism: Predictions From a Noted Economist*. New York: Norton.

Krauthammer, C. 1990. "Blest be the ties that bind," *Time*, 13 August.

Lukasiewicz, J., and Studnicki-Gizbert, K.W. 1977. "Aviation Activities in Global Perspective," *The Aeronautical Journal* (October): 451–59.

Schreiber, Jean Jacques. 1967. *Le Défi-Américain*. Paris: Éditions Denoël; *The American Challenge*, New York: Atheneum, 1968.

Skolnikoff, E.B. 1971. "Technology and the Future Growth of International Organization," *TechnologyReview* 73(8): 38–47.

U.N. 1973. *Multinational Corporations in World Development*. Department of Economic and Social Affairs, United Nations, St/ECA/190, New York, 195 pp.

U.S. 1976. *Science, Technology and Diplomacy in the Age of Interdependence*. Congressional Research Service, Library of Congress, U.S. Government Printing Office, 492 pp.

Williams, R. 1973. *European Technology*. London: Croom Helm.

6

Language in the Service of Identity — or Communication?

(Kaján Tibor: *Maglepő Táblák*, Budapest 1959)

ONE of the most sensitive and controversial aspects of the integrative pressures of industrial civilization concerns their impact on language. Among its many manifestations, three stand out: the use of foreign words and expressions for which native equivalents may or may not exist, the use of a foreign language in spoken and written communications, and the adoption of a phonetic system of writing and the Latin alphabet in place of native script. All of these developments enhance transnational communications but run counter to the traditional view of language as the main exponent of cultural and national identities, and as the repository of their historical base.

The biblical myth of the Tower of Babel demonstrated the necessity for people to have a common tongue to achieve a major task: the Lord confused the tongues of the presumptuous and proud builders to prevent them from erecting a tower which would reach the heavens. Unintelligibility was regarded as a calamity visited upon humans by the wrathful deity.

But in a traditional, nation-based culture, the primary purpose of language as a tool of communication is taken for granted and therefore overlooked. In such cultures the language reflects a society in which human interaction is largely confined to national, often ethnic, boundaries. Indeed, language has served as the criterion for the right to national self-determination and for establishment of geographical boundaries of nation states. Conversely, governments felt it necessary to suppress the language of other nationalities and impose their own, in order to exert effective political control as, for example, in Russian and German-occupied Poland before the First World War, or in the former Yugoslavia in the 1990s.

Similarly, in order to assert their sovereignty, or for political reasons, governments have arbitrarily given new names to towns and geographical features (such as rivers and mountains) without concern for the identification and information function fulfilled by the established names.

In Canada, Berlin (Ontario), a town with a population of largely German origin, was changed to Kitchener in 1916. Following the Bolshevik revolution of 1917, the names of many cities were changed in the USSR. In 1924 Petrograd became Leningrad, in 1932 Nizhni Novgorod became Gorki. After the dissolution of the USSR in 1991, many reverted to their original names: Leningrad became again Sankt Petersburg (which it was before 1914) and Gorki became again Nizhni Novgorod.

In 1973, the Soviet Union renamed a host of towns that bore names of Chinese origin, in a region of Far Eastern Siberia seized by the Czarist empire in 1860. Suchan was changed to Partizansk, Tetyukhi to Dalnegorsk,

Lifudzin to Rudny, Iman to Dalnerechensk. These changes, aimed at removing evidence that the region was once Chinese, satisfied the political objectives of Moscow rulers but irritated and inconvenienced the affected citizens and confused the outside world.

In the imploding world of industrial civilization the original, primary role of language as a tool of communication is expanding while its role as an attribute of cultural and national identity is being eroded. Language role conflict appears as one among many which accompany the process of modernization and global integration.

Latin: a Historical Illustration

There is abundant evidence which suggests that in a technological culture, based on efficient information transfer (rather than on transfer of material goods), language inevitably tends to assume its primary communication role, at the expense of its former role of national and cultural differentiation. The usage and evolution of Latin from Roman to Medieval times provide an early historical illustration of the paramount role of language as an agent of communication and integration.

Operation of the vast Roman Empire, sprawled over three continents, required the use of one common tongue. Latin, originally spoken only in and around Rome, performed this function. When the need for integration and cohesiveness disappears, so does the common language. The disintegration of the Roman Empire led to the emergence of Romance dialects and languages, eventually adopted by the nation states of Western Europe. Characteristically, each nation state — as an integral organism — elevated only one dialect to the dignity of a standard written language. Thus French is essentially the language of Paris, Italian that of Florence, and Spanish (Castilian) that of Old (Burgos) and New (Toledo, Madrid) Castile. It is interesting to note here that print technology — through standardization of text — played a significant role in the elimination of dialects and standardization of languages.

The role of Latin as a medium of communication and integration is also apparent in the history of the Roman Catholic Church. Latin provided the official language for the Church hierarchy and, until recently, for the liturgy. It assured highly efficient, unambiguous communications within the Church and standard, unalterable texts of its scriptures. Classical Latin was the tool which enabled the Church to develop, maintain, and control a transnational organization while a multiplicity of nation states was emerging. Even today, the Roman Catholic Church operates in more states than most multinational corporations. In recent years, it had to yield to national pressures in its total reliance on Latin, and—inevitably—its rituals have lost some of their former coherence.

The primary role of Latin as a tool of communication is also clearly visible in the development of intellectual activities in the pre-Renaissance West, when all scientific and literary endeavours remained the province of Latin, the universal language of the learned.

The Communication Imperative: India and Africa

The communication function of language asserts itself in spite of nationalistic pressures. Developments in India and Africa are powerful illustrations of this trend.

India is a nation of many "linguistic countries": the 1951 census listed 845 languages and major dialects. The constitution of 1950, which recognized Hindi and 14 other languages, provided for English as the official language, with Hindi to take over after 1965. However, the 1963 Official Languages Act assured continuation of the official status of English, in addition to Hindi.

The status of English, spoken by less than 3 percent of India's population and understood by no more than 15 percent, reflects the fact that English remains the dominant and cohesive national link in administration, education, business, and the courts. The bulk of work in the central offices of the government is carried out in English, and the government has to recruit people who have knowledge of English.

Hindi, the constitutionally designated native language of India, is the language of the north-central region (including New Delhi) and is understood by about 45 percent of the population. The late Prime Minister Indira Gandhi spoke English when she visited the south, and Hindi elsewhere. The parts of the country where Hindi is not spoken, especially in the south, fear that the imposition of Hindi will lead to permanent dominance by the north, placing them at an unfair advantage in terms of jobs and political influence. Riots and violence flared up in the 1970s when the government sought to press the use of Hindi. It is precisely the national and cultural identity of Hindi that prevents it from becoming the universal tongue of India, a role that can be assumed by English, in spite of its totally foreign and, moreover, colonial origin. Curiously, English, as a language spoken by many in the West, could be India's most valuable legacy of the colonial occupation, providing access to a large fraction of existing information and a key to modernization and development.

Also on a personal level, English provides the needed communication link in India. "I could never have married my husband without it," said one woman. "He comes from the North of India and speaks Hindi. I am from the West and speak Konkani. I still have trouble speaking to his mother."

The dilemma the native languages face in Africa parallels the one in India. Perhaps as many as a thousand distinct languages are spoken in Africa; the adoption of one tribal language in preference to many others spoken within a country (as in Nigeria with its one hundred languages) is inevitably unpopular and difficult to enforce. In fact, in the 1970s, 35 out of some 50 independent African countries used English or French as an official language, with Arabic being spoken in most of the others. While the overwhelming majority of people are fluent only in their tribal tongues and their communication is limited to the region where their ancestors lived, a small urban elite uses the European language in the conduct of government and business. In the schools, which reach only a small proportion of African children, the European languages predominate. The same is true of higher learning, the university libraries necessarily relying on foreign, mostly European and American, materials.

Knowledge of a European language is required to operate in one's own country, as well as in relations with other African and overseas countries. Knowledge of both English and French may be needed to ensure effective communication between francophone and anglophone Africans, a skill usually possessed only by the Europeans.

Since 1988, attempts have been made to achieve "linguistic liberation" of Africa through adoption of Swahili as the working language of the Organization of African Unity. Swahili is already an official language in Tanzania and Kenya, and is spoken in Uganda and Zaire. But in the long run Africans may be better served by the current practice of using European languages for inter-tribal communication and access to the developed world's pool of information.

The Communication Imperative: China and Japan

The benefits of communication in a modern European language, bestowed inadvertently by their colonial past on India and the countries of Africa, have been denied China and Japan. Politically independent but secluded for centuries from the influence of Western Civilization, China and Japan have not acquired fluency in any of the modern Western languages and, perhaps more importantly, have never developed an efficient technique for encoding the spoken word, *sine qua non* of effective communicating and information processing, among people and machines.

The Chinese system of writing, which originated in the second millennium B.C., uses complex "word signs" or logographs, which may contain elements derived from pictographs and ideographs (i.e., representations of things and ideas), as well as phonetic and signific signs. Because logographs contain indications of meaning, there are many more logographs than words. To record new words or meanings, new logographs must be devised. Thus the logographic system necessarily contains an enormous and continually increasing number of characters: 40,545 are listed in a 1716 dictionary, still much consulted; over 60,000 are in use today.

The Japanese originally adopted (starting in the 5th century A.D.) the Chinese logographic signs, in spite of a totally different structure of their language. By the 9th century A.D. a system of about 50 abbreviated Chinese signs (*kana*), used for phonetic value only was developed. Today, two such phonetically equivalent systems are employed (*hiragana* and *katakana*) in association with several thousands of Chinese *kanji* characters. Korean, whose structure resembles Japanese, uses a similar system.

The Chinese and Japanese systems of writing pose several obstacles to efficient handling of information and therefore to modernization.

The enormous number and the complexity of signs, and the appearance of new ones, make general literacy impossible, whether in the traditional sense of writing and reading, or in the modern sense of communicating with computers through the standard, Latin alphabet keyboard. The memorizing of thousands of symbols is beyond the intellectual capacity of the majority and, in any event, consumes years of effort. (Japanese children take eight years to learn the 2,000 *kanji* signs, but master the phonetic *kana* script by the age of six.)

The unwieldiness of written language leads to the development of an elitist society. As custodians of written records, the literate elites have privileged access to the past, learn the traditional ways of doing things, and thus strengthen the hold of tradition on society. They have no interest in reforms which would break with traditions, modernize the script, and expand literacy.

Efficient classification and retrieval of information, be it a telephone directory, an encyclopedia, or a computerized data base, relies on a standard alphabetical sequence. Such universal sequence does not exist in Chinese and Japanese, and in any case would be highly complex given the large number of characters (the traditional Chinese classification scheme uses 214 "radicals").

Machine handling and recording of Chinese and Japanese script is inefficient, slow, and expensive. Touch-typing, which requires only some forty keys to handle information in languages which use the Latin alphabet, is not possible given the thousands of signs required. A traditional Chinese "typewriter" consists of a matrix of several thousands characters; the "typist" must select manually (or, in the modern designs, electro-mechanically) the one to be printed. The technique is similar to typesetting, the process invented by the Chinese, in which individual characters are assembled to compose the text. While capable of handling only a small fraction of Chinese words, the technique is slow and must rely on memorizing thousands of character positions.

Just as the conventional typewriter, the telegraph—the first device capable of fast transmission of written language—also could not handle the Chinese script. The solution was to designate 10,000 Chinese characters by four-digit numbers, encode the message accordingly, transmit the numbers, and decode it back into Chinese. The method, which requires years of operator training, was recently improved through the introduction of ten-key decoding machines; however, the encoding continues as a manual process.

Machine-processing of Chinese script is no simple task

(Cable and Wireless)

Chinese typewriter handles 2,600 characters

The present-day Chinese typewriter has about 2,600 characters laid out in a flat-bed matrix. When the operator has selected the required character, a simple mechanical device lifts a metal slug out of its matrix position, uses it to print on the drum mounted paper, and then returns it to the board. The most proficient typists can achieve speeds of no more than 10 characters per minute, even when they are familiar with the positions of a working number of the characters. In practice there are about 400 characters used very frequently and these are generally grouped in the centre of the bed. The relatively slow speed of the operation is partly due to the tiny characters—about 3/16 inches square—and the fact that they are reversed type. The operator is aided by a small mirror attached to the selector arm.

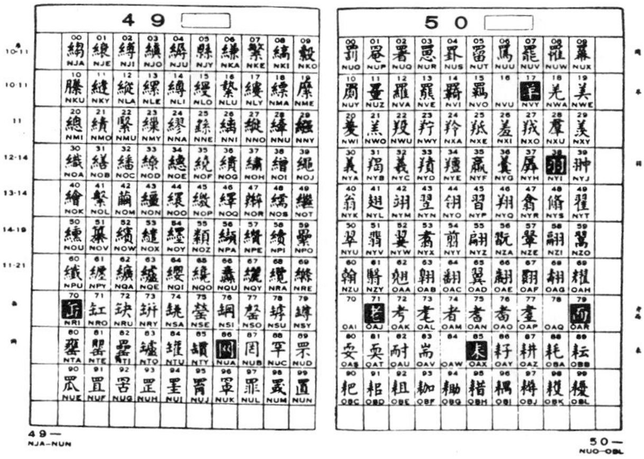

(*New Scientist*, 16 February 1978, 418–19)

A page from *The Chinese Telegraphic Code* book

In attempting to overcome the difficulties inherent in Chinese and Japanese systems of writing, two totally different approaches have been used: a reform of the written language through the adoption of phonetic script and the Latin alphabet, and application of sophisticated technology to allow more efficient handling (such as touch-typing) of traditional script.

A radical and comprehensive reform of the Chinese language was undertaken by the communist government soon after it came to power in 1949. The new rulers of China called for standardization of the spoken language, a reduction in the number of characters used and their simplification, and alphabetization of the written language. Chairman Mao was quoted as stating that "the written language must be reformed. It is necessary to take the road of phoneticization which is commonly adopted by other languages in the world." Alphabetic script was considered indispensable for achievement of universal literacy and the establishment of a modern industrial state. In 1958 an alphabet consisting of 26 Latin letters (i.e. modern European) was approved, with Peking Mandarin dialect as its standard pronunciation. In 1979, China officially adopted Pinyin (Chinese for phonetic spelling), or standardized spelling using the Latin alphabet, to be used for all diplomatic documents, passports, certificates, contracts, export catalogues, etc. In Pinyin, Peking is written Beijing, Canton becomes Guangzhou, Mao Tse-tung — Mao Zedong and China — Zhongguo. Today, Pinyin is taught in China's schools along with the traditional characters.

Some other countries have already travelled the road belatedly taken by China. In 1928, the Arabic was replaced by the Latin alphabet in Turkey, in accordance with the policy of modernizing the language itself and freeing it from dependence on Arabic and Persian.

In Japan, script has been simplified through adoption of standardized spelling and restriction of the number of characters for general use to less than 2,000. Also, two types of latinization have been adopted and are taught in elementary schools.

The above initiatives, drastic and farsighted, but culturally unacceptable, are being countered through application of sophisticated technologies to enhance the preservation of traditional Chinese and Japanese scripts.

Electronic computers and printers make it possible to construct Chinese and Japanese characters from fewer than thirty elements or "strokes." Such systems employ a relatively small number of keys (225 have been used in the English Monotype design), are not limited to a specific number of characters and allow a much higher typing speed. Japanese wordprocessors have a keyboard in *hiragana* and display a selection of possible *kanji* characters from which a choice is made according to the desired meaning.

Another recent wordprocessing technique relies on the display on the screen of Chinese characters which begin with the same sound (recalled from a memory of 6,000 according to the corresponding sound of a Latin letter); selection of the required one and its transfer to the line of text are carried out by touching the screen.

The development and increasing popularity of fax (facsimile) machines owes much to the complexity of Japanese script and wizardry of Japanese electronic companies. The ability of fax to transmit instantly any image is particularly useful when working with Japanese and Chinese scripts.

As the need for efficient handling of information grows and the volume augments, the pressure to devise standard practical systems of recording Chinese and Japanese languages, compatible with the Western alphanumeric system, is mounting. Clearly, this is an indispensable step in modernization, a development — in terms of Western progress — overdue by many centuries. And yet, paradoxically, it is the most modern technology that is deployed to assist in the preservation of antiquated systems and thus to delay modernization.

Toward Efficient Spelling

Western script, which uses a 26-letter alphabet, has been a marvellously efficient and simple system for recording language. Nevertheless, it too could be improved through rationalization of spelling (Yule 1982). However, in this case also, tradition stands in the way of efficiency.

The spelling of English, which was standardized in its present form over 200 years ago, reflects etymology and precedents which would not necessarily be acceptable today. Nevertheless, any changes of spelling are vehemently resisted because spelling — a method to record language — is confused with the language itself. Typically, in a survey conducted in France in 1989, a large majority of respondents agreed that the learning of spelling and grammar required a major effort by teachers and children. But, in the same poll, the majority was against introduction of simplified spelling and felt that traditional spelling must be preserved as a vital exponent of French culture.

A council appointed in 1989 has recommended only some cosmetic changes in spelling, such as omission of the circumflex accent on letters *i* and *u*, or writing *ognon* ('onion') instead of *oignon*.

A simpler spelling would make the language easier to learn, quicker to read and write, would reduce eye strain, and facilitate and speed-up machine processing.

Removal of surplus letters from words has already been taking place in an informal manner in America. The spelling of *catalogue, colour, labour, programme* and *draught* has been reduced to *catalog, color, labor, program,* and *draft*; *through, night* and *light* have been occasionally written as *thru, nite* and *lite*. The scope for elimination of surplus letters, which serve no apparent purpose for either pronunciation or meaning, is indeed vast.[1]

The difficulties of traditional spelling are being circumvented through introduction of English dictionaries in word processing programs so that spelling can be automatically checked and corrected. In this case also, sophisticated technology stands in the way of efficiency and progress.

English as the Modern *lingua franca*

The ease of communications enjoyed by the medieval intellectuals in the West was lost when modern tongues replaced Latin as the language of the educated, a process which started during the Renaissance period. The humanist Thomas More (1478–1535) and the philosopher Francis Bacon (1561–1626) both wrote in English and Latin; the astronomer Galileo Galilei (1564–1642) published in Italian and Latin. But until the early eighteenth century Latin was still widely used by intellectuals. The Dutch humanist Erasmus (c. 1466–1536), the astronomers Copernicus (1473–1543) in Poland and Kepler (1571–1630) in Germany, the physician Harvey (1578–1657), and scientist Newton (1642–1727) in England all wrote in Latin.

During the eighteenth century French emerged as the language of international relations and the second language of all educated persons. In central and eastern Europe the upper classes often preferred French to their native tongues; King Frederick the Great wrote his literary works in French; the *Almanach de Gotha*, an early (founded in 1778) and long-lived German yearbook of political and statistical information, was printed in French; and French was the official language of the academies of Berlin and Sankt Petersburg.

In this century, and particularly after the Second World War, the status of French as the language of international intercourse has been taken over and greatly expanded by English.

English has emerged as the closest thing to a *lingua franca*; it has taken over the role which once belonged to Latin in the West and to Chinese in East Asia. Some linguists believe that up to 1.4 billion people now speak versions of English, compared with an estimated 700 million in 1980. Non-native speakers probably outnumber born speakers 2 to 1. English is the main language used in all kinds of activities, from science, engineering, transportation, and communications to business, diplomacy, and pop culture.

But this is not to say that linguistic diversity does not continue to be an obstacle to efficient communication and organization as, for example, in the case of the European Economic Community. As already noted, large resources and much time is consumed by the Eurocrats from 12 member countries on operations conducted in the EEC's nine (!) official languages.

The Early Imperatives of Communication

Transportation has been one of the early activities in which communication requirements imposed the use of a single universal information system.

In simple situations, symbolic signs (shape and colour) have been used to convey the information. For many decades, standard road traffic signs have been in use in Europe, and are now being adopted world-wide. Clearly, car travel would have been unacceptably dangerous if drivers had to comply with regulations posted in languages unknown to them, or if a red light signal indicated a "stop" in one country, and "proceed ahead" in another. Through the use of traffic signs, a universal, symbolic language is being developed—a direct consequence of the widespread use of the automobile. Similarly, development of air travel has led to the use of universal sign language in airports.

More sophisticated activities require the use of a standard (spoken and written) language and terminology.

English became the universal language of marine and, later, of air operations. A single medium and a standard terminology of communications were needed not only to achieve efficiency, but also to preserve safety. Failure to comply would result in serious accidents and loss of life.

This was the cause of the world's worse mid-air collision, in which all 176 people on board perished in September 1976 over Yugoslavia. Contrary to standard regulations, the instructions to the Yugoslav plane were given by Zagreb controllers in Serbo-Croatian rather than English, and could not be understood by pilots of other aircraft in the area. The collision could have been avoided had the pilot of the British plane understood the messages being given to the Yugoslav aircraft.

In Quebec, in spite of the obvious desirability of using only English for air traffic control, the use of both French and English was introduced in the 1970s. Even in this strictly technical application, the government of Quebec viewed language as a cultural and national attribute first, and a tool of communication second.

A common language must also be used in establishing transnational voice communications. Again in this case, English has become the tongue of international telephone operators.

Even if only one language is used, standard and precise terminology is critical. When in March 1980 an Ottawa, Canada air controller told the snowplow operator to "clear the runway," he meant to order the vehicle off the runway as a jetliner was about to land. The snowplow operator took the instruction to mean he was to remove snow from the runway. A crash was narrowly avoided by an alert pilot.

In the spring of 1980 three aircraft were involved in a near-collision over Toronto because controllers failed to use phonetics in identifying the aircraft when talking to the pilots.

Science

The adoption of English by the practitioners of science, particularly (but not at all exclusively) in physical and life sciences, and in the disciplines dealing with the abstract, such as mathematics and logic, reflects the fact that the content of sciences and the activities of scientists are truly international. Clearly, national allegiance and geographical location of scientists are not relevant to their intellectual contributions.

As Louis Pasteur, the most international and yet the most French scientist remarked, "Science has no fatherland, but a scientist does." It makes no more sense to talk about French electronics, German chemistry, or Soviet physics than to classify animals and plants according to the political borders of nation states which may encompass or overlap their habitats. In all of these cases, the unity of a discipline or species transcends national and political divisions.

The overwhelming desire of scientists to communicate, rather than to emphasize, their separate, national allegiances, has been most evident in the evolution of their publication habits.

Traditionally, each country used to publish its own national journals in various fields of learning. World-wide integration of scientific, technological, and intellectual activities in general has now progressed to the point that national scholarly publications are no longer adequate. The objective of authors is to be heard by a large, competent and responsive audience—and this goal can be achieved only through publication in the journals patronized by the main body of contributors, in their language. Members of the "research front"—in any discipline—tend to publish in the journals foremost in their field, irrespective of the place of publication.

A study (Inhaber 1978; Auerbach 1978) of the publishing habits of Canadian scientists has shown that a majority of them prefer not to publish in Canada. In 1971, only one-third of papers by Canadian scientists were published in Canada; 43 percent were published in the United States. More significantly, just one-tenth of the "hot" papers (cited ten times in the same year, or in the year following publication) by Canadian scientists were published in Canada; two-thirds were published in the United States. Not a single "hot" paper from Quebec was published in French.

The inadequacy of national publications serving only a small constituency has led to publication of some journals in several languages and establishment of multinational or international journals aimed at a world-wide audience.

In many countries, scientific journals and papers are published in English rather than in the native language. This is particularly popular in Japan and Scandinavia, and reflects the recognition by these societies of English as the *lingua franca* of the sciences.[2] Even the French Pasteur Institute in Paris began publishing its scientific journals *Annales de l'Institut Pasteur* in English in the 1980s.

Some of the more popular magazines are issued in several languages. The monthly *Scientific American* is printed in English, German, French, Spanish, Italian, Hungarian, as well as Chinese, Japanese, Arabic, and Russian, the tongues used by over three billion people in 150 countries. *Saiensu,* the Japanese-language edition of *Scientific American,* is Japan's largest and most prestigious publication covering science and technology, with a circulation of more than 32,000 (in 1982).

American and other non-Russian scientists can subscribe to leading Russian journals published in English translation in the United States, and their Russian counterparts can read, in Russian, Western publications, printed in Russia. *Scientific American* is published in Russian (since 1983) and English-language copies of the weekly *Science* are imported.

Knowledge: the only frontier

The internationalization of scientific journals, the immediate dissemination of preprints of research papers by electronic mail and fax, and the plethora of international workshops and colloquiums, all bring together scientists who live, work and are paid under separate national systems.

To young scientists, national frontiers are increasingly meaningless as international travel grows easier, especially within Europe and between Europe, America and Asia ... science really does become the discourse of a global village.

To scientists there is only one frontier that matters, and that is the frontier of knowledge.

(M. Posner, *New Scientist*, 14 November 1992, p. 41)

The consolidation of five European astronomy and astrophysics journals into a single publication illustrates well the imperative of reaching a large body of authors and readers. Recognizing the inadequacies of nationally-based publications, which could not compete with the *Astrophysical Journal* published in the United States, the Scandinavian, Dutch, French, and German astronomers established in 1968 *Astronomy and Astrophysics, A European Journal*, an international journal with a "European flavour," supported by the participating countries in proportion to the gross national product of each. Characteristically, although the British declined participation, the new journal is printed in French and German, and in English, a language foreign to the founders but effective in the areas of astronomy and astrophysics (Steinberg 1971).

What is true of publications holds also for scientific and professional societies whose purpose is to provide mechanisms (such as publications and meetings) for dissemination and exchange of information. Again, national, regional, or other parochial bases for organization of professional groups are inadequate, the significant activities being conducted by the largest and most active groups which have, to a non-negligible extent, an international membership.

Although, as already indicated, progress is steadily being made toward integration of scholarly publications and professional activities among nation states, the conflict between a national versus international basis for such activities is not as yet generally resolved. Canada provides a good illustration of this situation. In spite of a common language and an economy essentially integrated with the United States, several Canadian professional societies parallel the much larger, and much more active American organizations. In some cases, which could be considered truly anomalous, there are branches of British societies operating in Canada — a carry-over from colonial times. Some of the Canadian journals, having a very limited readership, publish mainly survey-type and/or second rate material by Canadian and foreign (usually U.S.) authors, while first rate Canadian papers are published abroad. High cost to those Canadians who wish to belong to both the Canadian, and the other — usually American — society, and no professional gain are the net result of such activities.

Diplomacy, International Organizations, Business and Education

At the Versailles Peace Conference of 1919, English was already a major language of the pin-striper. Only one of the Big Four government leaders at Versailles, Italian Prime Minister Vittorio Orlando, did not speak English. Today, so many government leaders are fluent in English that even former French president Valéry Giscard d'Estaing was obliged to converse in English at summits.

English is the official language at meetings of countless international bodies, from the Olympic Committee to the Miss Universe pageant. Reporting on a North–South conference held in 1977 in Paris, *Le Monde* lamented that, "generally speaking, not only all the negotiations were conducted in English but it was easier at the press centre to find working documents in English or even Arabic than in French."

English is the tongue Japanese businessmen use to negotiate a deal with the Kuwaitis. It is how Swedes speak to Mexicans, Hong Kong bankers work in Singapore. In Mexico, English-speaking secretaries can increase their wages substantially; in Egypt their pay can go up ten times.

Many multinational corporations don't wait for their employees to learn English on their own. They offer English instruction to staff members on four continents and send executives for live-in conversation courses.

As English became a key to information access and to getting ahead (and getting out of, for example, the Soviet bloc), it has also become the most popular second language taught the world over. Qualified English teachers are among the best paid professionals in many countries.

In China, students in large cities can take nine years of English language studies before finishing high school. Chinese television broadcasts a dozen or more English classes each week. University students, studying science and engineering, as well as some other undergraduates, must study English for at least two years. Many Chinese students have excellent command of English, as became evident from TV reports of students' protests in Beijing in 1989.

In Japan, English is taught extensively in schools. Many Japanese scientists and engineers publish in English. In South Korean schools, English is a required subject from grade seven on.

The majority of Europeans — the French, the West Germans, the Swiss, the Scandinavians, and the Benelux citizens — choose English as their second language. They find a working knowledge of English essential in business, commerce, and travel, a common link in an increasingly internationalized society.

All the world's a stage

"All the world's a stage, and all the men and women merely players," says Jaques in Shakespeare's *As You Like It*, first produced in a theatre pointedly named The Globe.

"On the stage he was natural, simple, affecting: 'Twas only that when he was off he was acting" — Oliver Goldsmith, 1774.

In our day, the theatre is no longer a metaphor for the globe. The real world has become a theatre. And all the men and women are not "merely" players; they are players or nothing. The stage may have shrunk to the size of a TV screen, but the world is on it — or waiting in the wings.

(©Mavor Moore, *The Globe and Mail*, 16 January 1988)

Global Audience and Standards

The international character of creative and intellectual activities, at one time the hallmark of science, is evident today in all areas of culture. The process which started with movable print and growth of literacy, evolved to computer and satellite communications and has created, in the second half of this century, a world-wide audience eager to receive instantly any and all significant — and not so significant — information, irrespective of its provenance.

The 1991 war for Kuwait provided the most dramatic demonstration of the global reach and demand for news. The round-the-clock TV broadcasts (in English) by CNN (Cable News Network) were viewed in over 100 countries around the globe by a large fraction of the world's population. On occasions, even the coalition forces benefitted from CNN reporting which reached them ahead of the information transmitted through secure military channels.

The Moscow coup which failed to oust Soviet president Mikhail Gorbachev in August 1991 was another occasion on which the global reach of information was demonstrated. Cut-off from Soviet communications, Gorbachev depended on BBC radio for news of the coup.

Global communications have imposed global—rather than national—standards on the creative arts. The quality of a book, article, song, or film is measured by world-wide, rather than national, acceptance. Writing in his native tongue, a successful author of fiction or poetry is assured of a foreign-speaking audience who reads his work in translation, even though it may not match the beauty of the original. The writings by Aleksandr I. Solzhenitsyn, some of which have not been published in his native land for years, are a good demonstration of this situation. So is the first novel by a Canadian, David Adams Richards, which was published in Moscow in 1979 in 200,000 copies, about ten times the total Canadian sales of all four of his books.

The same tends to hold for pop culture: music, films, TV series. English pervades rock music the world over. Rock singers usually give the same reasons for singing in English: their own exposure to English lyrics. In December 1982, 13 of the top 20 LPs in Japan had English titles. West German rock songs average 56 English words a tune. When the Spanish punk group Topo released a record on learning English, it became a hit.

American film and TV programs command a large world-wide audience and represent a major U.S. export ($3.7 billion to Europe in 1993). American "cultural" exports became a major issue, particularly with France, at the final round of GATT negotiations in 1993. In spite of France's heavy subsidization of the film industry ($245 million a year), 60 percent of France's film box office comes from American productions. French TV is protected from invasion by American programs by a quota system, which requires 60 percent of programs to be of European origin (two-thirds of that French). Other members of the European Community impose a quota of 50 percent.

American audiovisual exports are not only popular in Europe but are also affordable. Again in this case, a very big domestic film and TV market provides the large resources needed to pay for audiovisual productions.

For France—in the words of Prime Minister Edouard Balladur—abolition of quotas and subsidies would spell "the end of European cultures" and put at risk not only "one's national soul" but also global intellectual freedom because "by sending its pictures all over the world, a country spreads a certain type of civilization."

Similar concerns are voiced in Canada, where 95 percent of film box office comes from U.S. productions.

The government prescribes a minimal national content of TV programs (but allows distribution of American TV through cable) and, since 1972, subsidizes publishing of Canadian authors.

Such measures run the risk of supporting inferior quality productions under the guise of satisfying national aspirations and, in view of the mass market demand, their success is uncertain.

In a world that increasingly approximates McLuhan's "Global Village" it is difficult to sustain productions (whether books, newspapers, magazines, films, or TV programs) of restricted or local interest only, in spite of the fact that such productions may have a high appeal and value for a limited audience.

Nevertheless, considerable efforts are made, particularly by France and Canada, to support national cultural industries. Canada has succeeded in obtaining cultural exemption from the North American Free Trade Agreement and the issue of cultural exports was not resolved by the 1993 GATT negotiations.

In 1965 the Canadian government introduced legislation designed to protect the domestic magazine industry. Canadian advertisers could no longer claim advertising in foreign (read: U.S.) magazines as a business expense and so called split-runs, in which the original editorial content is used with Canadian ads to produce an edition for export to Canada, were prohibited. These measures have been only partly effective and had little impact on foreign publications which could not have a viable Canadian equivalent. A Canadian skin magazine could not compete with *Playboy*: its readers are not interested in the nationality of the women it serves up and, moreover, a magazine of comparable quality for the small Canadian market would be prohibitively expensive. The scope is for periodical press which covers national, regional, and city news and issues, or highly selective topics which can command international readership.

The experience of *Time* weekly magazine clearly shows that many Canadians — *Time*'s readership is estimated at over two million — insist on access to world coverage of news. In response to tough legislation, *Time* abolished its Canadian edition, discontinued its special Canadian section, laid off most of its Canadian staff and raised the subscription rate from $18 to $30. *Time*'s circulation dropped from over 500,000 in 1975 to 350,000 in 1982 (compared to 650,000 of *Maclean's*, Canadian national newsmagazine), but, the volume of advertising has been maintained and *Time* remained in excellent financial shape. It has been publishing nine separate editions in Canada, containing the same editorial material but different advertisements, reflecting the region advertisers want to reach.

Today's electronic transmission technology allows total separation of editing and printing, and therefore may be by-passing the split-run restriction on importation of magazines from abroad. In 1993 *Sports Illustrated* announced publication of six Canadian editions per year, prepared in New York (including Canadian ads) and printed in Ontario. The market targeted by *Sports Illustrated* as a general sports magazine is not being served by a Canadian periodical. Because *Sports Illustrated*'s editorial costs are covered by its large U.S. run, it can offer attractive advertising rates in Canada, much lower than Canadian magazines.

In any event, in the age of satellite communications and electronic dialogue of computers, attempts to control production and distribution of printed matter are bound to fail in the long run and are equally impractical as control of the reach of television and radio broadcasts.

World coverage of news as provided by such publications as *Time* and *Newsweek,* is necessarily unavailable in a domestic publication such as *Maclean's,* designed to cover mainly national, rather than international, news. National publications, particularly those whose domestic markets are relatively small (as, for example, in Canada), cannot possibly afford their own world-wide news-gathering organization and have to rely on major established purveyors of news (such as Associated Press, United Press International, Reuters, *The New York Times,* etc.) which offer global coverage and operate in a global market. The same is true of radio and TV: reports by CNN, BBC, NBC, ABC, and CBS can be heard and seen on English language broadcasts anywhere (CNN TV reportage on 17 January, 1991, the first day of war with Iraq, was seen in over 100 countries by an estimated one billion people). Even the editorial comment and feature articles are often reprinted from major newspapers and magazines to enhance the quality of lesser publications and expand the range of topics they cover.

The internationalization of publishing has been progressing not only in the field of science. High quality magazines and newspapers, such as *Time, Newsweek, The Economist, The New York Times, Le Monde,* among others, have a significant international readership. *The Wall Street Journal,* printed in 12 plants in the United States (1.6 million circulation) also publishes the *Asian Wall Street Journal* in Hong Kong. The London *Financial Times* receives one-third of its revenue (in 1982) from overseas sales, and prints a European edition in Frankfurt. It also publishes the *World Business Weekly.* Aimed at the United States, this weekly contains more information about international business in one place than is available anywhere in American journalism.

Today, a successful artist or author commands an international, and often a global audience. This view was articulated by Mordecai Richler, a Canadian writer of international repute. Speaking in 1973 on "The arts and nationalism in Canada," Richler commented eloquently on the perils of chauvinistic nationalism as a "shield for mediocrity" and on the literature, that "is more than a local address."

Richler left Canada for London in 1951 and stayed there for almost two decades. As for the Canadian artists and writers who stayed at home,

> they did so out of necessity, not without self-apology, promising themselves that next year, or the year after, they would try London or New York, testing their talents against the larger world. Alas, next year, or the year after never came, and a decade later many felt themselves compromised, self-condemned, a big bat in the minors forevermore, until, with hindsight, they redeemed themselves in their own eyes by becoming the most impassioned of nationalists, declaring that for all seasons there is nothing like home, which, I fear, was nothing more than self-justification.
>
> And there were others, luxuriating in provincial celebrity, who were, I think, irresponsible. Take, for instance, that engaging poet, famous in Canada, largely unknown abroad, who has been playing the campus circuit for years telling the students that the best damn poetry in the world is being written here.
>
> Nonsense.
>
> The rest of the world does not suffer from a tin ear, and if the best damn poetry was indeed being written here, they would have heard and, furthermore, they would have clapped hands.
>
> Something else.
>
> If, in Paris, I was to discover many neophyte writers with all the faults of genius, that is to say they screwed and drank prodigiously, never paid the rent, and happily belted their wives about the room, but when you came down to it, still couldn't write or paint worth a damn: so, on many a return trip home, I found artists who were long, marvellously long, on integrity but conspicuously short on talent. Say the ebullient National Film Board or CBC drama director who assured me he would never, no matter what, sell out, as it were, to Hollywood, New York, or London. Or the journalist, equally charged with patriotic pride, who would not, come hell or high water, write for *Life*, *Playboy*, or *Esquire*.
>
> Nationalism was self-interest: not so much a badge of honour as a shield for mediocrity.
>
> My quarrel with the nationalists is that they—obviously thinking very little of us—would put barriers above all, erecting a great cultural wall of Canada, jamming the airwaves, sealing off the frontier, sheltering us from all things American, in the slender hope that something better, something distinctly our own would emerge from wilderness land we would be left to linger in. On the other hand, it is my case, that this is to licence mediocrity and twice-bless the second-rate, endorsing just about anything that is our very own.

Even as Canadians complain about American domination, points out Richler, they are quietly intervening in American mythology and pop culture.

> Were I the devil's advocate, I would even make out a case for unseemly Canadian manipulation of that very scene we claim is smothering us. Louis B. Mayer and Jack Warner, makers of the Hollywood dream, both emerged out of Canada. The popular myth of a couple of years ago, Love Story, was perpetuated on screen by a CBC-trained director, Arthur Hiller. And the most successful and well-loved western series ever, Bonanza, relied for its father figure on Canada's very own Lorne Greene.
>
> Amidst a plethora of obscene, drug-addicted rock'n'rollers, the last shining morning face in American entertainment is Ottawa's own Paul Anka. *The Police Gazette*, a time-honoured American Institution, is actually edited in Montreal. Harlequin doctor and nurse novels, written and published here, are devoured in small town America. Until *Screw, Swinger, Suck* and other salacious tabloids came along, *Justice Weekly* was in the vanguard. *Justice Weekly*, for many a year the only journal to publish endlessly saucy spanking letters. Out of Toronto, from hogtown with love, the pervert's *New Statesman*.
>
> [In the Global Village] one must not be diverted into chauvinism, a stagnant stream, and accept or burnish cultural wooden nickels, even if they are stamped with the Maple Leaf. Literature is more than a local address, or familiar street names, or good intentions. It's what, hopefully, makes our short passage here more endurable. And to my fellow artists I say eschew the cultural policy of the closed door, reject the proffered nationalist crutch: instead, seize the day.

Publish, perish or get an arts grant

I find it hard to figure out who we are protecting our culture against. In the debate over free trade between Canada and the United States, some of our most highly respected writers tried to make us believe that an entire generation of Canadian art would be crushed beneath the heavy hand of American cultural imperialism if not protected. For this theory to make sense, however, three things have to be taken for granted: we must assume that Canadian art is generally inferior to American; that Canadians do not generally want to read home-grown material; and, most important, that we have a right to force our own inferior product on the Canadian public via the financial bullying of the government.

I personally do not accept any of these premises. Those at the Canada Council, it would seem, do. They have no problem with deciding what is Canadian and what is valid, and then supporting it financially.

Another underlying argument is that we as a society should support the arts against a hostile domestic environment. In real terms, this means we pay for them with our tax dollars. How the government can justify taking money from people to support art that nobody really wants is an interesting question. Paying artists to do whatever they please reinforces the romantic misconception of the artist as outsider, or even as somehow morally superior to the rest of humanity (as evidenced by their inability to make a living).

Blaming society for an inability to earn a living benefits no one. Blaming society while at the same time taking its money is just plain stupid.

But what about those who don't get grants for whatever reason? They are forced to compete in a publishing arena increasingly controlled by public funding. Publishing houses must choose between producing books with funding, or those without. The decision, especially in today's financial climate, is obvious. Canadian artists are forced to compete in a scenario in which a small body, supported by millions of dollars, has happily relieved the public of the burden of deciding what they wish to read or view. It is also an issue of censorship: the grant-givers are in a position to encourage artists whose points of view they find agreeable.

(Rob McCleary, a 25-year-old writer. *The Globe and Mail*, 15 February 1994)

The impact of a "foreign culture" and the imposition of world standards, so acutely felt in Canada because of its proximity to the much larger and more dynamic U.S. society, are resented and resisted by many other countries. As examined in the concluding section of this chapter, attempts to constrain foreign influences, in a world of augmenting interdependence and integration, are not likely to succeed.

Internationalization of Vocabularies and Lifestyles

One of the important consequences of invention and innovation is the appearance of new words and meanings, usually in the language of the innovator. The adoption of such new terms by other languages serves the cause of efficient communication; attempts to substitute artificially contrived "native" terms in order to preserve the "purity" of one's language, have necessarily the opposite effect.

The examples considered here show how science, technology, and the lifestyles they bring on have influenced the vocabulary and infiltrated other languages. Again in this case the communication function — rather than the identity attribute — has been the winner.

As noted by Wallace Reyburn (1969), the ultimate tribute to man's inventiveness is to have his name incorporated into the language as a noun, without a capital letter — perhaps a tribute superior to that accorded explorers and astronomers through giving their names to geographical features and heavenly bodies. Such internationally accepted terms, as *ampere, coulomb, ohm, volt, watt, fahrenheit, curie, roentgen* (for physical units), *diesel* (for compression-ignition internal combustion engine) honour, in all languages, the pioneers of science and technology.

Names of more mundane inventions — such as *chesterfield, davenport, mackintosh, gladstone, stetson, bowler, macadam, wellingtons, bloomers, sandwich* — also immortalize the originators, often in languages other than their own (as with *macadam* and *sandwich* in French and many other tongues).

Such words as *distaff* and *spinster* have interesting and related origins. *Dis* in Old English means a bunch of flax. A *distaff* was a staff with a cleft end for holding flax or wool to be fed into a spinning wheel. This task was almost invariably performed by women. The *distaff* became a symbol of women's work, and evolved to mean women in general.

Spinning was also exclusively associated with women and produced the word *spinster*. Since working women were mostly single, *spinster* came to mean an unmarried female and eventually a plain, older and unmarriageable one.

In some cases, the impact of innovations on language has been much more complex and unpredictable.

There cannot be many Russians who know that *karandash*, 'pencil' in Russian, is a phonetic rendering of *Caran d'Ache*, a Swiss manufacturer of pencils, still in business. Or that *royal*, 'piano' in Russian, is the name of a French maker of pianos. Not many Poles realize that *rower*, 'bicycle' in Polish (pronounced *rover*), is the well known English manufacturer of bicycles and cars. And no doubt few Americans and Canadians are aware of the origin of the term *crapper*, and its derivatives, in common use in North America, expressions which pay tribute to Thomas Crapper, a British pioneer in the technology of sanitary engineering.

As told by W. Reyburn (1969), Thomas Crapper was the man "whose foresight, ingenuity and perseverance brought to perfection one of the great boons to mankind" — the water closet. He was born of a humble family in the Yorkshire town of Thorne in 1837 — "appropriately enough the year in which Queen Victoria came to the throne, the start of the Victorian Era to which he was to make such a splendid contribution."

> The firm old Thomas established did a lot of work in military hospitals and barracks in the first World War. The troops could not help but be made aware day after day that the sanitary arrangements were by T. Crapper,

Chelsea. If one casts one's mind back to the 1914—18 period one realizes that at that time in the hinterland of America they were not very advanced in what the *Plumbing Equipment News* calls 'sanitary sophistication'. American doughboys from the hills of Kentucky or an Idaho farm, where the privy was all they knew about, would be mighty impressed by Thos. Crapper's slick contraption. And they would be quick to pay verbal tribute to his inventiveness.

Thus it was that returning American troops spread the word. Going to the *crapper* got a great deal of use during the 1920s, so that eventually the *Dictionary of American Slang* was able to report that the term 'had come into common usage in America by 1930'.

American servicemen stationed in England during World War II took home the expression 'You've had it'. Their fathers in World War I took home *crapper.*

The only reason one can think of why British troops didn't follow suit is that the Crapper insignia was old stuff to them. It had been around for many a long year in this country which, after all, was the pioneer of this whole water closet business. It was no novelty to them.

The word crap was a fine old English word. The book *Slang & Its Analogues*, published in 1891, gave it a variety of unrelated meanings — 'to harvest', 'the gallows', 'printers' type in disarray' and 'to ease oneself'. But nowhere in that book or any other English dictionary I have searched through can I find the word *crapper*. The Americans alone have given the man his due.

And from that word they have derived others. To quote from the *Dictionary of Americanisms*:

> crappy — inferior, ugly, cheap, merchandise of inferior workmanship, inferior entertainment, *crappy* workmanship.
> *crap* — nonsense, cant, lies, exaggeration, mendacity, bull. 1939: 'Pally, I have never heard so much crap in such a short time in my life.' John O'Hara, *Pal Joey*. 1949: 'I'm not interested in stories about the past or any crap of that kind.' Arthur Miller, *Death of a Salesman*.

It is *crap* in this connotation which has drifted across the Atlantic from America to England in recent years. One hears it from time to time in this country, as in 'You're talking a lot of *crap*'. But the English are hesitant about using it in polite society, associating it in their minds with the good old Anglo-Saxon word.

Presumably *crap*, meaning nonsense, will also become acceptable here — a strangely round-about way of his fellow-countrymen at long last giving credit to Thos. Crapper, the W.C. pioneer.

In the early years of industrialization, every language was creating its own new vocabulary needed to describe new activities, innovations and their use. *Industry* (in the sense of manufacturers), *business, capitalism, commercialism*, and *working class* described the new kind of society emerging. In some cases, different terminologies were adopted in the same language by different countries. Although imported from Britain, *railway* became *railroad* in the United States and the two English-speaking societies developed very distinct vocabularies of rail transportation (and, to some extent, distinct rail technologies). *Baggage car, caboose, dining car, truck* are the terms used in the United States (and Canada); *luggage van, brake van, restaurant car,* and *bogie* are their British equivalents.

The introduction of the automobile has also led to the appearance of distinct British and North American vocabularies. When the British speak of *bonnet, boot, wing,* and *petrol,* Americans and Canadians talk of *hood, trunk, fender,* and *gas.*

As the rate of growth of science and technology increases, so do the new vocabularies that these activities create. Moreover, the new terms often gain universal acceptance, in all languages.

It has been said that there are twice as many names of chemical organic compounds as there are words in English. *Jane's Aerospace Dictionary,* published in 1980, contains more than 15,000 entries in the areas of aviation, space-flight and related subjects. Such words as *electron, telephone, radio, radar* (for "radio detecting and ranging"), *television, photograph, maser* (for "microwave amplification by stimulated emission of radiation"), *laser* (for "light amplification etc."), *holograph, jet, film, X-ray, transistor, penicillin, aspirin, antibiotic, nylon, teflon*—are typical of the international vocabulary. (Incidentally, *radio* has taken over in French from *t.s.f.* (telephonie/telegraphie sans fil), and *radar*—from *radiolocation,* used in England during World War II.)

Innumerable examples show that technological and scientific developments, which rely on good communication, enhance and often depend on the use of a single terminology or language.

As already noted, transportation and communications had to rely, early on, on the use of a single standard language. Today, producing, selling, operating, and servicing of a plethora of technological devices promotes similar skills and vocabularies. Clearly, IBM (International Business Machines Co.) or VW (Volkswagen) workers, salesmen, and technicians from various countries would experience little difficulty in communicating about their respective activities and products. Indeed, each internationally produced and marketed artifact creates an area of effective comprehension among those involved, irrespective of their native tongue.

The linguistic impact of inventions goes far beyond the creation of specialized, scientific, and technical terms. As innovations modify traditional activities and introduce novel ones, they bring about new vocabularies which quickly enter the popular culture and become universally accepted in all languages.

Such terms as *club, weekend, parking, credit card, gangster, kidnapping, holdup, best seller, sex appeal, camping, jeans, disco,* have gained world-wide currency, in all languages. The French talk about *les T-shirts, le marketing, le peep-show, le hamburger,* and *le take-over.* Germans read *Quick, Hobby, Men, Trend,* and *Manager Magazin,* watch *die Stripteaser,* shop at *der Supermarket,* fly *nonstop,* call for *eine Baby-sitter,* enjoy *ein Thriller,* learn *das Know-how,* and keep *up to date.* Americans try to keep their *sang froid* and to stay *au courant,* enjoy French *cuisine,* speak about *détente,* and keep a *laissez-faire* attitude. Russians fear *eskalatsiya,* like to watch *khokkei, futbol, voleibol,* and *beisbol* as they taste the *chuvingum,* fear *mass mediya,* do *export-import biznes,* drink *dzin* and *tonik,* and dance *tvist.* Greeks hold a *press-conference,* visit *topless clubs,* operate *bulldozers,* and hope for *air conditioning.*

The list of internationally adopted terms is inexhaustible and growing. As the global industrial civilization brings more and more common elements to all lifestyles, the vocabulary which is understood by everybody expands inexorably and enriches all languages.

Preservation of Linguistic Identity

As the role of language as a medium of international communications expands, attempts to preserve language as an expression of national and cultural identity also intensify. This has been particularly evident in France and Quebec, where increasing popularity of English terminology and expressions, and of English as a second language, have been aggressively resisted and opposed.

The French government's commitment to preservation of linguistic purity has been rooted in the belief that, since language and culture are always one and indivisible, the growing use of English would undermine the French culture and, without a cultural anchorage, France could not survive long as a politically independent country and would not fulfil its mission as a leading force in Europe.

For the more extreme French nationalists, as for the late General de Gaulle, for many humanists and philosophers the decline of France would spell the end of Europe as a major cultural and political influence in the world; for them, to maintain France's cultural and political dominance is to preserve Europe. "A European country which today turns its back on France betrays Europe"—wrote *Paris Match* in its 19 May 1974 issue. Such a country

> is resigned to be nothing more than subsidiary of a commercial empire; it may gain temporary material prosperity but it will inevitably lose the freedom of its soul.
>
> Neither English nor American are languages of Europe; they are merely the dialects of international commerce. ... Obviously, French is the language of Europe. Why? Because it is the French literature which for

> five centuries has given Europe its ideas and its philosophy. The German culture is much too young and much too fragmented, as is the Russian culture. ... There is no point to teach in schools basic English, only to have your children, when they grow up, become clerks and salesmen for American corporations.

Such extreme views, not uncommon in France, show a lack of appreciation of the communication imperative of language in the modern world. They have caused France to mount a considerable effort aimed at protecting the French from the onslaught of English. The communication imperative should be recognized, but should not detract from the importance of language as an exponent of cultural and national identity.

Until the 1960s, the "purity" of the French language was the responsibility of the French Academy. The "save the French language" campaign started in earnest in 1966, launched by General de Gaulle and pursued by his successor, the late President George Pompidou.

(Julius Lukasiewicz)

"Une baby sitter?" In the Paris metro, 1994

Committees and commissions for "the defense of French language" drew up lists of hundreds of French substitutes for undesirable (mostly English) terms (typically, *commercialization, gros porteur, prêt-à-manger* replacing *marketing, jumbo jet, fast food*); their use in government dealings was decreed compulsory; 200 foreign military terms were banned from the French armed forces vocabulary. Since 1975, French language must be used in the offer and sale of goods and services, in public services and buildings, and in radio and TV programs. The French government has been insisting on the use of French in publications and at meetings. Delegates to international conferences have often been instructed to lecture in French even to predominantly English-speaking audiences.

However, many French scientists do not support the government's chauvinistic policies and attempts to fracture the predominance of English in science. As one of them put it, "to do research you need the tools, one of which is English." Some argued that the French would not be so quick to press for "scientific French" if they saw the awkward, stilted, ungrammatical, unpoetical garble English becomes in the mouths of international scientists. "To defend the language of Molière (or Mitterand) the contrary is necessary: to forbid its use in international scientific meetings and publications."

Curiously, the preoccupation with the "purity" of the French language in the face of invasion by English appears to neglect the outcome of the earlier evolution which resulted in adoption of extensive identical vocabularies (including spelling) by the two languages. It is only necessary to open an English or a French dictionary to note hundreds of words which belong to both languages. The following is a small sample: *action, combat, grimace, flirt, nation, possible, route, secret, valet.*

It appears that earlier in this century, the French were not much concerned with the invasion of English words, but accepted them as functional and useful. The *Petit Dictionnaire Français,* published by Larousse in 1936, designated the following, among others, as "mot anglais": *nurse, railway, rowing, speech, side-car.* This designation is not even given many other entries, equally English, as, for example: *macadam, plum-cake, plum-pudding, speaker, trade-union, tweed, water-ballast, water-polo, week-end, water closet, yachting, yachtsman,* etc.

Over two decades of effort and bureaucratic zeal to keep the French "pure" while adapting it to modern social and technological developments have largely been a rear-guard action which, as noted before, has not eliminated the use of technical and trendy English terms. In 1981, two French lexicographers identified 2,600 Anglicisms and Americanisms commonly used in France. The famous French jeweller advertises his wares the world over as *les must de Cartier.* Frenchmen, who have succumbed en masse to American fast food (McDonald's hamburger dispensaries are all over Paris), have their own *restaurants rapides* called ... *Croissant-Show* (a Franglais pun on *chaud,* or "hot").

Stop sign a life saver

I have just been in Portugal. There I found that at intersections they have red and white octagonal signs that say "STOP." People who know only the one word of English do in fact stop.

I have found the same sign being obeyed in England, Scotland, France, Germany, Austria, Italy and Spain. I understand that it is universal everywhere except Quebec.

In the name of humanity we need a program to institute this sign in Quebec, or Québécois going abroad will kill or be killed in large numbers as the only people in the world who stop only for signs that say "ARRÊT."

James F. Hutchinson
Woodstock, Ont.

(*The Globe and Mail*, 14 February 1989)

In January 1993, the *Gazette Officielle du Québec* declared that *stop* is a French word, as is *arrêt*, and both can be used legally on road signs.

With French increasingly taking a back seat to English and German in Europe (a 1989 study has shown French to be the most widely taught in only two countries of the European Community: Britain and Ireland), initiatives to protect and promote the French language have again appeared in the 1990s. In March 1994, Prime Minister Edouard Balladur inaugurated a Higher Council of the French Language and the government introduced legislation which would put a barrier against further foreign incursions (the enemy, unnamed in the draft law, is English, of course). The use of foreign words would be banned from virtually all business and government communications, radio and television broadcasts, public announcements, and advertising messages whenever a "suitable equivalent" exists in French. Labels on products and instructions for using them would have to include French, and so would conferences and publications arranged by French citizens.

Within the European Community there are nine official languages but only two, English and French, are designated working languages. German may be added to counteract the hegemony of English.

The effort to preserve and expand the use of a language has been nowhere greater than in Canada. The 1969 legislation accorded equal status to English and French in all activities by and on behalf of the federal government. Since 1976 French has become the exclusive language in government and business in the province of Quebec. Access to

(Philip Pocock)

Köln, Germany, 1991

(Philip Pocock)

Limoges, France, 1991

(Philip Pocock)

Aylmer, Quebec, 1991

(Julius Lukasiewicz)

Georgeville, Quebec, 1993

The Québécois are the only people in the world who stop only for signs that say ARRÊT.

(Martyn Hayhow, *Associated Press*, January 1994)

In a linguistic compromise, the train which in 1994 will start moving motorists under the English/La Manche Channel is called *le shuttle*. The number of cars the Eurotunnel train will carry is seen arranged in London in the shape of the company's logo.

Le Shuttle

English-language schools has been restricted and immigrant children were required to be educated in French. On outside signs, only French has been allowed.

The language laws resulted in unreasonable "francization," duplication, and sometimes poor communication.

Quebec restaurateurs have been told to list *hamburgois, chien chaud* and *bière-à-la-pression* instead of the generally accepted in North America *hamburger, hot dog* and *draft beer* (this is as if the English were insisting on *crescent* instead of *croissant* on a breakfast menu!). Through inept translation, *pineapple* became *pomme de pin* rather than *ananas.*

However, even the Quebec government finds it necessary to use English on some occasions. Signs that say "Visitors Welcome to Quebec" greet motorists who enter La Belle Provence.

Drastic language legislation has been seen as contributing to the exodus of anglophones from Quebec, and a deterrent to foreign, particularly U.S., investment. In 1993 the Quebec government introduced legislation which would abolish the so-called language police, allow bilingual (but predominantly French) commercial signs, permit English immersion classes in French schools and some relaxation of the rule forcing children of immigrants to attend French schools.

Federal bilingualism has brought on extensive, costly, and often ridiculous duplication. Government publications are translated, printed in both languages, and distributed irrespective of the recipient's usage. "Bilingual" signs lead to pedantic repetition.

Seeing double?

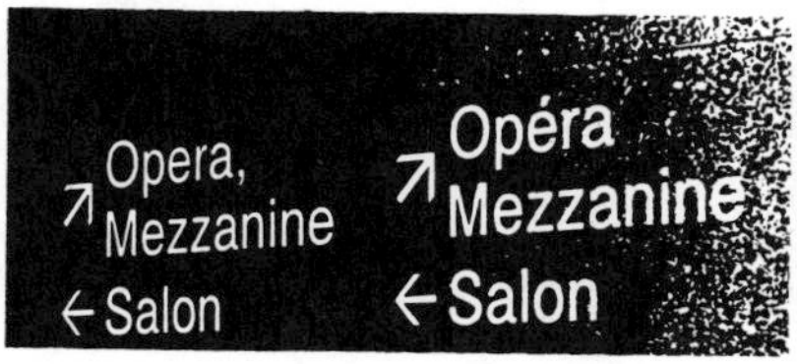

(Julius Lukasiewicz)

No! In Ottawa — the bilingual capital of Canada — eager bureaucrats have been "translating" identical English and French words lest the public at the National Arts Centre be confused.

In the short run, the French language campaign encourages development of Quebec by enhancing its distinct identity. In the long run, the

Protecting the French language from the onslaught of English is pedantic but not always successful

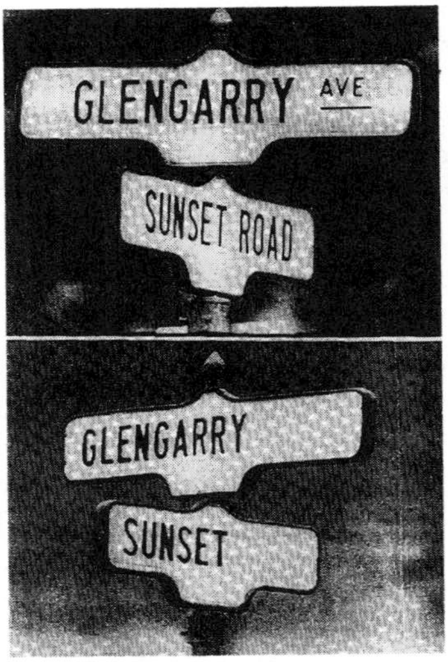

In the 1970s, Montreal street signs fell victim to the laws of language. Daubs of paint obliterated "Road" as well as "Ave," although the latter is truly bilingual. How can a stranger tell "Sunset Road" from "Sunset Lane" after the signs have been "purified"?

(*The Globe and Mail*, 17 August 1985)

"Must" sounds much better than its French equivalent.

(Advertisement in Canada, 1980)

preservation of francophone Quebec, a small enclave amidst an English-speaking continent, may prove difficult and may deter, rather than enhance, a full measure of development. Evidently, the conflicting demands of Quebec's modernization do not permit an easy solution of the language problem. Ideally, a true bilingualism would enable Quebec to preserve its identity and to participate fully in the life of North America and beyond.

The preservation of cultural identity does not require adoption of the extreme, militant language policies that have been pursued in France and Quebec. The use of a common language for the purpose of facilitating communications need not undermine the celebration of differences so essential to cultural identity.

Belgium is another country sharply divided along linguistic lines and burdened with the impact of English. Flemish is spoken in the north, French in the south; each area is rigorously unilingual and monocultural. Political parties are divided along language lines; language is the cultural issue which cuts across all other issues and loyalties. As in France and Quebec, attempts have been made to eliminate the usage of "franglais" and substitute French for English terms.

Mexico is among the latest countries concerned with the invasion of English. A commission established in 1981 has been emulating its French counterpart in trying to eradicate the epidemic of English.

Infiltration by foreign tongues and preservation of identity have not been a problem for English-speaking societies. On the contrary, English has freely adopted foreign words and expressions whenever they would bring new meanings and convenience and, in the process, has been greatly enriched. As France and Quebec fight the invasion of French by English terms, English speakers frequently use such words as *détente, tête-à-tête, rendezvous, élite, connoisseur, cuisine, bon vivant, croissant, fait accompli, savoir-faire, déjà vu, ambiance.* They borrow *kindergarten* and *kaput* from the German, *spaghetti, macaroni, pizza, lasagna* and *papparazi* from the Italian, *kimono* and *karate* from the Japanese.

Of course, all modern languages have borrowed heavily from each other and from older tongues, such as Latin and Greek. We could hardly speak about physics, literature, politics, mathematics, or any other field of knowledge without a generous use of Latin and Greek words or their derivatives, or about music without the use of universally accepted Italian terminology—and we could not contemplate substituting made-up "native" terms. Extensive foreign vocabularies have not prevented the nations of Europe from developing and preserving their cultural and linguistic identities but have enriched their languages and facilitated communication. In spite of efforts to the contrary, this process is likely to continue unabated.

Toward a Common Language

The exclusive use of different languages impedes communications; adoption of a "universal" language would facilitate them. This has been realized for many years and has led to several proposals, starting with the artificial idioms envisaged by Descartes and Bacon in the seventeenth century. Other suggestions included the revival of a "dead" language such as Latin, the use of semi-artificial languages such as Esperanto (published by L.L. Zamenhof in 1887), and the extension of a modern spoken language, in its current or modified (e.g., Basic English) form.[3]

The use of dead or artificial languages can be considered impractical[4] for a very basic reason: a language, as the repository of knowledge and information evolves naturally with the society and therefore cannot be devised separately as a static system independent of society's activities. As we have seen, actual developments are moving in the direction of modern language extension, with several languages obtaining increasing international currency, especially English (American), for obvious reasons of scientific, economic, and cultural output of English-speaking societies.

With the advent of computers, proposals have been made for a comprehensive, world-wide system for dissemination of scientific information using computer storage of all scientific information, machine translated into a common "metalanguage," and its retrieval in any desired language (Sullivan 1971). It could be perhaps argued that this kind of computer usage could detract from adoption of a common language by people. Moreover, it would obviously be more desirable to use a modern language, such as English, instead of an artificial metalanguage confined uniquely to computers.

While the processes of standardization of scripts and of languages are, in global terms, only in the early stages of development, the positional, decimal numeral system, using Hindu-Arabic characters, could be regarded as the first universal language devised by man. Introduced some 1,000 years ago in Europe, it has been accepted by all literate societies, irrespective of the language encoding systems they use — by China, Japan, India, Russia, Greece, etc. Its general adoption has been due to its functional advantages (the ease of numerical manipulation)[5] and to the need for efficient "quantitative communication" between people and nations.

Some other "symbolic languages" have also acquired universality, for similar reasons. For example, even the Chinese use western symbols for chemical elements.

In addition to a standard and efficient numeral system, efficient communication of quantitative information requires the use of standard units in which things are measured. The process of standardization of physical units dates back to 1801, the year France adopted the metre and the kilogram as the units of length and mass. By 1972, of the 141 countries of the world, some 131 (accounting for 85 percent of world trade) used the metric system or were proposing to change to metric.

A change to a different system of units, as from the English to the metric, presents little difficulty when it is a matter of straight information transfer. However, when products are involved, their physical characteristics necessarily reflect the system of units used by the producers (e.g., screws with metric versus inch threads) and, unless the same units are used, the products will be different and incompatible. Clearly, the use of standard units (including, incidentally, a standard monetary unit, currently often represented by the U.S. dollar) facilitates international trade and is a requirement for international production.

Today, the metric system is universally used in sciences; it has also been adopted in industry and commerce, with notable exceptions of the United States and Great Britain (it is being introduced in Canada independently of the United States; see Note 3, p. 172). Given the large capital investment in industry, in these countries the switch to the metric system is occurring gradually and is not likely to be completed for many years. It is a costly process which occasionally is also opposed on cultural grounds: identity and tradition are lost as pounds, feet, and gallons are abolished and metrication takes over.

As for a universal language, machines are ahead of people. In order to maximize access to information and programs, computers, irrespective of their "nationality"—have been designed to work in a number of standard "languages." Although Russia, Ukraine and Belorus would not consider, for ideological and political reasons, replacing the Cyrillic script with the Latin alphabet, they nevertheless make their computers compatible with the computer languages used in the West. When China uses American IBM computers in taking population census, it also uses American programs to handle the data. As with technology is general, the computer demands of people—their inventors and users—to match their ability to communicate through adoption of a common language.[6]

In parallel with this process, techniques of machine translation are being developed and perfected. They are now routinely used for translation of technical and scientific papers and abstracts, patents, weather forecasts, etc.; a word and sentence accuracy of up to 80 percent has been attained.

As with the Chinese logographic script, in this case the application of sophisticated technology also serves to preserve the traditional *status quo*. Clearly, the availability of cheap and accurate translations acts as a disincentive to learn other languages and therefore may deprive one of a much wider range of benefits resulting from fluency in an extensively used foreign language, such as English.

Notes

1. This is not the same as shorthand, where omitted letters must be reconstituted for reading.
2. Nevertheless, in Japan, a vast majority of some 10,000 science and technology journals are published only in Japanese, and therefore largely inaccessible to workers in the West. Bibliographic citations and abstracts in English are available through services supported

by the U.S. government, but they cover only about 60 percent of the journals and are expensive. Japanese to English machine translation programs are being developed.

3. Between 1880 and 1907, some 53 "universal languages" were proposed.
4. This is not to deny the importance of Latin, ancient Greek, and other dead languages in historical studies of various fields.
5. It is amusing to note how conservative and traditional even modern societies are. It was only in 1971 that the British — the pioneers of industrialization and large-scale international commerce — adopted the efficient decimal monetary system. The productivity of the British economy must have suffered under the traditional system in which — lacking computers — arithmetic operations could not be performed efficiently. The decimal system would have been most useful before the onset of computerization of finances, but, ironically, the switch to decimal money did not occur until then.
6. The issue of homogenization of society resulting from widespread use of computers has been addressed by Grant (1976).

References

Auerbach, L. 1978. "Scientists — a Case of Timidity." *Science Forum* (November-December) 11(4): 51–52.

Grant, G. 1976. "The Computer Does Not Impose on Us the Ways It Should Be Used." *Beyond Industrial Growth*, edited by A. Rotstein. Toronto: University of Toronto Press.

Inhaber, H. 1978a. "The Leading Edge of Science in Canada." *Research Policy* 7: 88–98.

Reyburn, W. 1969. *Flushed with Pride: A Story of Thomas Crapper*. London: MacDonald and Co.

Steinberg, J.L. 1971. "European Astronomers Decide to Consolidate Their Journals." *Science* 172 (30 April): 451–52.

Sullivan, W. 1971. "Scientific Research Conference Supports a Worldwide System for the Storage and Exchange of Data," *The New York Times*, 11 October 1971.

Yule, V. 1982. "Shorter Words Mean Faster Reading," *New Scientist* (9 December): 656–57.

7

Technology and War

(McLuhan, M. and Fiore, Q. 1967)

"We look at the present through a rear-view mirror"

AS already noted, the consequences of deployment of technology are often unforeseen and unpredictable. This has been particularly true of military applications.

It is a truism to observe that technology — from the stirrup that gave rise to cavalry, to the canon, machine gun, tank, aircraft, radar, ballistic missile and nuclear explosive — has governed the character of war. And yet, more often than not, the impact of new weapons has been poorly understood not only by the society at large, but also by the military and politicians, the professionals responsible for the procurement and deployment of weapons.

Marshall McLuhan, widely acknowledged as the most original cultural historian of this century, recognized that in the age of technological speedup, "when faced with a completely new situation, we tend always to attach ourselves to the objects, the flavor of the most recent past. We look at the present through a rear-view mirror. We march backwards into the future" (McLuhan and Fiore 1967, 74–75).

This is precisely how the military and the politicians of France and England were preparing in the 1920s and 1930s to march into World War II. Static trench warfare of 1914–1918 was their model of the future war, *Maginot Line*[1] of fortifications on the Franco-German border — their weapon. They did not envisage a significant role for motorized armour (although, ironically, the tanks were first used by the British and the French in World War I) and for aircraft in its ground and sea support, and long-range, strategic bombardment roles. The mistake turned out enormously expensive: a military defeat of French and British forces in Europe and a devastating six-year world conflict in which tens of millions perished.

The Cold War period provides the most recent example of failure to recognize the nature of a radically new weapon technology and the consequences of its deployment. Contrary to popular belief, the availability of nuclear weapons of global range has served — as here argued — to maintain peace between the superpowers and has thus prevented the outbreak of yet another world war.

General Mitchell's crystal ball

At the expiration of his term as assistant chief of U.S. Army Air Service in April 1925, brigadier-general William (Billy) Mitchell was sent to San Antonio, Texas, in the permanent grade of colonel, as an air officer of the 8th Corps. He continued to promote aggressively his views on the future of aircraft in war and advocated creation of an independent Air Force. The U.S. Army tried Col. Mitchell for "conduct and ideas prejudicial to the good of service"; in December 1925 he was convicted of insubordination and suspended from rank and duty for five years. Mitchell resigned from the Army in 1926 and died ten years later. Here are some excerpts from his court martial (as quoted in *Aircraft Engineering*, pp. 9–10, October 1970; see also, J. Lukasiewicz, "Letters," *Time*, 23 December 1991 and "Letters to the Editor," *The Globe and Mail*, 4 January 1992):

Prosecutor:	You say that "in future wars soldiers will invade by leaping in parachutes from aeroplanes." Would you care to reveal who gave you this startling information?
Mitchell:	Nobody gave it to me. It's quite obvious to anyone with the slightest foresight.
P.:	It is your actual belief that this country is vulnerable to attack from the air?
M.:	In the foreseeable future.
P.:	Colonel Mitchell, do you have any idea of the width of the Atlantic Ocean?
M.:	Approximately 3,000 miles.
P.:	And the Pacific Ocean?
M.:	I know what you are getting at and I tell you that it won't be long before aeroplanes will fly non-stop across both oceans.
P.:	You say that "aircraft travelling 1,000 miles an hour will fight each other in the stratosphere." Do you have any comprehension how fast a 1,000 miles an hour is?
M.:	Of course I do.
P.:	Do you know it is faster than the speed of sound?
M.:	Approximately 250 miles faster.

The prosecutor then reminded Mitchell that he foresaw an air attack on Pearl Harbor and had described in detail how it would take place. After saying Mitchell had no better basis for his views than "palmistry, table tipping and the reading of tea leaves," he asked sarcastically:

P.:	Does your crystal ball reveal by what enemy this mythical attack will be made? By whom, Colonel, by whom?
M.:	The attack will be made by the Japanese.

* * *

"It is significant that despite the claims of air enthusiasts, no battleship has yet been sunk by bombs" — read a caption for a photograph of the USS *Arizona* in the program for the Army-Navy game on 29 November 1941 (Walter Lord: *Day of Infamy*, 1957).

Eight days later, on 7 December 1941, the Japanese attacked the U.S. Navy base in Pearl Harbor from the air, sunk USS *Arizona* and three battleships, destroyed and damaged several other vessels and over 80 aircraft.

In 1946 the U.S. Congress authorized a special medal to be struck in Mitchell's honor; it was presented to his son in 1948 by the chief of staff of the newly created U.S. Air Force.

Nuclear Weapons: What Are They Good For?

Nuclear weapons, whose development has continued since they were first used in 1945, represent possibly a more radical change in weapons technology than any experienced before. But, in spite of a fundamentally altered situation, the traditional view of weapons and war persisted throughout the 1945 to 1991 Cold War period, a rear-view mirror of the irrelevant past. Even the most eminent among scientists, who had a profound knowledge of nuclear energy, misjudged the significance of nuclear weapons.

In 1946, an Emergency Committee of Atomic Scientists was formed in the United States under the chairmanship of Albert Einstein. The Committee declared that "if war breaks out, atomic bombs will be used and they will surely destroy our civilization," that "there is no solution to this problem except international control of atomic energy and, ultimately, the elimination of war," and that "these facts are accepted by all scientists." A year later, the Committee felt that "once stockpiles of atomic bombs have been accumulated by two national blocs in a divided world, it will no longer be possible to maintain peace." "Since the completion of the first atomic bomb nothing has been accomplished to make the world more safe from war, while much has been done to increase the destructiveness of war" — wrote Einstein in the November 1947 issue of the *Atlantic Monthly*.

Einstein and his colleagues saw world government and abolition of war as the only means of saving mankind from nuclear war and annihilation. In 1955, just before his death, Albert Einstein launched with Bertrand Russell a movement among scientists aimed at reversing what they believed was the "cold war" trend toward nuclear war. "Shall we put an end to the human race; or shall mankind renounce war" — were the only alternatives envisaged in the Russell–Einstein Manifesto.

Pyotr Kapitza (1894–1984), the eminent Russian physicist who moved with his Cambridge (England) laboratory to Moscow in 1934, resisted Stalin's pressure to work on nuclear weapons. For Kapitza, "to talk of atomic energy in terms of atomic bombs is like talking of electricity in terms of the electric chair."

cruis
greater
Navy ha
order, most
by 1944. Each
of approximate
to man its fifteen
four to eight planes
gray hull it carries four
turbines which turn up
100,000 horsepower, the pow
than 1,000 average automobiles

Right—A bow on view of the *U. S. S. Arizona* as she plows into a huge swell. It is significant that despite the claims of air enthusiasts no battleship has yet been sunk by bombs.

180

From the Army-Navy game program, November 29, 1941: ''A bow on view of the USS *Arizona* as she plows into a huge swell. ... despite the claims of air enthusiasts no battleship has yet been sunk by bombs.''

Eight days later — the USS *Arizona* exploding from direct bomb hit.

After the attack the shattered USS *Arizona* lies, a tomb for 1,102 men.

"No battleship has yet been sunk by bombs."

For J. Robert Oppenheimer (1904–1967), who led the development of the first atomic weapon in the United States during World War II, the work on weapons of massive destruction presented a moral dilemma. "The physicists have known sin, and this is a knowledge they cannot lose"—stated Oppenheimer in 1947.

Richard Feynman (1918–1988), who as a young physicist worked at Los Alamos on the atomic bomb project, felt that nuclear weapons were no good, that we would be living in fear of them for the rest of our lives, that they would not keep the world at peace. In 1946, Feynman left Los Alamos and cut his involvement with military projects.

The view that nuclear arms must inevitably lead to war was shared by prominent military men and their advisers. Sir Solly Zuckerman, chief scientific adviser to the British Ministry of Defence in the 1960s, considered the nuclear arms race to be foolish and immoral, even if nuclear weapons were to be used only if deterrence fails and NATO is attacked. His views gained support of Lord Louis Mountbatten, then chief of the Defence Staff, and senior people in scientific and political circles in the United Kingdom and the United States. "There are powerful voices around the world," said Mountbatten, "who still give credence to the old Roman precept 'if you desire peace, prepare for war'. This is absolute nuclear nonsense and I repeat—it is a disastrous misconception to believe that by increasing total uncertainty one increases one's own certainty."

To the end of the Cold War in 1991 many considered nuclear war unavoidable as long as nuclear arsenals existed, and advocated the elimination of nuclear arsenals as the only means of preserving peace. Fritjof Kapra (1981) in his review of the "state of the world" wrote that "Nuclear weapons do not increase our security ... they merely increase the likelihood of global destruction. The threat of nuclear war is the greatest danger humanity is facing today. ... " Zbigniew Brzezinski, who was national security adviser to President Carter from 1977 to 1981, felt in 1986 (p. x) that "a strategic posture that safeguards peace by the threat of annihilation ... is ethically troubling, morally corrosive, and dehumanizing ... such a posture may make a nuclear attack more rather than less likely." "The logical consequence of preparation for nuclear war is nuclear war"—wrote Dr. Helen Caldicott of Harvard University in 1984, former leader of Physicians for Social Responsibility, a nuclear-disarmament group.

As it turned out, since Hiroshima and Nagasaki the "absolute nuclear nonsense" has served peace and humanity well.[2] It is only in the 1980s, over forty years into the nuclear era, that the futility of the nuclear arms race was being gradually recognized and the process of containing it started as the doctrine of "reasonable sufficiency" began to slowly take hold.

The de-escalation of the arms race was dramatically accelerated following the 1989 anti-communist revolutions in Eastern Europe, the demise of the Warsaw Pact and, in 1991, the splintering of the Soviet Union. The Cold War ended with the capitulation of the Soviet Union, no longer a superpower. The United States, the NATO alliance, and members of the new Commonwealth of Independent States (CIS) agreed on massive cuts to their nuclear arsenals.

The nuclear confrontation and competition between the superpowers became history.

* * *

For a long time, a nuclear war, as all past wars fought with conventional weapons, has been considered—by the hawks and the doves alike—as a war which is likely to be precipitated by the superpowers.

For the hawks, a nuclear war has been a winnable proposition; therefore, superiority or at least parity in nuclear armaments has been deemed by them indispensable to maintaining the advantage required to deter aggression or, in the last resort, to secure a military victory.

The doves have also believed nuclear war possible and probable, but not winnable; they have viewed elimination of nuclear arsenals as necessary to prevent global suicide, to render life free of constant fear of a nuclear holocaust, and to guarantee peace.

In both cases wrong conclusions were arrived at through badly flawed reasoning, which failed to account for the extraordinary nature of nuclear—as opposed to conventional—warfare, and for the fundamental causes of military conflicts.

Had the hawks realized that a nuclear war is not winnable, they would have found that the nuclear arms race need not be pursued to the extent that it has been to maintain an effective deterrent; a relatively small arsenal of nuclear weapons would suffice to deter the enemy. The doves, on the other hand, would have realized that the presence, rather than the elimination of nuclear weapons, constitutes an effective guarantee of peace.

Indeed, the lethality of weapons at man's disposal has never been the cause of war. The most cruel violence has been committed by men with all kinds of primitive weapons. The source of war and of what we mistakenly call "inhuman behaviour" is human nature itself.[3]

With the appearance of the atom bomb in 1945 the explosive power of global range weapons was multiplied by thousands and then, with the thermonuclear (hydrogen) bomb in 1952, by millions. Destruction on a scale far beyond anything experienced before became possible, accompanied by uncontrollable, pervasive, and persistent poisoning of the environment.

It was estimated that a one-megaton bomb (i.e., equivalent to one million tons of the conventional TNT explosive, fifty times more powerful than the first atom bomb dropped on Hiroshima in 1945) exploded over a metropolitan area would kill up to two million people. As of 1988, strategic nuclear arsenals of the superpowers each contained over 10,000 warheads and 2,000 launchers, including hundreds of warheads in the 15- to 20-megaton range. Clearly, only a small number of nuclear warheads, and a very small fraction of those which were available, needed to be deployed successfully to literally wipe out the enemy. Many experts believed that 3,000 nuclear weapons on each side would have sufficed as an effective deterrent.

Grand Illusions of the Warrior Class

What self-respecting general wants to be told that the genius of modern technology has revised the grammar of warfare to such a radical extent that two ragged men driving a second-hand truck now can command the firepower of 37 armed divisions?

The current generation of dreaming tacticians (together with its vociferous claque in the media, the universities, the policy institutes and Congress) seems easily as fatuous as the crowd of French generals who so fervently believed in the impregnable beauty of the Maginot line.

(Lewis H. Lapham, *The Globe and Mail,* 11 August 1986)

This is the crucial fact that made nuclear war totally different from any type of war waged in the past. Using conventional explosives (TNT), thousands of bombs dropped from hundreds of aircraft, or hundreds of thousands of artillery shells had to be deployed in recurring attacks to inflict unacceptable damage on the enemy. This meant that successful defence was possible: if a large proportion of the aircraft or guns were destroyed, offensive operations could not succeed.

With nuclear weapons the opposite was true: even if a large proportion of them could be neutralized by the defense, the enemy could still be destroyed by the few weapons that got through. In other words, in a nuclear war the defense, to be successful, must be close to 100 percent effective. Consequently, since such effectiveness cannot ever be attained, effective defense against nuclear weapons is not possible.

In the absence of effective defense, to win a nuclear war, it would be absolutely necessary to prevent the enemy from executing a nuclear attack. This could only be done through a pre-emptive "first strike" which would completely destroy the enemy's ability to retaliate with his nuclear explosives. But here again a complete success of a first strike must be denied:

given the large number and variety of the enemy's weapon systems (land and submarine launched ballistic missiles, cruise missiles and bombers), inevitably enough of them would escape destruction in a first strike to make a successful retaliatory attack possible.

Thus neither an effective defense against a nuclear attack, nor a preemptive strike to render such an attack impossible, were feasible. Therefore, in a nuclear war, the aggressor as well as the victim risked losses in population and damage to the environment on a scale that they could not sustain and preserve the fabric of their society. There would be no winners in a nuclear war. Moreover, even if a nuclear aggressor were immune to nuclear retaliation, his would be a pyrrhic victory.

Any lands acquired by nuclear force would become barren and permanently uninhabitable. The acquisition of territory as the key, traditional objective of war, was no longer a viable goal in the nuclear era. Nor was subjugation of peoples, another historic percept of war, irrelevant in the nuclear age. For in this too, the destructiveness of nuclear weapons undermined their usefulness. And finally, since radioactive contamination cannot be contained (as demonstrated by the 1986 Chernobyl disaster), it could harm the aggressor as well as the victim.[4]

Nuclear weapons deter aggression and their own use. This is all they are good for. But for many years the impracticality of waging a nuclear war has not been appreciated by the superpowers. A winnable nuclear war has been the illusive goal of the U.S. and Soviet military, to be attained through continuing development of defensive and offensive systems.[5]

In the West, Dr. Edward Teller, who guided U.S. development of the hydrogen bomb in the 1940s and 1950s, and strategic defense systems in the 1980s, has been the most prominent advocate of the nuclear arms race. He envisaged a nuclear war that the Soviet Union could win by virtue of superior firepower and more effective civil defense.

The *Maginot Line* of the Space Age

The fundamental change, noted above, in the role defense can play in a nuclear as opposed to a conventional war has not been recognized.

A traditional view of defense was the basis of President Reagan's Strategic Defence Initiative (SDI, dubbed Star Wars) announced in 1983 as a system which would provide a totally effective "shield" against nuclear attack.[6] The widely publicized SDI project demonstrated once again how difficult it is to abandon old concepts in new circumstances. After ten years and the expenditure of about $30 billion, Star Wars was cancelled in 1993 by Clinton's administration.

(David Austin, *New Scientist*, p. 71, 14 April 1988)

Briefly, the focus of SDI was the destruction of the enemy's ICBMs (intercontinental ballistic missiles) and their warheads after they had been launched. This was to be achieved with surveillance/tracking systems and weapons deployed from the Earth's surface and/or satellite space weapons orbiting the Earth. All kinds of exotic techniques were being considered, including "kinetic energy weapons" launched by missiles on collision trajectories ("smart rocks" and "brilliant pebbles" which destroy through impact), "directed energy weapons" such as powerful lasers and particle beams, and nuclear weapons detonated in the path of approaching warheads. The cost estimates of the completed system varied widely, around the $100 billion range. Some typical estimates of the extent of the SDI system have been indicative of its complexity and impracticability.

The initial boost phase of ICBM's flight, from the Earth's surface into space, is the most vulnerable. Since each ICBM may carry ten or more warheads, the destruction of a booster eliminates several weapons. If rockets equipped with explosive warhead weapons were used to attack boosters, 300 rockets would have to be orbited for each booster, or 300,000 rockets maintained in orbit to enable 1,000 boosters to be intercepted.

The rocket-warhead proposal was superseded by a more sophisticated scheme of "brilliant pebbles" (descended from "smart rocks") — compact, one metre long rockets weighing only 100 pounds, carrying a two-pound "pebble" and no explosive charge, equipped with powerful — brilliant — computers. Parked in orbit, brilliant pebbles would sense missiles as they rise from silos or submarines, follow a collision trajectory and destroy on impact. Again, thousands of brilliant pebbles would have to be maintained in orbit.

In the mid-course above-the-atmosphere phase of missile flight, decoys would be deployed to confuse the enemy's defenses. If each missile carried 1,000 light balloon decoys, a million of them would be deployed by 1,000 missiles. To detect warheads among decoys by laser radiation, 1,500 satellites each carrying a 10-foot diameter mirror capable of targeting ten decoys per second would be required. Maintenance of a space-based missile network would require launching as much as 2,500 tons into orbit annually.

Defense against a warhead in the final portion of its flight, would be almost impossible: a 20 megaton warhead would set entire cities aflame even if detonated at 30 kilometres.

Given the large numbers of warheads, decoys, and defensive missiles involved in the short time available to track, discriminate, and destroy targets, the SDI would have to depend entirely on computers. It was generally agreed that the needed programming in terms of complexity and volume of instructions was not feasible and would be unlikely to come close to the near-perfect reliability required. Moreover, even the checking of all possible paths through the program, to guarantee that it contains no faults, would take years to complete.

Needless to say, space-based SDI defenses would provide easy targets for the enemy's anti-satellite weapons and space mines; in fact, the SDI system would be much more vulnerable and expensive than the offensive weapons it was designed to destroy. Clearly, its destruction would be the first step in a first-strike attack and therefore its presence would not affect the "balance of terror" situation.

To test defensive systems, such as the SDI, it would be necessary to simulate deployment of hundreds of missiles, warheads, decoys, and nuclear explosions — obviously an impossible task.

This has been only partly realized by the SDI Organization which intended to develop an "SDI National Test Bed" (NTB) — a complex of existing and future installations in Europe, North America, and the Pacific to perform as an "SDI truth machine," or a system with which SDI could be developed, tested, and evaluated. Although the NTB could have provided the best simulation possible, in the absence of nuclear explosions (prohibited under the 1963 Partial Test Ban Treaty and environmentally unacceptable) it would have inevitably fallen far short of a real war environment and would have been therefore of little help in ascertaining the effectiveness of defenses. Also, the NTB activities would have been, of course, closely monitored by the Soviets; the results of simulation would have been known to them and would have provided information necessary to develop effective countermeasures.

The SDI project has met with widespread criticism from scientists and engineers. But, surprisingly, it has been supported by some, with Dr. E. Teller being the most prominent among them. Teller has been pushing development of nuclear-pumped X-ray lasers. In 1984 he claimed that "a single X-ray laser module" could generate as many as 100,000 "independently aimable beams . . . quite lethal to a distant hardened object in flight." These weapons would be capable of destroying all Soviet land based missiles and shoot down all of the missiles launched from Soviet submarines — asserted Teller.

The SDI concept has been evaluated by the Office of Technology Assessment of the U.S. Congress. The OTA study, published in 1988, concluded that "there may always be irresolvable questions about how dependable BMD (Ballistic Missile Defense) software would be" and "there would be a significant probability that the first (and presumably only) time the BMD system were used in a real war, it would suffer a catastrophic failure."

Some of the recent experiences, in situations almost infinitely less demanding and complex than the deployment of an "SDI shield" against an onslaught by thousands of ballistic missiles and their decoys, would certainly support the OTA assessment.

On 29 May 1987 Mathias Rust, a 19-year old West German amateur pilot, flew unmolested, his small and slow, single engine *Cessna Skyhawk 172* plane from Helsinki to Moscow and landed in Red Square near the Kremlin Wall. He spent six hours crossing 400 miles of the most heavily guarded air space in the world, including the ring of anti-ballistic missile defenses around Moscow. In the wake of Rust's incredible exploit, the Soviet defense minister and commander of air defense were instantly dismissed, but could anybody be certain that an equally daring flight could not be executed again?

The answer came two years later when Warsaw Pact defense forces were unable to track a Soviet *MiG-23* fighter after its pilot ejected over Poland and the unmanned aircraft flew west, ran out of fuel and crashed in Belgium on 4 July 1989. Soviet officials did not know what had happened to the *MiG-23* until European news agencies reported the crash.

On a more sophisticated level, deployment of missiles by the U.S. Navy cruiser *Vincennes* resulted in the shooting down of an Iranian *Airbus 300* jetliner and killing all 298 people on board. On 3 July 1988 the USS *Vincennes*, while engaged in combat with Iranian speedboats, mistook the jetliner for an Iranian *F-14* fighter. Equipped with some of the most sophisticated radars available, the *Vincennes* was unable to tell an *F-14* fighter from an *Airbus* wide-body jet. Moreover, in a fast-paced and stressful situation, communications between crew members broke down.

In the *Vincennes* incident, deployment of state-of-the-art warfare technology failed in circumstances which again must be considered incomparably simpler than the ICBM onslaught scenario.

The missile systems game

(Fink/Rothco, *The Bulletin of the Atomic Scientists*, November 1980)

The air defense system, successful in winning the Battle of Britain in 1940 and denying the Germans the air superiority they needed to invade Britain, was used as an example with which the SDI should be compared. However, the analogy was grossly inappropriate. In the 1930s and 1940s we were dealing with conventional explosives and aircraft, and radar was the one decisive technical breakthrough which made effective air defense possible. In spite of the application of the most sophisticated technologies and techniques, no such breakthrough has been possible in the defense against ICBMs, which had to rely on a multiplicity of complex and vulnerable systems.

The SDI concept of a shield impervious to ballistic missiles bore no similarity to the Battle of Britain defenses. Rather, it was the space age equivalent of the elaborate *Maginot Line* fortifications, which provided the French in the 1930s with the illusion of impenetrability of their frontier with Germany. Half a century later, U.S. politicians and military, with support from the scientific and industrial community, wasted enormous resources on a defence scheme which, even to the non-specialist, represented an obviously absurd and unworkable concept.

As for offense, it was noted earlier that a first strike was not a guarantee against devastating retaliation. Deployment of submarine and air-launched weapons, and land-based missiles which eluded first strike destruction, would still inflict unacceptable losses on the enemy. The nuclear deterrent was not compromised by the inevitable vulnerability of land-based missiles.

This has not been the view of the military, who have considered it essential for maintenance of deterrent to make land-based strategic missiles invulnerable to a first strike — a task that has been an exercise in futility.

Obsessed with the idea of a totally invulnerable system, the U.S. military–scientific fraternity has spawned a plethora of harebrained designs which rival the naïveté of SDI schemes.

Since the vulnerability of silo-based missiles became an issue some 20 years ago, no fewer than 34 "basing" schemes have been considered. They all fell victim to protracted disputes over their effectiveness, cost, environmental impact, effect on arms-control negotiations, and political acceptability.

Invulnerability was to be achieved through deception and mobility, with designs that verge on Hollywood fantasies.

The so-called rail garrison scheme was the cheapest (estimated at $12 billion) among the options considered. Mounted on rail cars, ten-warhead *MX* missiles would be kept at some 11 garrisons on military bases. In a time of crisis, missile trains would disappear into 150,000 miles of commercial railway tracks. "They would be rusty, with peeling paint and would look just like all the other trains on the track" — noted General J. Chain, then chief of USAF's Strategic Air Command. The Soviets would have to barrage vast stretches of rail lines to assure destruction. But in the event of a surprise strike, attacked at their garrisons, the missiles might not survive.

A "road mobile" system would allow wider dispersion of truck-mounted *Midgetman* missiles, which could be moved more quickly to escape a surprise attack. But, with *Midgetman* carrying only one or two warheads, deploying the same number of warheads in a "road mobile" system would be much more expensive ($39 billion) than in the rail garrison scheme.

Pure deception was the basis of the "multiple shelter" proposal in the late 1970s. A small number of missiles would have been hidden among 4,600 shelters, all equipped with launch equipment to buttress deception.

In view of the high cost of mobile systems, "carry-hard basing" as an alternative to multiple shelters has been proposed. Capsules hardened against nuclear blast would be placed in thousands of cheap silos, with only a small number of them containing missiles. The aggressor would be forced to expend thousands of warheads to destroy only a small number of missiles.

As with the SDI, the search for an invulnerable "basing" scheme was futile, but the temptation to continue playing with various options at taxpayers' expense proved irresistible to the politicians, the military and their scientific collaborators. The game came to an end when President Bush unilaterally scrapped the rail garrison project in October 1991.

But it was only in 1993 that another fatuous project came to light. The U.S. Federal Emergency Management Agency spent $1.3 million over a decade to make the government a moving target during a nuclear war. Five mobile units of 300 vehicles each, which could operate for a month without support, were scattered at sites throughout the country. This scheme was to provide better protection than the enormous bunkers built in the 1950s.

The Supreme Deterrent

To paraphrase von Clausewitz, war is a continuation of politics by other means. But when war is no longer an effective tool, when by its very nature it defeats the objective, it is an option that is likely to be passed over. And this is exactly what the supreme destructiveness of nuclear weapons has achieved during the superpower confrontation after World War II. As noted by John Polanyi, the 1986 Nobel laureate, "nuclear weapons are in the process of relegating not only nuclear war but war itself to the junk heap of history."

During the Cold War which followed the end of World War II, peace was maintained through the monopoly of the United States (until the Soviet Union exploded its first atom bomb in 1949) and later clear superiority in the deployment of nuclear weapons of the NATO alliance (formed in 1949) over the Soviet Union. But as the arms race continued into the 1960s, parity in nuclear armaments was reached and mutually assured destruction (aptly called MAD) replaced massive retaliation as an effective deterrent. Throughout the Cold War, MAD's "balance of terror" has been totally successful in preserving peace between NATO and Warsaw Pact powers.

It is interesting to note that in 1934 the efficacy of the deterrent had already been envisaged by Winston Churchill. Acknowledging that there was no effective defense against bombers (as experience of World War I had shown), Churchill advocated offensive parity as a guarantee of peace, a view he presented to the House of Commons on 28 November.

> The fact remains that pending some new discovery, the only direct measure of defense upon a great scale is the certainty of being able to inflict simultaneously upon the enemy as great damage as he can inflict upon ourselves. Do not let us undervalue the efficacy of this procedure. It may

> well prove in practice — I admit you cannot prove it in theory — capable of giving complete immunity. If two powers show themselves equally capable of inflicting damage upon each other by some particular process of war, so that neither gains an advantage from its adoption and both suffer the most hideous reciprocal injuries, it is not only possible but it seems to be probable that neither will employ that means. What could they gain by it?
>
> We all speak under the certainty of the future, which has so often baffled human foresight; but I believe that if we maintain at all times in the future an air power sufficient to enable us to inflict as much damage upon the most probable assailant, upon the most likely potential aggressor, as he can inflict upon us, we may shield our people effectually in our own time from all those horrors which I have ventured to describe. What are the £50,000,000 or £100,000,000 raised by tax or by loan compared with an immunity like that? Never has so fertile and so blessed an insurance been procurable so cheaply.

The situation changed drastically when radar and fast fighters were developed, and Britain opted for a defensive strategy in preference to constructing a strategic bomber force. But Churchill's prescription for the preservation of peace worked well after World War II, when with the appearance of nuclear explosives and strategic delivery systems circumstances analogous to those England faced in 1934 were created.

One may well ask why is it that chemical and biological weapons failed to deter conflict after World War I? All of the main participants in WW II had large stocks of them, and the limited experience in WW I certainly indicated enormous capability of poisonous gases to kill and incapacitate people. Coupled with the progress in bomber performance, chemical weapons acquired unparalleled lethality, in many respects comparable to nuclear explosives. And yet, they failed to deter WW II and were never resorted to by the belligerants, even under the most desperate of circumstances.

As noted below, a deterrent can only be effective if the aggressor believes that the deterrent will be used. This is the essential element that was missing in the inter-war period. France and Britain were not prepared to risk war in order to preserve peace; rather, they were seeking to preserve peace through the appeasement of the aggressor. The opportunity to maintain peace through exercising the deterrent of chemical weapons was missed.

In the conflict that followed, gases were not used because, just as nuclear weapons, they deter their own use. Their effects are difficult to control and may harm the aggressor as well as the victim.

With the appearance of nuclear explosives, chemical and biological weapons lost their potential significance as deterrents of a world conflict. With war effectively deterred by nuclear weapons, they have also lost their utility as components of arsenals of the industrialized countries.

Nevertheless, it was only in 1993, after over twenty years of negotiations, that 131 countries agreed to ban chemical weapons (such agreement was concluded in 1972 concerning biological weapons). The ban will come into force in January 1995, if at least 65 states ratify the treaty within 18 months. A commission will establish procedures for verification of compliance with the treaty.

Because chemical weapons are cheap and easy to produce (they can be made in many types of commercial plants, such as fertilizer works, from easily procured raw materials or basic chemicals), they have become "the poor man's nuclear bomb": they narrow the gap in destructive potential between the Third World countries and the most technologically advanced ones. Smaller or more volatile states, which feel either under threat or are anxious to flex their military might, want chemical weapons (Iraq used them in 1987 against Iranian troops and its own Kurdish civilians; it threatened to use chemical weapons against Israel and the coalition forces when military operations to remove Iraqis from Kuwait began in January 1991). This is the real obstacle to a truly global ban on chemical warfare.

What Makes Deterrence Effective?

In addition to the destructive power of nuclear weapons, several other factors have contributed to the effectiveness of the "balance of terror" during the Cold War.

First, for deterrence to be effective, the adversaries must be well informed about each other's capabilities. Surprise, as a crucial element of victorious strategy,[7] is thus eliminated and the chances of success are diminished if not reduced to zero.

Even as recently as World War II, the size and capability of military forces were closely guarded secrets, as was all information on development, testing, and performance of weapons. But during the Cold War, the numbers and costs of missiles, aircraft, tanks, ships, and submarines were well known. Developments of new weapon systems, such as cruise and ballistic missiles, fighters, bombers and "stealth" radar-invisible aircraft, or Star Wars defenses, were well advertised, extensively discussed by media and treated as major public relations efforts. Results of tests, including failures, were duly reported and telemetered flight data were recorded by the adversaries. Under a treaty which came into effect in January 1987, each of the 34 signatories (which included NATO and Warsaw Pact powers) agreed to tell the others about any military activity involving 13,000 or more ground troops (about one division) and invite them to send observers to those involving more than 17,000 troops. Military exercises were not to be mistaken for aggression and their monitoring was to be facilitated.

The 1987 Intermediate Range Nuclear Forces (IFN) treaty provisions for intrusive on-site inspection provided important military information for the superpowers. The treaty called for examination by the opposite sides of bases from which missiles have been eliminated and for setting up of permanently staffed observation stations at one of the other's key missile factories.

Efforts to establish the feasibility of verifying compliance with nuclear test ban through seismic monitoring have been jointly sponsored by the Soviet Academy of Sciences and the U.S. National Resources Defense Council. U.S. teams have operated five seismic stations on Soviet territory and Soviet seismologists have visited the United States to observe a series of underground chemical explosions.

Most important of all, continuous world-wide surveillance by satellites provided the superpowers with instant information on the potential enemy's military and industrial developments, including location of military installations, and deployment and movement of weapon systems.

Espionage has been the traditional means of assessing military capability and war plans; large resources were being provided by major powers to spy on the potential enemy and to fight the enemy's espionage activity. But in a situation in which the military objective is to deter rather than to attack, espionage must be regarded as yet another means of keeping mutually informed, and therefore as an effective way to enhance deterrence. Indeed, Soviet and U.S. spies have helped to keep the military gap narrow and have thus done more for the maintenance of Cold War peace through "balance of terror" than politicians and diplomats. Paradoxically, support for, rather than prevention of, espionage must be regarded as desirable in the name of peace. But, in any event, the relative significance of espionage has been declining as more and more military information becomes available in the open.

The impossibility of carrying out realistic tests of nuclear weapons constituted a powerful second deterrent to their use.

With atmospheric, outer space, and underwater tests prohibited under the 1963 Partial Test Ban treaty, the effects of nuclear explosions on hardened launchers and systems of communications and command could not be determined and the effectiveness of a first strike ascertained. To test defensive systems, such as Star Wars (SDI), it would have been necessary — as already noted — to simulate deployment of thousands of missiles, warheads, decoys, and nuclear explosions — obviously an impossible task.

Third, to be deterred, the aggressor must believe that the other side is willing to wage war. John F. Kennedy proved it in Berlin and in the quarantine of Cuba. But when in the 1930s the resolve was missing, Hitler was not deterred to re-arm, remilitarize the Rhineland, occupy Austria and Czechoslovakia, and — in 1939 — invade Poland.

Surprisingly, the elements necessary to ensure the effectiveness of deterrent — information about weapons and the enemy's belief in readiness to use them — were not appreciated by South Africa, engaged in clandestine development of nuclear weapons since 1974. The veil of secrecy was lifted in 1993 with the announcement that six bombs were built and the program cancelled in 1990. It was stated that South Africa acquired the bombs as a deterrent and therefore never intended to use them.

Containing the Arms Race

Until the 1980s, the superpowers did not fully appreciate the significance of the nuclear balance of terror as a guarantee of peace. With nuclear war viewed as possible and winnable, they have been engaged — as noted earlier — in a futile arms race with no end in sight. This led to amassing by each side of nuclear arsenals capable of annihilating the other several times over, arsenals much larger than required for credible deterrence.

Given this posture, attempts to contain the arms race by legislating ceilings on numbers of weapons and limiting their development were not successful. The "limits" negotiated under the USSR–US SALT (Strategic Arms Limitation Talks) I (1972) and II (1979) agreements, provided for some trade-offs between the numbers of various missile types but essentially confirmed the *status quo*. In terms of destructive power, the "limits" exceeded by a large factor the explosive power of weapons already deployed.

It was only after 1984, with the new Soviet regime under Gorbachev in power, that effective steps were taken to contain and reduce nuclear arsenals.

The Soviet leadership realized that continuation of the arms race would further impoverish the already ailing Soviet economy. Also, the abandonment of expansionist moves guaranteed freedom from interference by the Western Alliance and therefore allowed the USSR to stay out of the arms race and even reduce its military forces, which no longer needed to play the role of a deterrent.

"Arms race in reverse" started with the signing by the United States and USSR in December 1987 of the Intermediate Range Nuclear Forces (INF) treaty.

For the first time, the superpowers agreed to eliminate specific categories of nuclear weapons. The INF treaty prohibited production and required destruction of all land-based U.S. and Soviet nuclear missiles that have a range from 500 to 5,500 km, and established procedures for compliance with the provisions of the treaty.

This was followed in 1990 by the treaty on Conventional Forces in Europe (CFE) between NATO and Warsaw Pact countries. The agreement fell apart when the Warsaw Pact and the Soviet Union did, and was renegotiated in 1992 by NATO's 16 countries, Russia, seven other former Soviet republics, and former members of the Warsaw Pact. The CFE treaty provided for cuts in tanks, artillery pieces, combat aircraft and helicopters, and other non-nuclear weapons.

Reduction in long-range nuclear weapons was legislated through the Strategic Arms Reduction Treaties (START) I (1992) and II (1993) concluded between the United States and Russia. By the year 2003, all land-based long-range missiles with multiple warheads would be eliminated, and U.S. and Russian arsenals would be limited to from 3,000 to 3,500 warheads each. The missiles held by the former Soviet republics of Ukraine, Kazakhstan and Belorus, which accounted for about 3,000 strategic nuclear warheads, would be dismantled and the three states would become nuclear-free by the end of the century.

As for the short-range nuclear weapons, the United States announced in September 1991 withdrawal from Europe of all nuclear missiles and artillery shells, and denuclearization of Navy ships and submarines (except those carrying ICBMs). In December 1991 CIS responded and agreed to move all tactical nuclear weapons to Russia by July 1992, where they would be dismantled; between 10,000 and 20,000 tactical nuclear weapons would be destroyed.

The Need for "Minimal Deterrent"

Since development of thermonuclear explosives, safety has been — in Winston Churchill's words — the "sturdy child of terror." As Britain's Prime Minister Margaret Thatcher noted in Moscow in April 1987, "a world without nuclear weapons may be a dream ... but you cannot base a sure defense on a dream. A world without nuclear weapons would be less stable and more dangerous for all of us."

Notwithstanding the accelerating "arms race in reverse" and possible further reductions of nuclear arsenals, "reasonable sufficiency" in nuclear weapons is likely to be necessary as an effective guarantee of peace. It may not be as yet irrelevant as a deterrent in relations between the West and other nuclear weapon nations such as China, and may deter aggression by other countries which could acquire nuclear arms in the future.

Several less developed countries have been seeking military superiority through development of nuclear, chemical, and biological weapons. To prevent or contain wars in which the less developed countries may engage, the need for the West to have at its disposal a credible, minimal deterrent will continue. The 43-day 1991 war in Iraq, which required only 100 hours of land operations to liberate Kuwait and secure a cease-fire, may serve as a useful reminder to those who contemplate armed intervention to further their political ambitions.

With the objective of nuclear arms reduction by the West and the former Soviet bloc essentially achieved, enforcement of nuclear weapon non-proliferation and the ban on nuclear tests become the major goals to be pursued for the maintenance of peace.

Notes

1. The *Maginot Line* (later called more appropriately *Imaginot Line*) played no role in World War II; the German armies went around it and marched into France in May 1940 through Belgium. In the 1970s some of the forts were auctioned by the French government and local farmers found the old fortifications ideal for growing mushrooms. An abandoned cruise missile base in Britain's Greenham Common met a similar fate in 1993: it was given to a real estate agent for disposal and its missile silos may be leased to mushroom growers.
2. The need to deploy atomic bombs in 1945 for securing the surrender of Japan has frequently been questioned. However, it can be argued that a demonstration of the destructive power of nuclear weapons was necessary to establish the credibility of nuclear deterrent, and that therefore the devastation of Hiroshima and Nagasaki was justified because it was instrumental in preventing for several decades a world military conflict.
3. As most recently demonstrated by the 43-day war which devastated Iraq and Kuwait in 1991. Iraq's dictator Saddam Hussein elected to fight rather than back off in the face of overwhelming superiority of the coalition forces led by the United States.
4. This is precisely the reason that, after limited experience with poisonous gases in World War I, chemical and biological weapons were not used in World War II even though both sides possessed large stocks of them. Neither were they used by Iraq in the 1991 war for Kuwait, in spite of the desperate situation of Iraq's army, which was well equipped with chemical weapons.
5. A detailed analysis of thermonuclear war "options" was given by Herman Khan (1961). He considered, for example, the survival of the remaining American population after the fifty largest cities had been destroyed, and viewed reliance on nuclear deterrence as wishful thinking.
6. Brzezinski (1986) gives a comprehensive analysis of the SDI.
7. As most recently demonstrated in the 1991 war in Iraq. Completely deprived of air reconnaissance and deceived by what movements of the coalition forces it could observe, the Iraqi army was totally unprepared for the flanking assault executed by the coalition.

References

Brzezinski, Z., ed. 1986. *Promise or Peril: The Strategic Defense Initiative*. Washington, D.C.: Ethics and Public Policy Center.

Kapra, F. 1981. *The Turning Point*. New York: Simon & Schuster.

Khan, H. 1961. *On Thermonuclear War*. Princeton: Princeton University Press.
McLuhan, M. and Fiore, Q. 1967. *The Medium is the Massage*. New York and Toronto: Random House.

8

Jettisoning the Harness of Biology

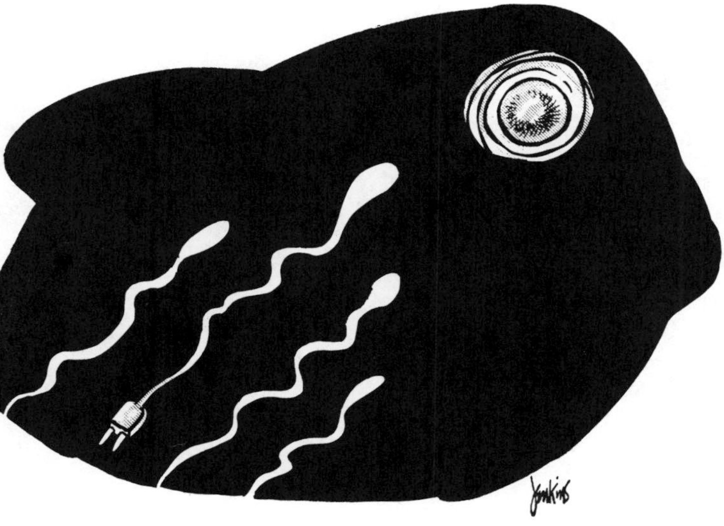

POSSIBLY the most difficult and intractable issues that confront industrial society are those created through direct intervention of science and technology into the biological nature of the human species.

In this case, the basic cause of our predicament is the difficulty of establishing unambiguous rational, moral, and ethical criteria for resolving the unavoidable conflict which occurs when the application of science and technology affects the characteristics and behaviour we have been endowed with by nature. Longevity, procreation, human genome, and sexuality are subject to the most obvious and significant interferences and interventions.

Prolonging Life — or Death?

In pre-industrial society death was viewed to be as natural as birth. Death was conquered and life extended through belief in everlasting afterlife. Christianity provided the means to control the quality of afterlife: good and moral behaviour on the Earth was an assurance of eternal happiness in Paradise.

As medical science and technology progressed, many natural causes of death, such as contagious diseases and childbirth — were essentially eliminated. But through application of ever more sophisticated medical interventions, it has become possible to prolong and sustain the biological life of people terminally ill and doomed to die, or those substantially incapacitated, mentally and physically — without concern for the unnecessary suffering inflicted on them and for the quality of life they would be forced to live. Transplantation of vital organs, replacement with artificial organs, artificial respiration and feeding, heart operations — are some of the techniques which may serve to "prolong" death rather than life. It is not possible to die with dignity when wired with tubes to every orifice and drugged to control the pain. Supporting life can create a caricature of human existence.

Quality of life is a matter of individual perception and judgment. Under the best of circumstances, it is the individual threatened with death that should be deciding his or her own fate. But what if, because of physical or mental condition, the patient is not competent to decide for or against death? Who is to decide for him and on what grounds?

We have been exercising, without restriction, the right to give life; have we the right to take away life? Are we entitled to assistance in living but not to assistance in dying? Should we be denied euthanasia or "good death," a comfortable and dignified death? Should "passive euthanasia" (i.e., death due to the original threat to life) be permitted as well as "active euthanasia" (i.e., death through introduction of a lethal agent)? How can euthanasia be administered and controlled, how can abuse be prevented? In some cases euthanasia may result from a faulty diagnosis, or would not be resorted to if a new treatment became available earlier. Can the risk be justified?

There are no unequivocal answers to these questions. Each case has to be judged on its merits, and the judgment is bound to reflect society's culture and traditions.

Some countries have already recognized their citizens' right to preserve dignity and minimize suffering in dying.

In 1993, the Netherlands adopted the most liberal euthanasia guidelines in Europe; the legislation guarantees physicians immunity if they follow strict rules for mercy killing. However, the Netherlands' experience indicates that euthanasia is difficult to regulate: a 1991 investigation found that about one-third of the patients who receive lethal doses of drugs from their doctors do not give their unequivocal consent.

In Canada, the law makes it a criminal offence (punishable by up to 14 years in prison) for someone to assist a suicide attempt. Thus a disabled person cannot legally obtain help in committing suicide, but it is perfectly legal for an able-bodied person to take his or her life, or for doctors to remove a life support system on request.

Sue Rodriguez, a 42-year-old British Columbia woman, terminally ill and disabled with ALS (amyotrophic lateral sclerosis), or Lou Gehrig's disease, requested the right to a doctor's help in committing suicide. In a statement presented in November 1992 to Parliament, she asked: ". . . if I cannot give consent to my own death, then whose body is this? Who owns my life?" and noted that "A law that states or implies that Canadians are not masters of their own fate, but belong somehow to the State or some other hypothetical authority, simply won't be tolerated much longer."

The Sue Rodriguez appeal reached the Supreme Court of Canada in May 1993. In September 1993, by a 4-to-5 margin, the court ruled that the law against assisting in suicides does not violate her constitutional rights. Thus ended any hope Sue Rodriguez had for dying legally with a doctor's help. Nevertheless, Sue Rodriguez controlled the time and manner of her death. She died in an assisted suicide on 12 February 1994, carried out furtively with the help of an unknown doctor. The issue of assisted suicide again became the focus of public debate and the justice minister announced that he favours a free vote on euthanasia in the House of Commons.

Possibly the most practical way to guard against "prolonged death" (as opposed to "prolonged life") is through the mechanism of a living will. This is an advance directive which details what should be done in the event of a life-threatening situation. The directive should be specific enough to include the majority of likely clinical scenarios and life-sustaining treatments, and several options (such a medical directive was outlined in 1990 in *The Journal of the American Medical Association*). Although situations not covered by a living will may always arise, in all cases the directive provides the family and the medical profession with a moral sanction to exercise their judgment to best reflect the wishes of the person whose life is threatened.

Beyond the physical, moral, and aesthetic aspects of quality of life and dignity of death, there is also the economic angle. The prolongation of death is an increasingly expensive procedure, a burden that a society may consider excessive and may wish to reduce and limit. A recent North American study estimated that half of all money spent on health care goes to sustain the last year of life. The trade-off between prolonging life and the cost to the society of prolonging death cannot be evaluated in any objective terms but is, nevertheless, very real. Clearly, the enormous resources required to prolong life when its quality is poor and death inevitable, could be better used for other purposes. For this reason also, a living will would be in order and would benefit society.

Playing God

"The key to achieving an eternally stable and happy society is to make people like their unescapable destiny." This would not be possible with naturally evolved humans who, capable of irrational, emotional, and unpredictable behaviour, could easily subvert the system. Moreover, their numbers resulting from viviparous reproduction could not be controlled.

"There is no social stability without individual stability." A different breed of people, produced in the required numbers, designed and conditioned to fit perfectly the occupational and social roles allotted them, would be needed.

The technology that makes this possible, and the resulting "World State" social system were described in 1932 by Aldous Huxley. In his *Brave New World* of "Our Ford" era, with procreation completely externalized, the principle of mass production is at last applied to human biology.

There is no longer any mutual involvement — physical or emotional — of men and women in the process of reproduction; sexual intercourse and pregnancy are eliminated. Human eggs are produced by ovaries removed from women who have undergone the operation voluntarily for the good of society and a salary bonus. At Hatchery and Conditioning Centres the ovaries are preserved alive and actively developing; each may yield over fifteen thousand adult individuals. Through "Bokanovsky's Process" an egg may be made to divide to produce up to ninety-six identical "twins":

standard men and women in uniform batches, a major instrument of social stability.

Immersed in a bath of free-swimming spermatozoa, the eggs are fertilized and the embryos grown under different conditions according to their social predestination — from the frightfully clever Alphas to the totally devoid of human intelligence, moronic Epsilons. Biophysical and psychological conditioning continues in the Hatchery after embryos develop into babies. "Sleep teaching" is an effective and widely applied technique.

Nevertheless, the sexual impulse and the ability to experience pleasure, anxiety, and depression have not been completely eliminated from the mass-produced population. Therefore, means were devised to control the undesirable and destabilizing behaviour.

Erotic play and unrestricted copulation continued to be enjoyed by and with "pneumatic" women. Strict birth control was routine and automatic. Girls from twelve to seventeen performed the necessary drill three times a week. Women carried regulation supplies of contraceptives in Malthusian belts.

When feeling strange, women would take "pregnancy substitute." "Violent passion surrogate" was administered regularly once a month as a harmless outlet for fear and rage. Going to the "feelies" would banish any unpleasant thoughts. Within minutes, a few tablets of delicious "soma" would overcome depression and take one on a holiday of any desired duration and destination, from a half-day to lunar eternity.

With total externalization of procreation, the notions of romance, lovers, husbands and wives, family, fathers and mothers, brothers and sisters, have vanished. In Our Ford era "everyone belonged to everyone else."

As the twentieth century draws to a close, industrial civilization has come a long way towards fulfilment of Huxley's vision.

All the fundamental obstacles to freeing the process of procreation from mutual involvement of men and women have been successfully overcome.

Just as in the *Brave New World*, eggs and sperm can be manipulated outside the bodies of the biological mother and father to produce new life. Through in-vitro (in-glass) fertilization (IVF), mature eggs removed from a woman's ovary are fertilized with sperm in a petri dish. The eggs are then returned to the uterus of the biological mother or another woman and, with luck, one or more will develop into an embryo, fetus, and baby. Eventually, the uterus of some other suitable primate could be used instead of a woman's. Should there be a shortage of donor eggs, they could be culled from aborted fetuses (in January 1994 it was announced that research to this end was underway in Britain).

Sexual intercourse is no longer necessary to produce offspring, and the biological mother need not undergo the discomfort of pregnancy.

So far, the chance of success of the IVF technique has been on the order of 15 percent. Since Louisa Brown, the first "test tube" baby was born in England on 25 July 1978, IVF has been used extensively to overcome infertility. If a low sperm count prevents conception through intercourse, pregnancy can be achieved with IVF using the partner's sperm. In other cases, in which the male partner is the problem, a donor's sperm may be used in IVF. In cases of female infertility, surrogate mothers are a possible remedy. In this procedure, a couple commissions a woman to have a child by artificial insemination using the male's sperm. The surrogate mother is often offered money in payment for her services. Such "contract motherhood" has been labelled "reproductive prostitution." Should both partners suffer infertility, it would be possible for them to contract for a donor's sperm as well as for a surrogate mother's uterus in order to acquire a baby. In general, IVF may be used solely as a means of avoiding the inconvenience of pregnancy or intercourse: lesbians and gays can become mothers and fathers.

Conversely, IVF technology allows postmenopausal women to become pregnant. By implanting eggs that have been donated and fertilized in a dish, a woman's normal reproductive life span can be extended.[1]

The natural sequence of conception through sexual intercourse, followed by pregnancy and birth, has been broken. With a variety of birth control techniques available and new ones being developed, the risk of pregnancy as a result of intercourse has been reduced or removed. The act of procreation has become one of merely recreation.

Should an unwanted pregnancy occur, or should it be determined that the sex of the fetus is not the one desired or that its development is abnormal, an abortion can be performed.

Through freezing of sperm, eggs, and embryos, procreation has been immortalized. The offspring may be 'born' long after its biological or legal parents have died.[2]

The availability and — albeit as yet limited — deployment of *Brave New World* technologies of procreation in a society still largely wedded to the traditional culture of viviparous reproduction within a family, has opened a veritable Pandora's box of dilemmas, from moral and emotional to legal and economic.

In the traditional natural system of reproduction, the biological bonds linking the parents and their offspring are the basis of deep emotional involvement of all members of the family and of their legal status, their responsibilities and rights. Through externalization of the biological process of procreation, the biological-emotional-legal linkage — until now the foundation of our social organization — has been severed and abolished.

When the father or the mother is not the biological parent, or when surrogate motherhood is used, the claim to one's "legal" offspring may no longer be based on its biological origin but only on contractual agreements. Conversely, a surrogate mother may develop a strong emotional bond with the baby she gave birth to but cannot legally claim to be hers.

The possibility of preservation of sperm, eggs, and embryos beyond the life span of one or both biological or legal parents opens the way for posthumous production of their offspring without their consent. Eggs from aborted fetuses would produce children whose mothers have never been born. What is the legal status of such progeny?

Women could conceive babies just to have abortions to sell their fetuses for culling of eggs (in Huxley's scenario human eggs were produced by ovaries removed from women).

A white woman's egg could be implanted into a black woman. "Designer babies" would be an option for mixed race couples.

Barring old males from fathering children has never been proposed; should postmenopausal women be treated differently? Should women, irrespective of age, have the right to have a child, or should the child's right to have a suitable home prevail? Can women who are 80 when their children are only 20 years old, be good mothers?

Should technology be used only to support nature when nature has failed (e.g., in the case of infertility), or should it also be used where nature has never been present (e.g., to make possible postmenopausal pregnancy)?[3]

As would be expected, the existing legal and social systems are not fit to cope with the consequences of the new reproductive technologies. As more and more "test tube" babies are produced, the responsibilities traditionally discharged by parents and families will have to be taken over by the state and society. Huxley recognized this as an inevitable outcome of externalizing human procreation; total conditioning of *Brave New World*'s population was his logical and effective answer.

The door to the biological conditioning of humans was already opened in 1953 with the discovery of the structure of DNA, the fundamental genetic material.

The next step is to determine the structure of the human genome, that is the complete set of instructions for making a human being that the nucleus of each human body cell (except red blood cells) carries, and to interpret its genetic message as it affects not only our body's physical characteristics, such as size, shape, and colour, but also intelligence, susceptibility to disease, life span, and behaviour. Such knowledge, to be acquired through the massive Human Genome Project launched in 1988, would provide us with a wide range of options, from therapy to eugenics, and would create many dilemmas.

Gene therapy can be used to treat a disease through repair and replacement of defective genes in human cells. It was applied for the first time in

1990 to cure a monogenic disorder, and may eventually be developed to treat many of some 3,000 such known defects, among them cystic fibrosis and sickle-cell anaemia. Extension to diseases which involve a plurality of genes is a matter for the more distant future.

The development of accurate genetic diagnostics through human genome research would allow us to perform extensive genetic screening. This could serve a variety of objectives, not all of which would be necessarily considered desirable on moral and ethical grounds.

Children could be screened for genetic predisposition to a disease, such as cancer or manic depression, and it might be possible to take preventive measures such as diet control. But, should someone destined to be stricken with a deadly genetic disease be told about his fate if a cure is not available? Should people be forced to live their lives under such a cloud?

Genetic screening could be seen as an invasion of privacy and lead to discrimination against the "genetically unfit." If such information were available many people would become uninsurable and unemployable. Families could be identified as carriers of genetic traits, parents blamed for "genetic errors" and handicapped people no longer seen as unfortunates worthy of special treatment.

Alteration of genes in somatic or non-reproductive cells is limited to the individual undergoing therapy and cannot be passed on to any children the patient may subsequently have. Genetic manipulation of germ or reproductive cells is a much more potent technique: it comes close to "playing God." It would allow the new genes to be transmitted from one generation to the next, and thus to shape the course of heredity and human destiny.

But who could we trust to play God and "improve" our species, make "perfect" babies and produce "superior" individuals? Wouldn't we have to resist the temptation of eugenics, which promises "purification of species" through genetic manipulation and selective breeding, and could be practised to create—as intended by the Nazi rulers of the Third Reich—a "master race"?

If we accept gene therapy for children, would we refuse germ cell therapy for their parents, so as to prevent children from inheriting the genetic disease in the first place? But genes that are detrimental under certain conditions may turn out to have hidden benefits. Genetic engineering could also be used as "cosmetic surgery" to improve genes that are not defective but merely mediocre.

As genetic prognostication develops it will become increasingly difficult to distinguish between genetic abnormalities and normal human variability. Application of genetic engineering could lead to reduction of genetic diversity, a necessary ingredient of the survival of a species.

Genetic and other techniques provide opportunities for intervention during pregnancy. It is possible, through a variety of prenatal tests, to determine the sex of a child, whether it will be retarded or crippled, or subject to some fatal genetic defect. If such information were available to parents, they may opt for abortion. Justified in cases of major disorders, it could be abused if practised to get "a perfect baby" or to select its gender.[4]

Some societies have a strong preference for male offspring, a practice motivated by economics and religion. In India, the East Indies, and China parents typically go on having children until they have at least one boy. In such cultures gender detection and abortion of female fetuses — viewed by some as racist and sexist — would go far towards solving the two most important and obdurate problems of the Third World: overpopulation and the low status of women.

As the number of reproducing females would fall, the population would tend to level off. Capital could be saved rather than consumed, demand for labour increased, educational opportunities and standard of living raised.

Wherever women have reproductive choice, they opt for fewer babies. They would no longer be required to function as baby producing machines and domestic servants. As the number of available women fell, their value would go up, their social status would improve, they would become more secure economically and more likely to be educated.

In a society which has preference for male offspring, letting parents choose the sex of their children appears to be beneficial and desirable. But, more generally, what criteria should govern the exercise of gender choice? How could we guard against selection for frivolous and trivial reasons?

* * *

Within half a century of its publication, Huxley's utopia has turned into a prophecy of uncanny realism and accuracy. We can now produce babies of desired sex without direct involvement of their biological parents and we are quickly learning how to manipulate genes. We are being increasingly reduced to nothing more than the chemical elements of our bodies. Do we want to continue our brave march towards the New World just because it may be possible to do so, or should we stop interfering with the natural biology of human reproduction and heredity?

We already find it difficult to face up to the social and legal consequences of the technologies we elected to develop. If deployed on a grand scale, they will call for psychological and societal changes more radical than ever experienced before, perhaps of a kind envisaged by Huxley. Are we prepared to go that far?

The Tyranny of Sexual Gratification

Through science and technology we have succeeded in eliminating the biological purpose of a sexual relationship: it is no longer necessary to have sex to produce new life. We have been freed from the reproductive necessity of sex and — through birth control techniques — from its natural consequences. But the psychological and social impacts of sexuality have not been jettisoned, the biological sexual impulse has stayed with us and has continued to provide us with emotional fulfilment and the ultimate pleasurable experience of romancing and love making.

Sexual activity is considered to be right and necessary; to control and restrict it is to deprive people of independence and freedom. Women have been liberated from the "tyranny of their reproductive biology" and have attained sexual equality with men. Pregnancy has become a burden, and unwanted pregnancy is tantamount to enslavement.

Abortion is the remedy, to be freely chosen by women who have the right to "control their bodies." Characteristically, they are not expected to control their bodies' desire to make love and have sex; it is only when such activities lead to unwanted results that women are willing to assume *ex post facto* "control."

Politicians who advocate anti-abortion laws are engaged in a similarly inconsistent exercise: not capable of legislating love making, they attempt to prohibit deployment of a technology which helps women to avoid the outcome of a legal activity, when women consider such outcome undesirable.

Protection of human life has been the basic purpose of criminal law. But for those who advocate wide access to abortion, freedom of choice is the supreme good in a free society. For unconstrained feminists, sexual equality means rejection of woman's biological nature with its risk of pregnancy.

There are also those who object to birth control and abortion on moral grounds. To submit to the biological urge of sex and to create life in any circumstances, even when conditions needed to sustain life after birth may be lacking or a modicum of life quality cannot be assured, is right and moral; to prevent birth — except when the mother's life is threatened — is sinful and criminal.

Society's attempts to come to terms with the issue of abortion have not been successful. They have often hinged on the obviously specious ruling as to when a fetus becomes a person and can therefore enjoy the protection of law.[5]

If society does not deny women the freedom to get pregnant, should it also not allow them to end pregnancy?

Sexual equality has been extended to cover homosexuality, euphemistically referred to as "sexual orientation." With a heterosexual relationship no longer necessary to ensure reproduction, homosexuality and bisexuality are regarded on par with heterosexual behaviour as outlets for gratification of a biological and emotional urge.

The ancient Greeks and some primitive societies accepted homosexuality as normal, just as it is accepted by many animal species. This view is increasingly shared in the West. Even though the specific basis of homosexuality — whether biological, psychological, or environmental — has yet to be determined,[6] homosexuality is seen as a natural variation of sexual behaviour, a condition to be catered to and protected, with homosexual unions afforded the legal and social status of heterosexual couples.[7]

Although deprived of its monopoly on reproduction, sexual activity remains an essential ingredient of our civilization and continues to exert an enormous influence. It is exploited commercially as a powerful tool of advertising and it is the eternal theme of much literature and art.

We view the world around us through the lens of sexuality. How else could one account for our fascination with the shape of the female body? Would it be considered aesthetically appealing or even remarkable if it did not convey a sexual message?

Robbed of its traditional biological purpose, sexuality does not promote satisfactory management of human relations. Sexual equality provides the opportunity to meet many more partners, but may not facilitate the establishment of more meaningful and durable relationships. Increasing incidence of divorce, teenage pregnancy, abortion, single parenthood, child and woman abuse, and homicide signify a lack of success in the conduct of interpersonal relations.

Sexual impulse often controls the behaviour of an otherwise rational people. The promise of sexual pleasure — even of just the company or the sighting of the loved one — may be the source of extreme devotion and sacrifice, the deepest, purest and most altruistic feelings, the motivation to excel in creative achievements. The denial — may generate violent passion to the point of insanity, cruel abuse and crime. Even the most cool-headed, educated, moral and rational among us may find it impossible to control their sexual urge and may cause — in objective retrospect — untold suffering and commit totally unreasonable, unwarranted and hideous acts.

The scientific and technological part of human sexuality equation has largely been solved; the societal component has yet to evolve. The organization of society and the constraints it imposes on human sexuality will have to reflect the changing role of sex.

Notes

1. As a result of such a procedure, reported to have cost $6,000, a 59-year-old British woman gave birth to twins in December 1993; she was believed to be the oldest mother of twins in history. Two days later a 63-year-old Italian woman announced that she was 3 months pregnant.
2. For an annual fee, freezing and storing services are already offered by sperm banks. Since the 1991 Persian Gulf War, departing servicemen have been making sperm deposits so that they may be able to father one or more children after they are dead or become sterile.
3. In their 1993 report, Canada's Royal Commission on New Reproductive Technology argued against extension of the human reproductive life span.
4. Another technique of gender selection with more than the customary 50 percent probability relies on sorting out the father's sperm according to whether they carry an X chromosome (which will result in a girl) or a Y one (a boy) before artificially inseminating the mother.
5. Since 1990 there is no legal sanction against abortion in Canada.
6. Although homosexuality occurs naturally, it is not normal and biologically desirable. While considerable activity is devoted to accommodate and protect it, little is done to determine its causes and devise remedies.
7. Not satisfied with protected enjoyment of their sexual preference and denied natural progeny, gay and lesbian couples demand the "right" to have children through adoption or the use of another person's sperm or uterus. The natural right of children, whether adopted or biological, to a heterosexual family is of no concern to them.

9

Has Vision Been Lost?

Peace Tower (West side),
Parliament Building, Ottawa

Philip Pocock

"Where there is no vision the people perish"

THE scientific revolution of the sixteenth and seventeenth centuries and the industrial revolution which soon followed gave birth to modern science and technology. The science of Classical Antiquity and the scholastic philosophy of the Middle Ages were destroyed, the fundamental laws of nature were discovered, the required analytical tools developed and, through a rapid succession of inventions, technologies of thermal power, electricity, and mass production were created. As large scale industrialization took off, the future possibilities of science and technology appeared to be almost boundless; they gave rise to many imaginative explorations by science fiction writers.

Most of the prophesies addressed technical developments, with little or no concern for the more subtle and profound effects of industrialization. Many technical advances were correctly predicted, as by Jules Verne who wrote in the 1860s about space and underwater travel. Imaginative utopias described future societies of high technology. The scenarios devised by H.G. Wells at the close of the nineteenth century and by Buckminster Fuller in the 1960s, relied on romantic extrapolations of existing technologies. These authors naïvely assumed technology to be perfect in every respect, free of all harmful consequences. What appeared technologically possible was also the most desirable.

Much more incisive and illuminating visions of our future were painted in this century by Orwell[1] (1949) and Huxley (1932). Their anti-utopias described techniques of controlling people to achieve a stable society in which "nothing can go wrong."

Although different, Orwell's and Huxley's visions of humanity's future were equally dark. In Orwell's *1984*, people are controlled by punishment and the threat of punishment. In Huxley's *Brave New World*, non-violent manipulation and rewards for desirable behaviour are used; people are deprived of their capacity to think through technologies which inflict pleasure. As Neil Postman (1985) noted, "Orwell feared that what people hate will ruin them; Huxley feared that what they love will ruin them."

Orwell's vision was influenced by the emergence of fascist and communist totalitarian regimes after the First World War, in a period of vigorous scientific and technological development which culminated in the first nuclear explosion in 1945. But post-1984 history does not confirm Orwell's forecasts. On the contrary, as the twentieth century drew to a close, we witnessed the disintegration of the Soviet empire, the collapse of the Soviet Union and the growth of democratic—as opposed to totalitarian—systems of government.

Orwell's, Huxley's and other scenarios suffered from a common deficiency: they all depicted static societies whose development has been arrested and where humans have lost creativity, their most distinctive attribute.

Huxley's scenario did expose some trends characteristic of our industrial society. It correctly reflected our almost infinite appetite for distraction, for products that amuse us, a tendency to lead passive existence in a consumer culture. It pointed to the disappearance of the family as the fundamental unit of social structure, a consequence of tampering with human biology.

Has Western Society allotted too much leisure time to the masses?

> The golden, glittering, brave new information superhighway is actually the road to hell, paved with good intentions. . . .
>
> I became an Internet junkie two months ago. . . . Something went awry almost immediately. I pulled onto the highway and got mired in a traffic jam of newsgroups. Oh, it is a noisy, congested, filthy and degrading mess of some of the most bogus tripe you have ever seen. It is also incredibly addictive . . . .
>
> Humanity spins completely out of control on "alt.barney.dinosaur.die.die.die." Any semblance of common sense or rationality disappears once you enter the world of Barney. . . .
>
> It does not take a Barney War to hint that perhaps our civilization is coming under attack and is crumbling from the sheer weight of too much amusement. As I sit at my keyboard for hours at a time, surfing from newsgroup to newsgroup, I wonder if perhaps it isn't too late to exit at the nearest electronic off ramp and trade in my computer for a dog-eared copy of Thoreau's *Walden*.
>
> (Sean Silcoff: "Information superhighway is littered with sleaze," *The Globe and Mail*, 7 April 1994)

Indeed, Western societies have already been experiencing significant erosion of family ties and increasing reliance of individuals on institutional and professional services for coping with personal problems. The responsibility among family members for providing mutual support and counsel is being largely replaced with processing of personal problems through a host of social workers, marriage consultants, lawyers, stress and grief managers, psychologists, psychiatrists, and the like.

Men and women appear to be incapable of handling their own troublesome situations that develop between the sexes. A firm and decisive attitude may be all that is required to deal with insignificant and common incidents. But, even in such cases, we tend to rely on law, sexual harrassment committees, and similar bodies to control our behaviour. The responsibility for dealing with one's own problems is being externalized and people are being deprived of gaining experience and developing the ability to cope with totally normal but difficult and stressful situations. Taking care of family is increasingly considered a collective, rather than an individual responsibility.

The same tendency has been apparent in the way children are being brought up. Pre-schoolers are increasingly relegated to day care centres. Many parents, and society at large, expect the school to provide, beyond education, everything that a child should most effectively acquire at home. Here belong moral and ethical values, social manners, work habits and responsibility for one's actions among others. Teachers become *de facto* social workers because children's home lives are a mess.

The abdication of responsibility for one's own life has been encouraged and facilitated in industrial nations through development of extensive social safety nets, which, while performing a needed humanitarian role, take care not only of the unemployed, the old and the sick, but also of those who abuse the system or who suffer as a result of their own behaviour. A failure to balance employment and family responsibilities, teenage and single motherhood are some of the typical situations. Moreover, as noted before, the cost of safety nets usually exceeds the ability of the society to pay for them (see Chapter 3).

Drop drunk or drop out: it is your right

Mr. E. Phillips, a labourer at the Metro Toronto Housing Authority, planned to attend a wedding on the weekend of January 26–28, 1992. On the Friday before, he called his employer to report that he would not be at work on Monday because he would be sick that day.

The clerk asked Mr. Phillips, how could he know that he would become ill? He explained that he would be attending a wedding on Sunday and that he would have a hangover which would prevent him from being able to work. He did not want to take a vacation day but wanted to take a sick day.

On Monday, Mr. Phillips called that he would not be in for work because he had a hangover.

The Authority refused to award Mr. Phillips sick leave because getting drunk was a premeditated and self-inflicted condition. A provincial arbitration panel rejected the Authority's position and concluded that Mr. Phillips was too sick to work and awarded him sick pay (he receives $15.60 an hour).

* * *

"We've got to restore a feeling that the 18-year-old dropout has as much right under the rules of fairness to get access to a good, secure job over time as does the Queen's University economist who's working for a stock firm." — Human Resources Minister Lloyd Axworthy

(*The Globe and Mail*, 25 January 1994)

The second half of this century saw a dramatic increase in the awareness of difficulties that Western civilization has to face, ranging from the physical effects of economic growth on nature to its impact on political process, ethics, and values.

Limitations to industrialization and consumption, exasperated by a quickly rising population, have challenged unimpeded economic growth as the all-important criterion of the success of industrial society. It became clear that the by-products of industrialization and consumption may exceed the carrying capacity of the environment and inflict long-term or perhaps even irreversible damage. The same activities led to over-exploitation of natural resources (both renewable and non-renewable) and could tax society's ability to adapt to shortages or switch to substitutes.

The distant future — as noted in Chapter 3 — is necessarily the domain of great uncertainty. Often reluctant to admit our ignorance, we have only a limited understanding of the long-term impacts of massive industrialization on nature and therefore lack the wisdom required to take appropriate action. This is not a deficiency that enlightened leadership and willingness to opt for long-term objectives in preference to short-term ones can overcome.

The second difficulty concerns the inability of the political process as we know it to assume global responsibility for the far-away future.

As noted by Jonas (1974), immutability of nature can no longer be taken for granted. Man's intervention, possibly irreversible, now encompasses the whole planet. Nature can no longer be viewed in separation from human society; it has become a human trust, whose time horizon is indefinite future.

The sphere of human interaction — just as human intervention in nature — has become global in scope and requires collective action, a goal which, as related in Chapter 5, even the most advanced countries find difficult to attain. To achieve collaboration among nation states whose degree of development ranges from primitive to highly industrialized presents a still greater challenge.

The globally enlarged space-frame must be viewed in a time-frame which reaches far beyond the present. But politics is concerned with the present, has no obligation towards posterity. "The non-existent has no lobby, and the unborn are powerless ... accountability to them has no political reality behind it ... in the present decision making, and when they can make their complaint, then we, the culprits, will no longer be there"—observes Jonas.

Clearly, conventional politics is ill-suited to serve the new, greatly expanded in space and time, human responsibility. To fulfil it, politics needs to acquire a new moral dimension and individuals an ethics concerned with the future well-being of mankind and nature rather than with the dealings between people and the immediate consequences of their actions.

The GNP per capita is an example of how inappropriate criteria, which reflect only the present, have been applied to measure the standard of living and wealth. As pointed out by Gore (1992) and others, nature has not been part of economics and calculation of the GNP has not been taking into account the depreciation of nature due to pollution and depletion of resources. Indeed, reckless exploitation of resources, be it forests, fish, minerals or oil, would cause the GNP to increase as nature and our future are impoverished.

Other, possibly more significant and dangerous threats to industrial civilization may come from a different quarter: from the subversion of the very values and mechanisms that assured the success of industrialization.

In the liberal democracies of the West, economic growth has led to the emergence of a permissive society,[2] characterized by erosion of traditional moral standards and lack of a common set of values, in which the notions of right and wrong have little meaning, with each individual being the ultimate authority of his conduct, with personal pleasure the guide and gratification of one's desires the objective, with material wealth considered the only measure of success.

Such attitudes are not compatible with the workings of industrial society, which must rely on structured and efficient organization, personal responsibility, reliability, and ethical behaviour.

As pointed out in a perceptive essay by Schafer (1987), a liberal free market society can only survive if competition is governed by the values which predate the marketplace. When ruthless and rampant self-interest and ambition prevail over public spiritedness, mutual cooperation, family bonds and honesty, when the value of work is measured only in terms of monetary gain and consumption, when GNP per capita is the sole measure of quality of life and social welfare—internal corruption and social disintegration may menace the very existence of industrial civilization.

As participants in the revolution of rising expectations, we are competing for things which, if available to everybody, would not deliver the very benefits we expect from them. "When everybody achieves a home with a view, the view is likely to be of each other's homes" — says Schafer. Universal ownership of fast cars leads to traffic jams moving at a snail's pace; the advantage of graduate education diminishes when everyone holds a graduate degree. As the gap between expectations and reality grows, so do frustration, alienation, and cynicism. No society can survive "when its citizens are all engaged in a furious competition to carve up the spoils," warns Schafer.

Abuse of the environment and ruthless exploitation of resources, as well as the morality of self-interest in the marketplace, will increasingly affect democratic industrialization. Its well-being and survival will depend on its ability to contain and curb these trends, so that it can evolve into a sustainable socio-economic system.

A large share of technical and economic effort will have to be devoted to restoration and preservation of environmental quality, development of more benign technologies, conservation of resources through substitution, renewal, and re-use. The necessary shift from the pursuit of individual self-interest towards public interest will inevitably require more regulation and control in the marketplace,[3] more government, and less personal freedom. Coupled with the need to contain the excesses of permissive society, a delicate balance will have to be struck between democracy and the powers of state.

On a more fundamental level we are moving towards Huxley's scenario with the role of the family being continually eroded through progress in biomedicine and genetics. Biologically bonded, traditional social structure will have to be replaced with yet to be evolved different mechanisms.

Beyond the environmental, resource and socio-economic issues, industrial civilization faces the immediate challenge of complexity and constant, rapid change. As noted earlier (Chapter 4), industrialization has created an environment whose enormous complexity and dynamics tax our ability to manage it. Beliefs and ideologies — religious or political — can no longer define goals and provide guidance and motivation needed to achieve them.

As scientific knowledge brought rational comprehension of the workings of nature, it eroded religious creed as man's anchor in the universe, as a norm of his morals and determinant of his destiny.

Reliance on religion gave way to political ideologies which were to take man into the promised land of plenitude, justice, and happiness. Some, such as Marxism and communism, claimed historical and scientific validity for their prescriptions of achieving a universally perfect society.

But, as noted in the first chapter, at least since World War II, all ideologies — from extreme left to far right — have demonstrated their inability to deliver on their promises. Fascist movements perished in a war that was to gain for them world rule. Communist regimes, which staked the highest claims, have totally failed and, except for Cuba and China, have vanished.

As for the industrial democracies, they all experience economic recessions, unemployment, inflation, urban poverty, crime, and deterioration of the environment, but also deliver an affluent life style and extensive social services — irrespective of the political orientations of their governments.

There are no ideological prescriptions for prevention of difficulties and assurance of achievements; the complexity of industrial society does not admit such simplistic solutions. The most we can hope for is to deal with each issue on its merits, based on informed evaluation rather than what might be deemed ideologically appropriate.

However, a totally rational and objective approach to industrial society's problems is not a substitute for ideology. It does not satisfy man's eternal search for life's significance, it is not a source of motivation in his life's journey, it provides no vision of the future. It is exactly because the reality of the industrial world is too complex to be comprehended by anyone that a visionary world-view is needed. As noted by Sowell (1987):

> It would be good to be able to say that we should dispense with visions entirely and deal only with reality. But that may be the most utopian vision of all. . . . Visions are like maps that guide us through a tangle of bewildering complexities. . . . Visions are indispensable — but dangerous, precisely to the extent that we confuse them with reality itself.

Development of the industrial democracies has rendered traditional visions and ideologies irrelevant — but has yet to evolve new ones capable of cutting through "the maze of bewildering complexities."

It was the thesis of Arnold Toynbee's *Study of History* that a civilization without challenge must perish. As limitations of industrialization and consumerism in a free market system are increasingly felt, industrial civilization is being challenged on a broad front. To survive and prosper it must meet the challenge and free itself of the mechanisms that in the long run can lead to its own ruin. This would mean re-orientation of the values of consumer society and re-definition of the standard of living, with environmental quality and preservation of resources being counted as well as consumption.

At the end of this road is the bright vision of a stable and affluent industrial civilization which co-exists in harmony with the Earth's environment and its finite resources. Environmental decay, ruthless competition and disintegration of the fabric of society could be the alternative dark future.

Notes

1. Orwell's *1984* was directly influenced by Zamyatin's *We*, written in 1920–21 and first translated into English in 1924 (Zamyatin 1972).
2. Jonas (1974) and Mishan (1980), among others, have addressed this issue.

3. Paradoxically, as in the 1970s and 1980s the Marxist or communist governments were trying to catch up with their more successful competitors by discarding some of the Marxist dogma and adopting the incentives of free market economy, the technologically saturated capitalist societies found it necessary to expand controls and regulations to cope with their own success.

References

Gore, A. 1992. *Earth in the Balance: Ecology and the Human Spirit*. Boston, New York, London: Houghton Mifflin Co.

Huxley, Aldous. 1932. *Brave New World*. New York: Doubleday.

Jonas, H. 1974. "Technology and Responsibility: Reflections on the New Tasks of Ethics." In *Philosophical Essays*, 3–30. Englewood Cliffs, N.J.: Prentice-Hall Inc.

Mishan, E.J. 1980. "The Growth of Affluence and the Decline of Welfare." In *Economics, Ecology, Ethics*, ed. H.E. Daly, 276–81. San Francisco: W.H. Freeman.

Orwell, George. 1949. *Nineteen Eighty-Four*. London: Secker & Warburg.

Postman, Neil. 1985. *Amusing Ourselves to Death*. New York: Viking Penguin Inc.

Schafer, Arthur. 1987. "Morals in the Rat Race," *The Globe and Mail*, 27 February 1987.

Sowell, Thomas. 1987. *A Conflict of Visions: Ideological Origins of Political Struggles*. New York: Morrow.

Zamyatin, Yevgeny. 1972. *We*. New York: Avon Books (A Bard Book).

Subject Index

Name Index

Authors of references are not listed except where extensively quoted in the text.

Yousuf Karsh

Julius Lukasiewicz, professor of Mechanical and Aerospace Engineering at Carleton University in Ottawa, Canada, has developed and directed aerospace laboratories in the U.S., England and Canada, has been a member of the NATO Advisory Group for Aerospace Research and Development, and consultant to the U.S. Academy of Engineering and aerospace industry. A forerunner of studies in Society, Technology and the Environment, Dr. Lukasiewicz has lectured on this continent and overseas, and has been a frequent contributor to the Op-Ed page of the Globe and Mail, Canada's national newspaper. His publications include some eighty papers and two books:

Experimental Methods of Hypersonics (1973) and *The Railway Game: A Study in Socio-Technological Obsolescence* (1976).